RELIGION AND AFRICAN CIVIL WARS

NIELS KASTFELT

editor

Religion and African Civil Wars

HURST AND COMPANY, LONDON

First published in the United Kingdom by
C. Hurst & Co. (Publishers) Ltd,
38 King Street, London WC2E 8JZ
© Niels Kastfelt and the Contributors, 2005
All rights reserved.
Printed in India

The right of Niels Kastfelt and the Contributors to be
identified as the authors of this publication is asserted
by them in accordance with the Copyright, Designs
and Patents Act, 1988.

A Cataloguing-in-Publication data record for this book is
available from the British Library.

ISBNs
1–85065–456–5 *cloth*
1–85065–455–7 *pbk*

FOREWORD

The chapters of this book were originally presented as papers at a conference on 'Religion and Social Upheaval in Africa' held in December 1999 at Tune Landboskole outside Copenhagen and organized by the University of Copenhagen. It was part of a series of conferences, seminars and other initiatives under the North-South Priority Research Area of the University of Copenhagen which has been set up to facilitate and coordinate research at the university on North-South issues. I wish to thank the steering committee of the North-South area for sponsoring the conference and the publication of the papers. I also wish to thank Hanne Sørensen for her efficient assistance in organizing the conference and Maj-Britt Johannsen for her effective and patient work on making the papers ready for publication.

The interview with 'Rose', which appears in Paul Richards' chapter, is transcribed from the BBC programme 'Sierra Leone Rose' and published by kind permission of the BBC Africa Service.

Copenhagen, January 2004   NIELS KASTFELT

CONTENTS

vii

THE CONTRIBUTORS

René Devisch is Professor of Anthropology and Director of the Africa Research Centre, Department of Anthropology, Catholic University of Louvain, Belgium. His publications include *Weaving the threads of life: the khita gyn-eco-logical healing cult among the Yaka* (University of Chicago Press, 1993) and *The law of the life-givers: the domestication of desire* (Amsterdam: Harwood Academic Publishers, 1999, with C. Brodeur).

Sharon Hutchinson is Associate Professor in the Department of Anthropology, University of Wisconsin-Madison. She has published *Nuer Dilemmas: Coping with Money, War and the State* (Berkeley: University of California Press, 1996) and numerous articles on the Nuer and the southern Sudan.

Christian Kordt Højbjerg is a Lecturer in the Department of Ethnology and Archaeology at the University of Copenhagen. His PhD dissertation from 1995 is on Loma ritual and cultural knowledge, and he has published articles on religion and politics in the Upper Guinea forest region.

Niels Kastfelt is Lecturer at the Institute of Church History and the Centre of African Studies, University of Copenhagen. He has written *Religion and Politics in Nigeria: a Study in Middle Belt Christianity* (London: British Academic Press, 1994) and edited *Scriptural Politics: The Bible and the Qur'an as Political Models in the Arab World and Africa* (London: Hurst, 2003).

Timothy Longman is Associate Professor of Political Science and Africana Studies at Vassar College and Director of Rwanda Research, Human Rights Center, University of California, Berkeley. His publications include *Proxy Targets: Civilians and the Civil War in Burundi* (New York: Human Rights Watch, 1998) and *Commanded by the Devil: Christianity and Genocide in Rwanda* (Cambridge University Press, forthcoming).

David Maxwell is Lecturer in International History at Keele University in England and the senior editor of the *Journal of Religion in Africa*. He is the author of *Christians and Chiefs in Zimbabwe: a Social History of the*

Hwesa People c. 1870s–1990s (Edinburgh University Press, 1999) and the editor (with Ingrid Lawrie) of *Christianity and the African Imagination. Essays in Honour of Adrian Hastings* (Leiden: Brill, 2002).

Paul Richards is Professor of Anthropology, University College London, and Visiting Professor, Technical Centre for Agricultural and Rural Co-operation, Wageningen, the Netherlands. His has written *Indigenous Agricultural Revolution: Ecology and Food Production in West Africa* (London: Hutchinson, 1985), *Coping with Hunger: Hazard and Experiment in a West African Farming System* (London: Geo. Allen & Unwin, 1986) and *Fighting for the Rain Forest: War, Youth and Resources in Sierra Leone* (Oxford: James Currey, 1996).

Andrew Wheeler is a historian with many years of experience in East Africa. He is the co-author of *Day of Devastation, Day of Contentment. The History of the Sudanese Church across 2000 Years* (Nairobi: Paulines Publications Africa, 2000) and has edited *Land of Promise: Church Growth in a Sudan at War* (Nairobi: Paulines Publications Africa, 1997) and *Announcing the Light: Sudanese Witnesses to the Gospel* (Nairobi: Paulines Publications Africa, 1998).

RELIGION AND AFRICAN CIVIL WARS
THEMES AND INTERPRETATIONS

Niels Kastfelt

INTRODUCTION

The many civil wars in contemporary Africa have raised important questions about the causes and cultural meaning of civil wars and other forms of violent conflict. Masked soldiers in Liberia, the proclamation of the war in the southern Sudan as a *jihad*, the formulation of the Hutu Ten Commandments in Rwanda and the establishment of a Truth and Reconciliation Commission in South Africa have all provoked questions about the role of religion in these conflicts. The claim behind this book is that many African civil wars have religious dimensions which are sufficiently important to deserve to be studied in their own right without, of course, thereby ignoring their social, economic and political context.

Geographically, the contributions to this book focus on four areas: the southern Sudan, Central Africa, the Sierra Leone-Liberia-Guinea region, and southern Africa. Other zones of conflict have had to be left out, including some which are relevant to our central theme. This is the case of Uganda, for instance, where Alice Lakwena's Holy Spirit Movement and the Lord's Resistance Army of Joseph Kony are both prominent examples of movements with a strong religious element. Other areas which might have been included would be Somalia, Mozambique and Angola as well as those countries—like Nigeria—in which the religious dimension of politics has escalated during the last decade without ending in actual civil war. Nor have cases from Islamic Africa been included because, with the notable exception of Sudan, Islam plays a relatively small role in the type of conflict we are discussing.

Modern civil wars in Africa have revived or strengthened old stereotypes of Africa and Africans. The continent is again portrayed as being steeped in superstition and tribal warfare whose nature escapes the kind of rationality usually applied in analysing warfare and social conflict. To avoid this line of interpretation—aptly called the New Barbarism thesis

1

by Paul Richards[1]—we need to discuss African civil wars and conflicts in their proper historical and conceptual context.

We should first of all be careful not to see contemporary African civil wars as peculiar to post-colonial Africa and therefore requiring exclusively African explanations. African conflicts do, of course, have local reasons but we should avoid an African exceptionalism in at least two respects. We should, firstly, keep in mind that globally the twentieth century experienced more systematic killing and violence than any other century in history. So while African wars are indeed African and have African roots, they take place in the most violent century in world history, in the 'age of massacre'.[2]

Secondly, we should be careful not to exoticise post-colonial violence in Africa and thereby, by implication, normalise colonial violence. For instance, the region from the southern Sudan through northern Uganda to Rwanda, Burundi and Congo—now the scene of brutal civil wars and genocide—has a long history of colonial violence in the form of slave trading, slave labour, plantation terror and a violent gun culture which all have to be taken into account when explaining the contemporary situation.[3] This should also remind us that what may appear to be an exceptionally high occurrence of civil wars in contemporary Africa may be new manifestations of old conflicts, both regarding the social and political substance of the conflicts and their cultural and religious dimensions.

A final comment should be made on conceptual exceptionalism. Much as we should contextualise African civil wars and conflicts in their global and historical dimension, we should also reflect critically on the very concept of civil war. We can define civil war as armed conflict between two or more parties within the boundaries of a single state. This may do as a working definition, but it clearly raises serious problems of delimitation, not least as to what level of armed conflict it takes to talk about a civil war. We should also bear in mind that by focusing on the very notion of civil war we risk seeing civil wars and their cultural and religious context as too exceptional phenomena. Civil wars may indeed be exceptional in that they represent an unusual level of violence and scale of conflict, but they are frequently continuations of old conflicts whose political substance and cultural expression are also found in times of peace. In many cases it is more useful to see 'war', 'civil war' and 'peace' as positions on a scale, which would imply that we should constantly reflect on the balance between continuity and change in situations of civil war and serious civil conflict. This also raises a question related to the specific place of religion in civil wars. We may ask if there is a substantial difference between religious phenomena in civil wars and in times of peace. Many of the religious phenomena observed in civil wars are not exceptional to a war situation but are found in everyday religion in times of peace. Nevertheless, as the contributions to this book show, wars are often extreme social situations in which religious phenomena occur in more radical forms than in times of peace, and where the breakdown of social relations is often accompanied by religious change on a scale unseen under more peaceful circumstances.

RELIGION AND CIVIL WAR IN AFRICA: HISTORY AND TYPOLOGY

The conflicts discussed in this book all belong to the contemporary post-colonial African world, but we may find comparable cases in the colonial period, especially in some of the large anti-colonial rebellions like the revolt in southern Rhodesia in 1897, the clashes of the Mahdist state with the British in the Sudan in the 1890s, the Maji Maji rebellion in Tanganyika in 1905–7, the Nyasaland rising of 1915, or the Mau Mau revolt in Kenya in the 1950s.[4]

However, with the possible exception of the turmoil and rebellions in the Congo between 1960 and 1965[5], the earliest parallel in independent Africa to the civil wars of the 1990s is the Nigerian civil war of 1967–70, which may serve as a historical paradigm of the conflicts discussed in this book. It was one of the first major national upheavals in the post-colonial Africa of the 1960s and contained many of the elements, including significant religious ones, which later resurfaced in other conflicts across the continent. It had a fundamental ethnic character, as it was fought between the Igbo and the Nigerian federation. It was an ethnic competition for state resources, it was a battle over natural resources (oil), and it was fought with unprecedented violence. As in contemporary conflicts starvation was used as a deliberate tactic, the war was publicly debated as genocide against the Igbo, and it quickly became a highly internationalised conflict involving debates about the conditions of international intervention in an internal African conflict.[6]

Like the conflicts discussed in this volume the Nigerian civil war had significant religious dimensions, both because religious ideas, rituals and institutions played an active role in the course of the war, and because the war produced important religious changes. Religion was a decisive element in the social identity of the fighting parties, not the least the predominantly Roman Catholic Igbos. On the Biafran side Christian ideas and images were crucial in the war propaganda. The war was presented as a battle between the Christian nation of Biafra and the Muslims of northern Nigeria who launched a *jihad* against the Igbo, and this image was employed systematically in the effort to create sympathy for Biafra in the West.[7] Biafran newspapers and war songs were full of Biblical references and images,[8] a common idea being that the war was a battle between David and Goliath and to claim parallels between the fate of the Jewish people and that of the Igbos.[9] Churches and Christian missionaries also played an active role in the war. Roman Catholic missionaries stayed with their parishes in the war zones inside Biafra, organising fasts and prayer meetings and reporting to the outside world on conditions there. The Vatican was active in international diplomacy trying to bring the war to an end, and churches of many denominations were involved in humanitarian assistance to Biafra.[10] Inside Biafra the war also brought about religious change and innovations. Some Igbos turned to traditional sacrifices or to traditional 'doctors' who were expected to be able to influence the cause of the war,[11] and new religious movements, rituals and churches were created in response to sufferings during the war.[12]

In the 1970s and 1980s African countries experienced new civil wars and insurgencies which form part of the background to the contemporary situation: the fresh outbreak of war in Sudan; the civil wars and liberation conflicts in Mozambique, Angola and Guinea-Bissau; the wars of liberation in Namibia and Zimbabwe; the guerrilla war in Uganda and the conflict between pro- and anti-apartheid groups in South Africa.

During the 1990s some of these wars continued and new ones appeared, many of them with a significant religious dimension. In a study of African insurgencies Christopher Clapham has distinguished between four main types, which fit most of the studies of this book.[13] *Liberation insurgencies* aim at achieving independence from colonial or minority rule; in the cases of the present volume this would include Zimbabwe and South Africa. *Separatist insurgencies* represent the interest of ethnic groups or regions within an existing state and aim at achieving secession from or autonomy within the state; this would include the case of the southern Sudan. *Reform insurgencies* seek radical reform of the state, and the case of Rwanda may be seen as a particular example of this type. *Warlord insurgencies* aim at changing the leadership of the state without necessarily wishing to create a new state radically different from the existing one, rather being directed against creating a personal political fiefdom within the state; cases of this would be Liberia, Sierra Leone and Congo.

RELIGION AND CIVIL WAR IN AFRICA: INTERPRETATIONS

The scholarly interest in the role of religion in civil wars and other forms of conflicts is inseparably linked with the colonial situation. In the wake of the Second World War anti-colonial resistance and rebellion forced colonial authorities and scholars alike to reflect on the logic of rebellions in both Asia and Africa, and scholars began to point at the importance of understanding cultural and religious dimensions of the conflicts. This political and intellectual development created the conditions for the emergence of new kinds of understanding of civil war and rebellion. In Asia, for instance, the French scholar of Buddhism and Vietnam, Paul Mus, stressed the crucial role of Confucian and Buddhist ideas and action in the Vietnamese war against the French,[14] and similar approaches emerged in Africa, first of all in connection with the Mau Mau revolt in Kenya from 1952–6.

With Mau Mau emerged some of the debates on religion and war in Africa, which have resurfaced in the 1990s. A common public view in Europe was that Mau Mau was a reflection of 'the latent terror-laden primitivism in all Africans, the Kikuyu especially'[15] and 'that it was a form of collective psychopathology and that it was akin to devil-worship'.[16] These images and the terror of colonial warfare urged some analysts to try to understand the rationality of such conflicts. In that respect the Mau Mau conflict had a great general impact. Max Gluckman challenged the view that Mau Mau was a 'reversion to African pagan religion and magic'[17] and rather saw its religious aspects as a 'magic of despair' in a situation of rapid urbanization, land shortage and lack of a united political leadership.[18] Gluckman's ideas were developed in association with the work of historians and anthropologists like Norman Cohn, Peter Worsley and Eric Hobsbawn who shared an interest in the cultural and religious ideas inherent in wars and rebel movements, whether in Europe, the Pacific or Africa. Out of this work grew such well-known and influential books as Cohn's *The Pursuit of the Millennium*, Worsley's *The Trumpet Shall Sound* and Hobsbawn's *Primitive Rebels*[19] that were all to influence the work of later generations of scholars studying wars and rebellions in Africa and elsewhere.

Mau Mau and colonial Kenya were not the only parts of Africa where scholarly and political attention was drawn to the religious aspects of war and rebellion. Throughout the continent in the 1950s and 1960s both African and European scholars working within the emerging nationalist framework were increasingly interested in religion and its political importance in colonial Africa. This interest was not only applied to African traditional religions, but also to African Christianity. African independent churches, prophetic and millenarian movements were seen as proto-political movements in an age where Africans were denied formal political activity by the colonial states, and Christianity was seen as an important source of political inspiration and imagery.[20] A similar perspective was applied to African Islam, emphasising the great political potential of Mahdist ideas and Sufi brotherhoods.[21]

This approach to the religious dimensions of politics, or to the political aspects of religion, had two implications that have also characterised many later studies, including much contemporary research on religion and civil wars. Firstly, it applied a functional and intellectualist approach to religion by focusing on those aspects of it which were political in the modern Western sense, and by concentrating on religion as an intellectual system which Africans use to make sense of their lives and the world around them.

Secondly, the view was introduced that there is a direct correlation between people's access to state power and the political significance of religion: the more access to state power, the less the political importance of religion, and vice versa. Religion became politically important because Africans could not act in legal political organisations, which were part of the political system of the state. It became 'the weapon of the weak'[22] against the state, and this view is still powerful.

Research in the 1970s and 1980s followed much of the main program of the nationalist tradition, but new approaches were added. A new interdisciplinarity emerged, combining history, anthropology, sociology, political science and religious studies in new ways and applying this approach to contemporary guerrilla movements and civil wars.

The first major works along these lines grew out of the liberation war in Rhodesia/Zimbabwe and were not the least linked to Terence Ranger's work. Ranger's sustained interest in understanding the African voice in both pre-colonial, colonial and post-colonial politics and religion was embedded in the nationalist tradition, but he applied its perspective to new contexts. His *Peasant Consciousness and Guerrilla War in Zimbabwe*[23] stands out as a significant work, which opened new lines of interpretation. Ranger pointed at religious traditions going back to the nineteenth century, which were being activated according to changing political circumstances. Prophetic traditions and spirit mediums, for instance, formed a long tradition of symbolic order and a resource of resistance that was drawn upon in the struggle against the whites in the late nineteenth century and again in the war of liberation in the 1970s.

More generally Ranger's work was important because it placed the theme of religion and war in a new context. He saw it as an aspect not only of African political history, but also of the history of African religions. In this understanding civil wars and other conflicts became formative moments in African intellectual and religious history.

Another new development in the 1970s and 1980s was the growing interest among anthropologists in studying contemporary civil wars. David Lan's *Guns and Rain* appeared at the same time as Ranger's book and also dealt with the civil war in Zimbabwe.[24] Lan argued that during the war in rural Shona areas there was a remarkable alliance between spirit mediums and guerrillas. The spirit mediums assisted the guerrilla soldiers, thereby creating a synthesis between the ancestors and the living, between past and present, and like Ranger, Lan placed religious traditions at the very core of the civil war.

A parallel to this work was done by the French anthropologist Christian Geffray whose book *La cause des armes au Mozambique* deserves to be better known than it is.[25] It is an anthropological study of the war between FRELIMO and RENAMO in Mozambique in the 1970s and 1980s, as it was experienced in a local rural region. The book is not primarily about religion but it plays an important role in it. Geffray explains, for instance, how religion was important in determining rural views of FRELIMO and RENAMO. FRELIMO was opposed, not least because its officials imposed a centralized political control over the villages and did their best to ridicule and suppress traditional religion and social structure, whereas RENAMO's policy of indirect rule better enabled the villagers to maintain their traditional way of life and religion.

The work appearing in the 1970s and 1980s also included important studies of the place of Christianity in civil wars and insurgencies, for example in Zimbabwe,[26] and the struggle over apartheid in South Africa produced new insight into the interplay of religion and armed conflict. Much of this research focused on two main themes: firstly, the relationship between church and state, both as this materialised in Christian churches acting as institutions of legitimation in relation to the state and as platforms of resistance to minority rule in southern Africa; and secondly the political and ideological uses of Christian dogmatics, whether as delivering theological justification of the apartheid system or as offering theologies of resistance and liberation.[27]

THEMES

The 1990s have seen the publication of a long series of studies of African civil wars and other forms or violent social conflict. Most of the conflicts studied in this literature, as well as most of its approaches and themes, are represented in the eight studies collected here.

The book opens with two essays on the civil war in Sudan by Sharon Hutchinson and Andrew Wheeler, both discussing the dramatic religious changes taking place in the context of the civil war. This is followed by two studies of the Great Lakes region, one by Timothy Longman on the role of Christian churches in the ethnic violence in Rwanda and Burundi, the other by René Devisch discussing Christian healing churches and the domestication of violence in Kinshasa. The two West African contributions focus on the civil wars in the Sierra Leone-Liberia-Guinea region, Paul Richards discussing the Revolutionary United Front in Sierra Leone within the perspective of the anthropology of religion, and Christian Kordt Højbjerg analysing the complex problems involved in understanding the connections between cultural traditions, ethnic violence and politics. The book ends with a chapter which deals with the place of religion in post-war situations. David Maxwell discusses the relationship between religion and war in a longer time perspective, including both the liberation war and the post-war period in Zimbabwe.

Their geographical and empirical differences apart, the contributions to the book share some common underlying themes:

1. *Religion, rationality and war.* This concerns recent debates about the rationality of African civil wars and not the least the extreme use of violence in some of the wars, including the particular role of religious factors in this violence.
2. *War, meaning and religious change.* This covers two main dimensions, firstly the use of religious ideas in describing, debating and making sense of violence and civil war and, secondly and related to that, the religious changes taking place as a consequence of war.
3. *Religion and the legitimation of war.* This deals with the use of religious ideas and institutions in justifying civil war and violence.
4. *Religion, war and reconstruction.* This relates to the various uses of religious ideas, rituals and institutions in attempting to create social reconciliation and reconstruction in communities that have gone through civil wars.
5. *Religion and civil war in time perspective.* This puts the theme of religion and civil war into a wider perspective by discussing it both chronologically and structurally. In that way we may get a better understanding of which phenomena are specific to civil war situations and which are found in other contexts as well.

These themes are discussed in the perspective of different academic disciplines—history, anthropology, political science and theology. They are also studied through different analytical approaches. Some see them in the context of a cognitive and intellectualist understanding of religion, focusing on the use of religion in creating meaning and symbolic order in the face of the extreme violence of civil wars. Others focus on the personal and spiritual aspects of the theme, discussing the significance of civil war experiences for the personal spiritual life of individual Africans. Other contributions put a special emphasis on the institutional and organized dimension of the theme. Yet others approach the theme historically, trying to understand the interactions between religion and civil wars through their historical development.

RELIGION, RATIONALITY AND WAR

Contemporary African civil wars have renewed old discussions and images of Africa and Africans. As European settlers, colonial administrators and others in the 1950s saw Mau Mau and related phenomena as manifestations of African primitivism and barbarism, so influential voices of the 1990s have described contemporary African civil wars in similar terms. And as anthropologists, historians and other scholars in the 1950s insisted upon finding rational explanations of apparently irrational political behaviour, so their heirs in the 1990s and 2000s have struggled to find the rationality of contemporary African civil wars. This debate can be illustrated by ongoing discussions of the civil wars in Sierra Leone and Liberia, both wars with forceful religious and cultural manifestations and displays of extreme violence. To mention two prominent contributors, the work of Paul Richards on Sierra Leone and Stephen Ellis on Liberia has highlighted some of the general issues involved in the debate.

The civil war in Sierra Leone, beginning in 1991, has attracted great international attention. In his important book *Fighting for the Rain Forest* Paul Richards has taken up the whole debate about the war and offered an alternative interpretation that is highly relevant to the theme of the present book.[28] Richards's book is a critique of the 'New Barbarism' thesis, which sees wars in the post-cold war period as small-scale conflicts fought with cheap arms easily available to small religious, cultural and criminal organisations. Culture clash, resource competition and environmental breakdown produce small localized wars whose participants are not traditional soldiers but criminals and bandits who revert to 'old, superstition-riddled forms of violence',[29] 'juju warriors, influenced by the worst refuse of Western pop and ancient tribal hatreds, and battling over scraps of overused earth in guerrilla conflicts that ripple across continents and intersect in no discernible pattern'.[30]

Opposed to this picture Richards places the young warriors of the Revolutionary United Front (RUF) in Sierra Leone in the 'hybrid and globalized world of Atlantic commerce rather than the 'traditional' subsistence world of the African bush', drawing upon the symbolic resources and cultural hybridisations of globalized modernity.[31] He also opposes the view of the rebels as being irrational bandits soaked in superstition and primitive violence. He rather sees them as being led by 'excluded intellectuals' who react to the crisis of the patrimonial state, which Sierra Leone experienced in the 1980s and 1990s. He sums up:

I consider it plausible, and useful, to think of the rebel movement in Sierra Leone as a sectarian intellectual response to the perceived corruption of a metropolitan patrimonial elite. Far from random, the violence is an expression of the social exclusion of a group of educated exiles determined to force patrons 'in town' to imagine what life is like for the young minds stranded 'in the bush.'[32]

In his contribution to the present book Richards elaborates his interpretation of the RUF and his attempt at making sociological sense of the behaviour of the young soldiers and 'the world the RUF made' in its camps. In this contribution he approaches the theme more explicitly within the perspective of the anthropology of religion in an attempt to understand its sectarian and religious dimensions. Basing his analysis on a neo-Durkheimian functionalist approach Richards focuses on the ways in which the social intelligence of humans 'works on the raw material of social interaction to develop a world of spirit forces, symbols and rituals through which we interrogate, comprehend, defend or change key values, relationships and institutional arrangements'.[33]

From this starting point Richards argues that in order to understand the behaviour of the RUF soldiers we have to look at how their world was first pulled apart by social exclusion and capture and then put together again through initiation and social control in a violent and highly egalitarian forest camp world. The camp world the RUF made was that of a 'circumstantial sect' based on meritocratic rank and mechanical solidarity, with clear millenarian overtones and a typical sectarian leadership based on charismatic, or messianic, authority and 'oracular saintliness', personified in Foday Sankoh. Richards sees the RUF forest camp society of the young soldiers as a kind of primary boarding school under siege where bigger boys and girls with guns maintained order while the 'teachers' were away for long periods of time. This type of society developed its own religion, its distinct rituals and worship that served as functional values in the making of camp life. Richards does not wish to let a neo-Durkheimian sociological functionalism obscure religious creed altogether and he especially emphasizes the millenarian character of the RUF world. Yet this is also interpreted in neo-Durkheimian terms in which millenarianism is not seen as social action driven by a vision, but rather reversely as a vision sustained by a particular kind of social organization—that of young soldiers locked in a forest camp world of meritocracy and egalitarianism and with little prospect of escape.

As in Sierra Leone the civil war in neighbouring Liberia has produced attempts at understanding the rationality of extreme violence and its distinct cultural and religious expressions. The most wide-ranging interpretation, Stephen Ellis's important work *The Mask of Anarchy*, is partly a detailed reconstruction of the course of the Liberian civil war in the 1990s, partly a study of its special cultural and religious style.[34]

Like Richards, Ellis makes his point of departure the public image of the Liberian civil war and not least the lack of understanding of its religious dimension. Ellis argues that most of the protagonists of the war claim to have been in direct communication with God and other religious forces during the war, and that these claims have to be taken seriously. For instance, Samuel Doe was widely believed to be impervious to bullets, to be able to disappear in the face of danger, and to make use of the special skills of a great number of 'juju men' from throughout West Africa. In order to maintain the strength of his power he was believed to drink the blood and/or eat the foetuses of pregnant young girls. Consequently, Ellis argues, in Liberia we are dealing with a political order rooted in religious beliefs, and if we wish to understand the breakdown of such a political order, we must take these beliefs into account and reconstruct and interpret their historical changes in order to understand their present meaning.[35]

Ellis pays special attention to the practice of human sacrifice and cannibalism widely said to be practiced in the Liberian civil war. He argues that these practices did actually take place and proceeds to explain their use in the war historically.[36] Human sacrifice and cannibalism are linked to a particular notion of power rooted in an idiom of eating and described through a vocabulary of digestion. Earlier in the twentieth century the production of power through human sacrifice and the eating of humans took place in the rituals connected with secret societies and other religious organisations. Through the twentieth century the institutions and political culture of the Liberian state and those of rural secret societies and rural political institutions were assimilated by one another, as the central government penetrated the hinterland and the people of the rural areas penetrated the institutions of the national government, culminating in Samuel Doe's take-over of the government in 1980.

In this process the earlier constitutions of both the republican institutions and the secret societies were eroded from within. In both cases there was a tendency for the institutional checks and balances that prevented the abuse of power to fall into decay. What was subverted was not just the legal constitution of the Republic of Liberia, but also the spiritual constitution of the secret societies, Islam and the churches alike. Power, whether local or national, was increasingly unregulated other than by factional intrigue.

One consequence of the centralization of power and of its contestation by intense factional manoeuvre was an inflation in the vocabulary by which power was expressed and understood, including that of sacrifice and eating. The practice of human sacrifice was taken out of the hands of officials of traditional secret societies and used by heartmen, independent commercial entrepreneurs who obtained human organs and sold them for monetary gain to those who believed that they could acquire wealth and power by their ritual use and even consumption. In fact, it was privatised.[37]

The civil wars in Sierra Leone and Liberia have both served to highlight and renew scholarly interest in the religious dimension of African civil wars. Richards' and Ellis' work, however, also shows radically different ways of approaching this dimension. Richards applies a strictly sociological approach to RUF religion, seeing beliefs and rituals as functional values emerging under particular social circumstances, echoing the Durkheimian view that where there is society there is religion. Ellis, on the other hand, argues that the religious dimension of the Liberian civil war must be understood historically, as the product of long-term religious and political change. Where Richards' sociological interpretation stresses the general nature of guerrilla camp culture, Ellis' historical analysis emphasizes the specific and the local and places the religious aspects of the civil war into the context of religious and political history.

WAR, MEANING AND RELIGIOUS CHANGE

Civil wars, like other wars, are not only about destruction. They are also sources of innovation and creativity. Scarcity, poverty and the lack of material goods often facilitate technological innovations, but civil wars may also produce important religious innovations. The same is the case with other forms of extreme social situations such as famine and drought—throughout the history of Africa, for instance, the lack of rain has been one of the most significant sources of religious change producing new rituals, beliefs and religious movements. As a particular type of extreme social situation civil wars have similar effects, and as several of the contributions to the present book show, these religious changes do themselves become important factors in the course of the wars. Wartime religious changes are not the least cognitive responses to radical social change. Long held religious views are abandoned and substituted by others seen to be better able to make sense of the wars and their evils and to make apparently incomprehensible suffering meaningful.

The connections between war, meaning and religious change can be seen in many of the contemporary civil wars in Africa. We see at least two different types of situation. In some cases, such as northern Uganda, established religious traditions are applied to new social conditions resulting in religious innovations being created on the basis of existing traditions. In other cases, as in the southern Sudan, wars produce fundamental social changes, which in turn erode the whole social context of religion and lead people to abandon their established religion and turn to new beliefs and rituals.

The first type of situation is seen in the rebel movements of Alice Lakwena and Joseph Kony in northern Uganda in the 1980s and 1990s.

Both movements emerged from years of military rule, ethnic conflict and social turmoil; both were perceived by their leaders and followers as prophetic spirit movements, as armies of God fighting the evils of this world; and both were rooted in local religious traditions which they renewed in the face of war and upheaval. The Holy Spirit Movement of Alice Lakwena was based on traditional Acholi religion and on Christianity and became a prophetic healing movement in which Alice received her healing gifts from God and the spirits, which enabled her to cure individuals of disease and society of social ills.[38] Alice worked with the help of well-known local spirits, as well as of the Holy Spirit and new spirits, which she introduced herself. On this basis her movement was a traditional witchcraft eradication movement, both aimed at fighting internal evil in the shape of soldiers, witchcraft and sorcery and external evil in the shape of the National Resistance Army of Uganda. The Holy Spirit movement was both an Acholi and a supra-ethnic regional cult which served as an effective basis of northern Ugandan armed resistance against the Ugandan state.

Unlike Alice Lakwena's movement the Lord's Resistance Army of Joseph Kony is a regular guerrilla army fighting the National Resistance Army and the state.[39] Kony claims to be sent by God to make people follow God and lead them to a new world. His is a cleansing movement aimed at eradicating witchcraft and unbelief, and this is partly done on a Biblical basis through the powers of the Holy Spirit, partly by potent new spirits working through Kony.

Both Lakwena's and Kony's movements are based on local religious traditions which they have renewed through the eclectic and dynamic use of prophetism, healing and spirits. In both cases it makes good sense to understand their religious dimensions historically, as the result of a long historical process. However, Kony's movement in particular has strong similarities with the RUF in Sierra Leone, and the type of religious innovation found in Kony could be understood along the lines suggested by Paul Richards. Little is known of the kind of guerrilla camp society found in Kony's camps, but what we know suggests that it could be seen as the type of sectarian enclave society described by Richards.[40] The camp culture of the Lord's Resistance Army was clearly based on charismatic, prophetic authority, on a strong millenarian eschatological vision, and on a strict maintenance of symbolic boundaries upheld through initiation rites and commensality.[41]

We now turn to situations of war-related religious innovation which has made people and communities change established religion and turn to new religious belief and practice. This is shown in Sharon Hutchinson and Andrew Wheeler's contributions to the present volume. In her book

Nuer Dilemmas. Sharon Hutchinson has already demonstrated some of the radical cultural and religious consequences of the Sudanese civil war for the Nuer communities of the southern Sudan.[42] The social disruption caused by the war, as well as the introduction of Christianity, has changed the sacrificial significance of cattle, which have been turned into a commodity. The war (together with the introduction of Western bio-medicine and of Christianity) has produced new interpretations of illness and death, a growing scepticism and internal religious debate, a secularisation and individualization of important parts of Nuer social life, and growing divisions between Christians and non-Christians.

In her contribution to this book Hutchinson focuses on the dynamic interplay between militarism, Christianity and indigenous prophecy as forces of religious change in Nuer communities in the period 1991–9. She shows that the war has simultaneously produced religious innovation and spiritual intensification as well as secularism and militarism, and that both processes are related to changing Nuer interpretations of fundamental religious and moral ideas. She also demonstrates how religious forces tending both towards unity and towards division have been constantly interacting in the Nuer communities during the war.

Hutchinson's basic point is that the rise of southern Sudanese militarism in the shape of the Southern People's Liberation Army (SPLA) of John Garang and the 'SPLA-Nasir' (later the Southern Sudanese Independence Movement) of Riek Machar has had serious secularising effects, first of all through stripping homicide of its spiritual dimensions. SPLA leaders convinced their soldiers that their power over life and death operated completely independently from the powers of God, that homicide was impersonal and free of pollution. To this secularising militarism, however, was added a new attitude towards religion after the split in the SPLA in 1991. Riek Machar turned to the help of indigenous Nuer prophets, and both he and John Garang had to face the remarkable growth of Christianity which had begun in the Nuer communities from the mid-1980s. Many began to interpret the sufferings of the war as a sign of God's anger, and among southern Sudanese Christianity was increasingly seen as a potential basis of regional identity and of unified resistance against the Khartoum government. Christianity, however, was not only a source of unity. Growing denominational divisions created what Hutchinson calls a 'segmentary Christianity', which was deepened by the channelling of incoming foreign aid through specific denominations. Since 1998 the potentially unifying force of religion has re-emerged. Three successive regional conference, actively supported by the New Sudan Council of Churches, have tried to promote peace between the conflicting Nuer, Dinka and other southern Sudanese communities and have simultaneously promoted ecumenical tolerance, especially through the initiative of Nuer prophets. The turn towards Christianity, though, has not been shared by all Nuer, particularly not by Nuer soldiers, many of whom have continued to turn to indigenous prophets and other spiritual leaders, thus contributing to a religious split between an increasingly Christian civilian population, a secular military hierarchy and a more prophet-oriented group of rank-and-file soldiers.

A different perspective on religious change in the southern Sudan is offered in Andrew Wheeler's contribution. His focus is on the development and role of Christianity during the war, and he especially discusses those 'narratives of significance', through which Sudanese Christians find meaning in their lives in the face of civil war and destruction. A main point in Wheeler's interpretation is that the war is not only destructive, but is also promoting a richer religious life for individuals and leads thousands of southern Sudanese to Christianity. To them the war has become one of the most significant agents of religious innovation in the modern history of the southern Sudan. For example, to many young Sudanese, abducted into the so-called Red Army and taken to SPLA camps in Ethiopia, this experience became a crucial step in their spiritual development, eventually turning the Red Army into a Christian army which came to play an important evangelising role when they returned to Sudan after the SPLA's expulsion from Ethiopia in 1991.[43] Hutchinson also discusses these events in the contribution and stresses that while many of the child soldiers turned to Christianity, others became alienated misfits

The dramatic spread of Christianity during the war has had different cultural effects. In the Bor Dinka community perhaps as many as 90% of the people defined themselves as Christians at the end of the 1990s, most of them having done so after the Nuer raid against the Dinka in 1991. This mass movement was accompanied by a systematic destruction of indigenous shrines and cult objects marking a radical break with the past in order to move forward. Among the Azande, on the other hand, the Episcopal Church took upon itself the role of guardian of traditional Zande culture.

To many southern Sudanese Christianity provided a key to conceptualising and making sense of the war. The destruction of traditional shrines, for instance, signalled that the old religion had to be removed in order to follow God who was punishing the Sudanese with the civil war. In that perspective the growth of Christianity became an important religious dimension of the course of the war. However, it also became a crucial element in the history of religious innovation in the southern Sudan and in the history of the domestication of Christianity in the region through different forms of contextualised Christianity.[44]

RELIGION AND THE LEGITIMATION OF WAR

The use of religion as a means of legitimating war is a classic field, and modern Africa shows many examples of this, as when the Afrikaners of South Africa drew on the Bible to construct a particular ethnic theology of apartheid, or when the government of Khartoum justifies its war against southern Sudan as a *jihad*. One of the most dramatic examples in the 1999s of the legitimising role of religion is the Rwandan genocide in 1994 in which we saw both an intellectual and an institutional use of religion—intellectually, by using particular religious ideas as a way of justifying political action, and institutionally through a close alliance between churches and the agents of the genocide.

Timothy Longman's contribution to this book demonstrates that the genocide in Rwanda implied a strong polarization of ethnic categories (Hutu, Tutsi and Twa) which were promoted and sharpened during the colonial period and in which the Biblically-derived Hamitic hypothesis played a crucial part in providing the ideological basis for a still more rigid ethnic hierarchy. The use of the Hamitic hypothesis, originally introduced into Central Africa by Europeans, led to the opposition between a superior, light-skinned, pastoral race of Hamitic Tutsi who had migrated into the region and the inferior, dark-skinned, agricultural Hutu.[45] After the Rwandan revolution of 1959 the Hamitic myth was transformed into a political ideology and re-emerged dramatically during the genocide of 1994:

Filtered through the lens of a rabidly anti-Tutsi, anti-monarchical ideology, the Hamitic hypothesis underwent a striking metamorphosis. What Europeans naively perceived as a superior brand of humanity was better seen as the embodiment of the worst in human nature: cruelty and cunning, conquest and oppression. Where missionaries invoked Semitic origins, as a source of racial superiority, Hutu ideologues saw proof of foreignness; where anthropologists detected contractual exchange based on reciprocal benefits was now condemned as social domination enforced by ruse and coercion; what most Europeans perceived as feminine grace was now denounced as yet another ploy designed to subjugate the Hutu.[46]

The Hamitic myth was blended with other racist ideas—including the notorious Hutu Ten Commandments from 1990, which were a celebration of Hutu superiority over the Tutsi—into that political and ethnic mythology which was systematically promoted as part of the coming genocide in the spring of 1994.[47]

Institutionally, religion was also important in the genocide in Rwanda, as appears from Timothy Longman's contribution to the present book. Longman focuses on the role of Christian churches in the genocide, and although the churches did not always legitimise the genocide explicitly they formed a close alliance with the Hutu groups that carried it out and thus shared an institutional responsibility for it. Longman's discussion helps us to understand how such a role of the churches was intimately linked with general church policies and also helps to remind us that Christian churches have not been champions only of civil society and democratisation in Africa but also of social destruction.

The complicity of the churches in the genocide sprang from their structural position in Rwandan society and this, in turn, was the product of the early missionary strategies of Catholic missionaries in the colonial period. They aimed deliberately at converting the Rwandese through their political elite and consequently developed an intimate alliance with the royal court and with local chiefs who converted to Christianity in growing numbers, so that by the 1930s being a Catholic was a virtual prerequisite for obtaining political office. Longman argues that the alliance between church and state was so close that Rwandan Catholics could later take part in the genocide of 1994 believing they were acting in accordance with the teachings of the church. From the early colonial period church leaders were also actively promoting the Hamitic hypothesis and began to reserve positions in schools and churches for the allegedly superior Tutsi, while new generations of missionaries after the Second World War increasingly began to cultivate a Hutu counter-elite. With the extreme ethnic violence being committed in Burundi and Rwanda in the early 1990s the churches generally remained passive, because they had much to lose by going against the state: if they challenged the ethnic structure which they had themselves helped to create they risked undermining the close link between church and state and also alienating broad sections of the population. Consequently the church hierarchy generally accepted the ideological legitimation of ethnic violence in both Burundi and Rwanda, whereas both countries saw more examples of individual clergy trying to stop the killings or saving the victims of genocide.[48]

RELIGION, WAR AND RECONSTRUCTION

This book ends with a contribution by David Maxwell discussing a country where civil war and violent ethnic conflicts have come to an end. In both Zimbabwe and South Africa the post-war situation has raised vital questions about how to make society move on after years of destruction. In other African countries—in Uganda, Sierra Leone, Liberia and elsewhere—similar questions are being discussed: how do countries promote reconstruction of broken social relations, of local communities, of families and individuals after years of suffering? How are child-soldiers abducted into guerrilla armies brought back to a tolerable social life? How can former enemies learn to live together again? How should war criminals be dealt with?

The attempts at solving these fundamental problems have taken different forms. In some cases war criminals are taken to court as in Rwanda; in others, truth commissions are set up to uncover the past in order to make it possible to live with it. This has been the solution in South Africa, and a similar one has been applied in post-war Sierra Leone. Parallel arrangements are found in Rwanda where perpetrators can have their sentences reduced if they confess their crimes to a council of elders, the so-called *gacaca* system,[49] or in Nigeria where the Human Rights Violation Investigation Commission is organising nationwide hearings on the abuse of human rights during Nigeria's years of military rule.[50]

Handling the post-war situation is a matter not just of legal procedures, but also of achieving what Wole Soyinka calls a 'sense of closure'.[51] This adds a moral, psychological or religious dimension to post-war reconstruction, as it should lead people to feel that the time of war is over and that they can put the troubled past behind them as a pre-requisite for moving forward. If we see this process as a ritual of transition, the post-war period is the time for rituals of incorporation through which social and personal relations are restored or established in new ways, enabling individuals and communities to live together. The most common elements in this process have been rituals of healing and cleansing and religious notions of truth, forgiveness and reconciliation.

Postwar Zimbabwe has had a long experience of ritual healing of national and personal wounds.[52] Not only spirit mediums but also traditional healers, *n'anga*, played a significant role during the liberation war, and the healers continued to be important in the restructuring of the post-war period. They performed rituals of expurgation, which functionally came to serve as rituals of incorporation, and likewise most churches developed healing rituals after the war. The *n'anga* had to settle the spirits of people who had not been properly buried during the war. Children who had witnessed bloodshed and death in the war had to be healed and reintegrated into their families and local communities. Men and women who returned from the war had to be cleansed through the rituals of the *n'anga*, and many of these rituals were based on the premise that they would only be purified if they told the truth about their deeds during the war. In this way purification, healing, truth and reconstruction were connected, and the rituals were turned into historical rituals, a ritualised means to uncover the historical truth about the war.

The interplay between purification, truth and reconstruction was also seen when South Africa began its process of reconstruction in the 1990s after the end of the apartheid system. Where the Zimbabwean system was widely based on indigenous religious traditions, the South African solution was framed within a Christian language. The Truth and Reconciliation Commission (TRC) was set up by a government act in 1995, and its very name claimed a direct link between uncovering the truth and promoting social reconciliation and reconstruction, echoing the words of St. John 8, 32 that the truth shall set you free. The South African faith communities played an active role in the work of the TRC from the beginning, occasionally leading to criticism that the churches were over-represented in the commission and that it imposed a Christian morality upon the whole reconstruction process. The TRC developed its own liturgy, used at many hearings, consisting of hymns, prayers, readings, lighting of candles and presenting of olive branches,[53] and the faith communities continued to play a crucial spiritual role in the work of the TRC, not the least through its chairman, Archbishop Desmond Tutu.[54]

RELIGION AND CIVIL WAR IN TIME PERSPECTIVE

The religious phenomena seen in African civil wars are frequently found in other contexts as well. This raises important questions of whether these phenomena are specifically shaped by the extreme conditions of the civil wars. Three contributors to this book—David Maxwell, René Devisch and Christian Kordt Højbjerg—discuss cases where war and violence are analysed either in a wider time perspective (Maxwell) or a wider structural perspective (Devisch and Højbjerg).

In his contribution David Maxwell discusses patterns of continuity and change in the religious and political history of the Katarere chiefdom in northeast Zimbabwe. By following the area both before, during and after the liberation war Maxwell is able to give a finely nuanced discussion of the role of religion in the war and of the long-term religious impact of the war.[55] He notes the flourishing of religious life after the end of the war, both in Christianity and in 'traditional' religion, which has been explained as a legacy of the liberation war. Maxwell questions this and argues that religious adherence rather than being seen as a product of the war must be linked to long-term tensions in rural society in relation to gender, generation, faction and status, as well as being a response to the social transformation taking place since independence. He also sees the religious development during and after the war as part of a recurring pattern of religious change and revival, which can be observed over the last century. Although serious religious change took place during the war, he argues that once the war was over old tensions re-emerged. This forms the background to the fast growth in the area after independence of

Pentecostal churches which had a special appeal to women and young people. He concludes that the religious changes in northeast Zimbabwe can only be partly explained by the war and by post-independence developments; they are also part of a century-long process of religious change.

Africans experience violence not only in the civil wars of the continent, but frequently as an integrated part of their daily life. Studying responses to violence inside as well as outside civil war contexts helps us to a better understanding of the spectre of violence and its cultural manifestations, and this is one of the aims of René Devisch's contribution to this book. Devisch focuses on Kinshasa and the Congo, an area victim to large-scale violence and war over long periods of time. His concern is to understand the cultural means which people use to come to terms with rampant violence and the collapse of the state and the market economy—not least the extreme outbursts of urban violence in Kinshasa in the early 1990s—thus placing people's coping with violence in the broader context of social collapse, and not only in that of civil war. Devisch especially emphasizes the role of independent prophetic healing churches and matricentric neighbourhood support networks in settling violence and creating new forms of community. He argues that these communities settle violence and resist globalism and individualist modernity through communitarian religious celebrations such as divination, ritual healing and funeral ceremonies, thereby mobilizing cultural resources for creating new communities and cultural revival. In that way religious communities become one way of domesticating extreme violence and the consequences that follow from war.

Christian Kordt Højbjerg's contribution takes us back to some of the issues raised in the beginning of this introduction. His analysis of cultural traditions, ethnicity and political violence among the Loma on the border between Guinea and Liberia discusses religion and civil war in a new perspective. His point of departure is the use of masks in some of the violent clashes between Loma and Mandingo in the late 1990s, and he uses this for discussing whether Loma mask symbolism legitimises or makes sense of radical political violence. Højbjerg's analysis is a critique of those interpretations which see acts of terror (like in the civil wars in Liberia and Sierra Leone) as a direct consequence of the symbolic and real violence displayed in the rituals of those secret cult associations which are common throughout the region. In other words, religious practices of the past are not models for contemporary acts of terror. Rather than seeing masking traditions as vehicles for ethnic violence Højbjerg stresses that the use of masks is first of all related to situations of transition from one state to another and is therefore a means used to cope with change and transformation in Loma society and to handle relations between Loma and other ethnic groups. There is little basis, therefore, for an instrumental understanding of the use of masks in the ethnic conflicts between Loma and Mandingo. On the contrary, the violent use of mask performances is atypical of Loma practice, and most ethnic clashes between Loma and Mandingo occur without any masking being involved. By way of conclusion Højbjerg turns the 'religion as idiom of violence' thesis on its head, arguing that it is not 'traditional' religious practice which explains contemporary acts of terror, it is rather the brutal violence of rebels and government soldiers which informs traditional religion and makes it more violent.

Højbjerg's conclusion becomes a timely warning against claiming any simple connection between religious traditions and civil war behaviour. Religion is indeed an important element in many of the contemporary African civil wars, but just as religion may give civil wars their particular cultural style, so civil wars are capable of transforming African religions.

NOTES

1. Richards 1996, pp. xiii ff.
2. This expression is from Hobsbawn 1996, p. 24. When reflecting upon the global context of African civil wars it is useful to turn to Hobsbawn's chapter on 'The Age of Total War', *ibid.*, pp. 21–53.
3. See, for instance, Martin 1983; Behrend 1999 and the survey in Hochschild 1999; cf. the comparative perspective on colonialism and terror in Taussig 1987.
4. See Ranger 1967; Holt 1970; Iliffe 1979, pp. 168–202; Shepperson and Price 1958; Berman and Lonsdale 1992.
5. See Young 1965; Fox, de Craemer and Ribeaucourt 1965–6 discuss the Kwilu rebellion of 1964 and include an interesting analysis of the religious dimensions of the rebellion.
6. General accounts of the war include St. Jorre 1972; Stremlau 1977; Tamuno and Ukpabi 1989.
7. See Stremlau 1977, pp. 110–17 and St. Jorre 1972, pp. 352–3.
8. For newspapers see Walls 1978 and for war songs Agu 1991.
9. Kirk-Greene 1971, pp. 171–2.
10. Stremlau 1977, pp. 118–23, 240–5, 280 ff.; Harneit-Sievers, Ahazuem and Emezue 1997, pp. 124–5.
11. Harneit-Sievers, Ahazuem and Emezue 1997, pp. 124–31.
12. See the interesting account in Gbulie 1989, pp. 108–60.
13. Clapham 1998, pp. 6–7.
14. Mus 1952. Characteristically, Mus was both a scholar and for a time a political adviser to general Jacques Philippe Leclerc, the leader of the French forces in Vietnam after the Second World War. See the brief biography of Mus in Thion 1981.

15. Lonsdale 1990, p. 421.
16. Cooper 1988, p. 317, n. 13.
17. Gluckman 1963, p. 139.
18. *Ibid.*, pp. 144–5.
19. Cohn 1957; Worsley 1957; Hobsbawn 1959. Cf. Gluckman's comments on this development in Gluckman 1963, pp. 137–8.
20. Influential works in this tradition include Sundkler 1948; Shepperson and Price 1958; Ajayi 1965; Ayandele 1966; Welbourn and Ogot 1966.
21. See, for instance, Hodgkin 1956, ch. 3; Abun-Nasr 1965; Kaba 1974; cf. the earlier study by Evans-Pritchard 1949 which pointed in the same direction.
22. Scott 1985.
23. Ranger 1985.
24. Lan 1985.
25. Geffray 1990.
26. See, for instance, Linden 1980. More recent research on the role of religion in the Zimbabwean war includes Bhebe and Ranger 1996; Kriger 1992; McLaughlin 1996; Maxwell 1999, Bhebe 1999 and, for a wider context, Alexander, McGregor and Ranger 2000.
27. See Walshe 1991.
28. Richards 1996.
29. Richards 1996, p. xvi.
30. Kaplan 1994, p. 14. Richards sees Kaplan's article as the prime example of the New Barbarism thesis. For the influence of Kaplan's article see Richards 1994, p. xiv and Ellis 1999, pp. 18–20.
31. Richards 1996, pp. 12, 13.
32. Richards 1996, p. xxv. See also the remarks on Richards in Ellis 1999, pp. 20–1.
33. Richards, pp. 124–5.
34. Ellis 1999.
35. Ellis 1999, pp. 23–5.
36. For the following see Ellis 1999, pp. 220–80.
37. Ellis 1999, pp. 265–6.
38. This account of Alice Lakwena's movement is based on Behrend 1999, *passim*.
39. For Kony's army see Behrend 1999, pp. 179–90 and Doom and Vlassenroot 1999.
40. Richards' discussion of the enclave or sect society is partly inspired by Douglas 1993 and Sivan 1995 who both offer comparative conceptual discussions of great relevance for the understanding of religious dimensions of African guerrilla armies, not least related to the use of notions of purity in the establishment of an exclusive sectarian community.
41. See the accounts by children who were abducted by Kony's army and later escaped, in Human Rights Watch/Africa 1997, pp. 30–9.
42. Hutchinson 1996, pp. 299–350.
43. The experiences of the children have been described in Oostland and Berkvens 1998 and in Zutt 1994.

44. For other examples of this religious development see Nikkel 1992 and 1995, and the contributions in Wheeler 1997.
45. On the historical development of the Hamitic hypothesis see Sanders 1969. The history of the Hamitic myth in Rwanda is discussed in Taylor 1999, pp. 55–97; Prunier 1995, ch. 1; Lemarchand 1999.
46. Lemarchand 1999, pp. 13–14.
47. See Des Forges 1999, esp. pp. 65–95 and Article 19 1996.
48. For the role of the churches see also McCullum n.d.
49. Reyntjens 1999, pp. 14–15.
50. See Adeshida 2000.
51. Soyinka 1999, p. 30.
52. For the following see Reynolds 1996, pp. 41–68; Schmidt 1997.
53. Meiring 2000.
54. On the role of the faith communities see *Truth and Reconciliation Commission of South Africa Report* 1999, vol. 4, pp. 59–92; Cochrane, de Gruchy and Martin 1999.
55. Cf. Maxwell 1999.

BIBLIOGRAPHY

Abun-Nasr, Jamil M. 1965, *The Tijaniyya: A Sufi Order in the Modern World*, London, Oxford University Press.

Adeshida, Emma 2000, '"Truth commission" reconciles enemies', *West Africa*, 20–6 November, pp. 16–17.

Agu, Oganna 1991, 'Songs and War: The Mixed Messages of Biafran War Songs', *African Languages and Cultures*, vol. 4, pp. 5–19.

Ajayi, J. F. Ade 1965, *Christian Missions in Nigeria 1841–1891: The Making of a New Elite*, London, Longman.

Alexander, Jocelyn, JoAnn McGregor and Terence Ranger 2000, *Violence and Memory: One Hundred Years in the 'Dark Forests' of Matabeleland*, Oxford: James Currey.

Amadiume, Ifi and Abdullahi An-Na'im (eds) 2000, *The Politics of Memory: Truth, Healing and Social Justice*, London: Zed Books.

Article 19 1996, *Broadcasting Genocide: Censorship, Propaganda and State-Sponsored Violence in Rwanda 1990–1994*, London: Article 19.

Ayandele, E. A. 1966, *The Missionary Impact on Modern Nigeria 1842–1914. A Political and Social Analysis*, London: Longman.

Behrend, Heike 1999, *Alice Lakwena and the Holy Spirits. War in Northern Uganda 1985–97*, Oxford: James Currey.

Berman, Bruce and John Lonsdale 1992, *Unhappy Valley. Conflict in Kenya and Africa*, Book II: *Violence and Ethnicity*, London: James Currey.

Bhebe, Ngwabi 1999, *The ZAPU and ZANU Guerrilla Warfare and the Evangelical Lutheran Church in Zimbabwe* (Studia Missionalia Upsaliensia, LXXII), Gweru: Mambo Press.

Bhebe, Ngwabi and Terence Ranger (eds) 1996, *Society in Zimbabwe's Liberation War*, Oxford: James Currey.

Clapham, Christopher 1998, 'Introduction: Analysing African Insurgencies', in Christopher Clapham (ed.), *African Guerrillas*, Oxford: James Currey, pp. 1–18.

Cochrane, James, John de Gruchy and Stephen Martin (eds) 1999, *Facing the Truth. South African Faith Communities and the Truth and Reconciliation Commission*, Cape Town: David Philip Publishers.

Cohn, Norman 1957, *The Pursuit of the Millennium. Revolutionary Millenarians and Mystical Anarchists of the Middle Ages*, London: Secker and Warburg.

Cooper, Frederick 1988, 'Mau Mau and the Discourses of Decolonisation', *The Journal of African History*, vol. 29, pp. 313–20.

Des Forges, Alison 1999, *'Leave None to Tell the Story'. Genocide in Rwanda*, New York, Human Rights Watch.

Doom, Ruddy and Koen Vlassenroot 1999, 'Kony's Message: A New *Koine*? The Lord's Resistance Army in Northern Uganda', *African Affairs*, vol. 98, pp. 5–36.

Douglas, Mary 1993, *In the Wilderness. The Doctrine of Defilement in the Book of Numbers*, JSOT Supplement Series 158, Sheffield: JSOT Press.

Ellis, Stephen 1999, *The Mask of Anarchy: The Destruction of Liberia and the Religious Dimension of an African Civil War*, London: Hurst.

Evans-Pritchard, E. E. 1949, *The Sanusi of Cyrenaica*, Oxford: Clarendon Press.

Fox, Renée C., Willy de Craemer and Jean-Marie Ribeaucourt 1965–1966, "The Second Independence': A Case Study of the Kwilu Rebellion in the Congo', *Comparative Studies in Society and History*, vol. 8, pp. 78–109.

Gbulie, Ben 1989, *The Fall of Biafra*, Enugu: Benlie Publishers.

Geffray, Christian 1990, *La cause des armes au Mozambique. Anthropologie d'une guerre civile*, Paris: Karthala.

Gluckman, Max 1963, *Order and Rebellion in Tribal Africa: Collected Essays with an autobiographical introduction*, London: Cohen and West.

Harneit-Sievers, Axel, Jones O. Ahazuem and Sydney Emezue 1997, *A Social History of the Nigerian Civil War. Perspectives from Below*, Enugu: Jemezie Associates.

Hobsbawn, E. J. 1959, *Primitive Rebels: Studies in Archaic Forms of Social Movement in the 19th and 20th Centuries*, Manchester University Press.

Hobsbawn, Eric 1996, *The Age of Extremes: A History of the World, 1914–1991*, New York: Vintage Books.

Hochschild, Adam 1999, *King Leopold's Ghost: A Story of Greed, Terror, and Heroism in Colonial Africa*, Boston, MA: Mariner Books.

Hodgkin, Thomas 1956, *Nationalism in Colonial Africa*, London: Frederick Muller.

Holt, P. M. 1970, *The Mahdist State in the Sudan 1881–1898: A Study of its Origins, Development and Overthrow*, Oxford: Clarendon Press.

Human Rights Watch/Africa 1997, *The Scars of Death: Children Abducted by the Lord's Resistance Army in Uganda*, New York: Human Rights Watch.

Hutchinson, Sharon 1996, *Nuer Dilemmas: Coping with Money, War, and the State*, Berkeley: University of California Press.

Iliffe, John 1979, *A Modern History of Tanganyika*, Cambridge University Press.

Kaba, Lansiné 1974, *The Wahhabiyya: Islamic Reform and Politics in French West Africa*, Evanston, IL: Northwestern University Press.

Kaplan, Robert D. 1994, 'The Coming Anarchy', *The Atlantic Monthly*, vol. 273, no. 2, pp. 44–76 (quoted from http://www.theatlantic.com/atlantic/election/connection/foreign/anarcf.htm).

Kirk-Greene, A. H. M. 1971, *Crisis and Conflict in Nigeria: A Documentary Sourcebook 1966–1970*, vol. II, *July 1967–January 1970*, London: Oxford University Press.

Kriger, Norma 1992, *Zimbabwe's Guerrilla War: Peasant Voices*, Cambridge University Press.

Lan, David 1985, *Guns and Rain: Guerrillas and Spirit Mediums in Zimbabwe*, London: James Currey.

Lemarchand, René 1999, *Ethnicity as Myth: The View from Central Africa*, Occasional Paper, Centre of African Studies, University of Copenhagen.

Linden, Ian 1980, *The Catholic Church and the Struggle for Zimbabwe*, London: Longman.

Lonsdale, John 1990, 'Mau Maus of the Mind: Making Mau Mau and Remaking Kenya', *The Journal of African History*, vol. 31, pp. 393–421.

Martin, Phyllis M. 1983, 'The Violence of Empire', in David Birmingham and Phyllis M. Martin (eds), *History of Central Africa*, vol. II, London: Longman, pp. 1–26.

Maxwell, David 1999, *Christians and Chiefs in Zimbabwe. A Social History of the Hwesa People c. 1870s–1990s*, Edinburgh University Press for the International Africa Institute.

McCullum, Hugh n.d., *The Angels Have Left Us: The Rwanda Tragedy and the Churches*, Geneva: WCC Publications.

McLaughlin, Janice 1996, *On the Frontline: Catholic missions in Zimbabwe's liberation war*, Harare: Baobab Books.

Meiring, Piet 2000, 'The *Baruti* versus the Lawyers: the Role of Religion in the TRC Process', in Charles Villa-Vicencio and Wilhelm Verwoerd (eds), *Looking Back Reaching Forward. Reflections on the Truth and Reconciliation Commission of South Africa*, University of Cape Town Press, pp. 123–31.

Moosa, Ebrahim 2000, 'Truth and Reconciliation as Performance: Spectres of Eucharistic Redemption', in Charles Villa-Vicencio and Wilhelm Verwoerd (eds), *Looking Back Reaching Forward: Reflections on the Truth and Reconciliation Commission of South Africa*, University of Cape Town Press, pp. 113–22.

Mus, Paul 1952, *Viêt-Nam: Sociologie d'une guerre*, Paris: Le Seuil.

Nikkel, Marc 1992, 'Aspects of Contemporary Religious Change among the Dinka', *Journal of Religion in Africa*, vol. XXII, pp. 78–94.

——— 1995, 'The Cross of Bor Dinka Christians: a Working Christology in Face of Displacement and Death', *Studies in World Christianity*, vol. 1, pp. 160–85.

Nuttall, Sarah and Carli Coetzee (eds) 1998, *Negotiating the Past: The Making of Memory in South Africa*, Cape Town: Oxford University Press.

Oostland, Rolanda and Ronald Berkvens 1998, *Sudanese Life Stories. Voices from Kakuma Refugee Camp*, Utrecht: Churches in Action and Pax Christi.

Prunier, Gerard 1995, *The Rwanda Crisis 1959–1994: History of a Genocide*, London: Hurst.

Ranger, T. O. 1967, *Revolt in Southern Rhodesia 1896–7: A Study in African Resistance*, London: Heinemann.

Ranger, Terence 1985, *Peasant Consciousness and Guerrilla War in Zimbabwe: A Comparative Study*, London: James Currey.

Reynolds, Pamela 1996, *Traditional Healers and Childhood in Zimbabwe*, Athens: Ohio University Press.

Reyntjens, Filip 1999, *Talking or Fighting? Political Evolution in Rwanda and Burundi, 1998–1999*. Current African Issues No. 21, Uppsala: Nordiska Afrikainstitutet.

Richards, Paul 1996, *Fighting for the Rain Forest: War, Youth and Resources in Sierra Leone*, Oxford: James Currey.

———— 2001, '"Witches", "Cannibals" and War in Liberia', *Journal of African History*, vol. 42, pp. 167–9.

Sanders, Edith R. 1969, 'The Hamitic Hypothesis: its Origin and Functions in Time Perspective', *Journal of African History*, vol. X, pp. 521–32.

Schmidt, Heike 1997, 'Healing the Wounds of War: Memories of Violence and the Making of History in Zimbabwe's Most Recent Past', *Journal of Southern African Studies*, vol. 23, pp. 301–10.

Scott, James C. 1985, *Weapons of the Weak: Everyday Forms of Peasant Resistance*, New Haven: Yale University Press.

Shepperson, George and Thomas Price 1958, *Independent African: John Chilembwe and the Origins, Setting and Significance of the Nyasaland Native Rising of 1915*, Edinburgh University Press.

Sivan, Emmanuel 1995, 'The Enclave Culture', in Martin E. Marty and R. Scott Appleby (eds), *Fundamentalisms Comprehended* (The Fundamentalism Project, vol. 5), University of Chicago Press, pp. 11–68.

Soyinka, Wole 1999, *The Burden of Memory, the Muse of Forgiveness*, New York: Oxford University Press.

St. Jorre, John de 1972, *The Nigerian Civil War*, London: Hodder and Stoughton.

Stremlau, John J. 1977, *The International Politics of the Nigerian Civil War 1967–1970*, Princeton University Press.

Sundkler, Bengt G. M. 1948, *Bantu Prophets in South Africa*, London: Lutterworth Press.

Tamuno, Tekena N. and Samson C. Ukpabi (eds) 1989, *The Civil War Years* (*Nigeria Since Independence: The First Twenty-Five Years*, vol. VI), Ibadan: Heinemann Educational Books.

Taussig, Michael 1987, *Shamanism, Colonialism, and the Wild Man: A Study in Terror and Healing*, University of Chicago Press.

Taylor, Christopher C. 1999, *Sacrifice as Terror: The Rwandan Genocide of 1994*, Oxford: Berg.

Thion, S. 1981, 'Paul Mus (1902–1969)', *Hommes et Destins*, tome IV, pp. 531–3 (quoted from http://abbc.com/totus/1981–1990/152biomus.html).

Truth and Reconciliation Commission of South Africa Report 1999 [1998], vols. 1–5, Cape Town: Truth and Reconciliation Commission.

Walls, A. F. 1978, 'Religion and the Press in "the Enclave" in the Nigerian Civil War', in Edward Fasholé-Luke, Richard Gray, Adrian Hastings and Godwin Tasie (eds), *Christianity in Independent Africa*, London: Rex Collings, pp. 207–15.

Walshe, Peter 1991, 'South Africa: Prophetic Christianity and the Liberation Movement', *Journal of Modern African Studies*, vol. 29, pp. 27–60.

Welbourn, F. B. and B. A. Ogot 1966, *A Place to Feel at Home: A Study of Two Independent Churches in Western Kenya*, London: Oxford University Press.

Werbner, Richard (ed.) 1998, *Memory and the Postcolony: African Anthropology and the Critique of Power*, London: Zed Books.

Wheeler, Andrew C. (ed.) 1997, *Land of Promise. Church Growth in a Sudan at War*, Nairobi: Paulines Publications Africa.

Worsley, Peter 1957, *The Trumpet Shall Sound: A Study of 'Cargo' Cults in Mela - nesia*, London: MacGibbon and Kee.

Young, Crawford 1965, *Politics in the Congo: Decolonization and Independence*, Princeton University Press.

Zutt, Johannes 1994, *Children of War: Wandering Alone in Southern Sudan*, n.p., UNICEF.

SPIRITUAL FRAGMENTS OF AN UNFINISHED WAR

Sharon Elaine Hutchinson

While the entire population of South Sudan has been engulfed in a devastating civil war since 1983, rural Dinka and Nuer communities of the Upper Nile, Bahr-el-Ghazal and Jonglei Provinces have suffered most intensely.[1] These two ethnic groups, the two largest in the South, have supplied the bulk of the southern military forces seeking to overthrow the northern-dominated, national Islamic state in Khartoum. Since 1991, however, intensifying leadership struggles and violent confrontations among South Sudanese themselves has devastated their traditional homelands. Whereas the political and economic forces fuelling these conflicts have been analysed from a wide variety of perspectives,[2] this paper concentrates on religious dimensions of, what has become, the world's longest surviving and most lethal civil war. To what extent have these people succeeded, if at all, in maintaining a sense of spiritual hope, a sense that God still cares and that all of these deaths are not meaningless? More specifically, this paper traces the dynamic interplay between militarism, Christianity and indigenous prophecy as contemporary forces of religious change in South Sudan, with special reference to rural Nuer communities of the Western Upper Nile during the 1991–9 period. It shows how this war has simultaneously promoted processes of religious innovation and spiritual intensification and processes of secularism and militarism. Both trends, I argue, must be understood in terms of deeper shifts in Nuer interpretations of the nature of homicide, the meaning of death and the role of Divinity in maintaining human morality.

CONTEMPORARY REALITIES

Having lost much of their homeland population to the ravages of war, famine, disease and displacement since the Sudan People's Liberation Army (SPLA) the main opposition guerrilla movement—exploded into two warring factions in 1991, contemporary Nuer and Dinka men and women alike complain of being 'exhausted by death'. Civilians on both sides of this ethnic divide desire nothing more than an end to the military stalement between the SPLA leader, Dr. John Garang, and his arch rival, Dr. Riek Machar, so as to protect 'the few [people] who are still alive'.

Between 1983 and 1991 Dr. Garang, a Dinka from Bor, and Dr. Machar, a Nuer from the Western Upper Nile, fought side by side against a common foe: the national Islamic state in Khartoum. However, in August 1991 Dr. Machar and two other discontented SPLA officers launched an unsuccessful coup against their commander-in-chief, Dr. Garang. After failing to gain control of the entire movement, they broke away to form an independent rebel movement, known at first as 'SPLA-Nasir.' Garang immediately rallied his supporters to form the 'SPLA-Torit' or 'SPLA-Mainstream' faction.

The 'two doctors' divided initially over the question of whether or not the SPLA should abandon its declared aim of creating a 'united, democratic, secular Sudan' in favour of 'political independence' for the South. Calls for internal political reform had also been building within the movement for years. However, it was not long before these leadership struggles took a bitter 'ethnic' turn. What followed were years of anarchic South-on-South violence that destroyed scores of Nuer and Dinka communities throughout the greater Upper Nile, Jonglei and Bahr-el-Ghazal Provinces. The region's economy—based on a mixture of pastoralism and horticulture, strengthened by seasonal fishing—rapidly collapsed. And whatever semblance of law and order existed before the SPLA split soon dissolved.

The Khartoum government avidly stoked the flames of these southern military conflicts in order to reassert its control over the enormous oil reserves located in the Western Upper Nile Province. The collapse of southern military unity also played into the hands of government propagandists who have sought to portray 'the problem of the South' as rooted in internal tendencies toward 'tribalism' rather than in the government's own discriminatory policies.

As the southern death count mounted between 1994 and 1997, the Government of Sudan (GoS) began to tighten its noose around Machar and other dissident SPLA officers. Offering Machar arms and ammunition to continue his fight against Garang, the GoS succeeded in luring him into signing a separate 'Peace Agreement', under the banner of building 'peace from within'. The 'April 1997 Peace Agreement' committed Machar and other southern signatures to grafting their remaining forces on to the national army, as the Southern Sudan Defence Forces (SSDF). In return, the government promised that southern Sudanese 'rights of self-determination' would be recognized through a southerner-wide referendum to be held after an 'interim-period' of four (or more) years.

This Agreement, however, brought anything but renewed peace to Nuer regions nominally under Machar's control. Commander Paulino Matiep Nhial, a Bul warlord formerly allied with Machar, rebelled against him in 1998 after his favoured candidate for the governorship of the Western Upper Nile was denied the position. Commander Matiep proceeded to vent his rage by burning down the bustling market centre at Ler, Machar's hometown, in June 1998 and by causing general havoc in the Western Upper Nile.

The immediate life circumstances of rural Nuer and Dinka civilians continued to spiral downwards through 2000, as a deeply fragmented and increasingly predatory southern military elite lost control over the esti-mated 1.2 billion barrels of proven oil reserves in the Western Upper Nile. With the aid of some 20,000 Chinese labourers, the GoS completed a 1,110 km oil pipeline in 1999 to carry southern crude to newly con-structed oil refineries and export depots in the North. Moreover, the cen-tral government has started to channel the profits of this 1.6 billion-dollar oil development program into the domestic construction of sophisticated weapons factories in order to bolster its seventeen-year-long assault on South Sudan and other politically marginalized regions.[3]

Although many Nuer men and women I interviewed during 1998 and 1999 remained committed to fighting against the Khartoum government, indefinitely if necessary, they were becoming rapidly disillusioned dur-ing that period with the political savvy of Riek Machar. Moreover, they were deeply frustrated by the seeming unwillingness of John Garang and Riek Machar to resolve their personal and political differences for the greater good and unity of the South.

By November 1999 there was a significant realignment of Nuer forces in which many groups abandoned the government's side and formed an independent, anti-government, military alliance, the Upper Nile Provi-sional Military Command Council (UNPMCC). Other Nuer forces split off from Machar to join with Garang's 'SPLA-Mainstream' faction. Charging the central government with violating both the terms and spirit of the 1997 Khartoum Peace Agreement, Machar finally resigned from the government in February 2000 and made his way to Nairobi, where he is currently struggling to salvage some of his former political prominence.

Whatever optimism flows through the hearts of Nuer and Dinka civil-ians at present stems from peace agreements forged by leading Nuer and Dinka chiefs and religious leaders aimed at ending, as one chief put it, 'this nasty little war that the educated [southern military elite] makes us fight'. With financial and logistical support from the New Sudan Council of Churches, three grassroots peace conferences were held between June 1998 and May 2000 aimed at ending all South-on-South violence and at restoring an atmosphere of intra- and inter-ethnic peace and trust. Nevertheless, it remains to be seen if this civilian drive for peace and reconciliation will triumph over intensifying governmental efforts to provoke further South-on-South military confrontations in order to consolidate its hold over the tremendous oil wealth of the South.[4]

PART ONE: THE RISE OF SOUTHERN MILITARISM

From the SPLA's inception, John Garang and other high-ranking SPLA officers adopted a profoundly secularist vision of their fight against the Islamicist zeal and racialist policies of the Khartoum government. The popular desire in the South was to secede from the North. However, the stated policy of the SPLA leadership was to liberate the entire Sudan and to establish a democratic, secular state.

The willingness of southern civilians to bear the cost of feeding and housing an unpaid guerrilla army was simply assumed from the outset. Consequently, early SPLA leaders devoted very little energy to clarifying their political objectives for rural civilians. Indeed, this would have been difficult, considering Garang's efforts to couch the movement's political aims in terms acceptable to his principal ally during the 1980s, Mengistu's Ethiopian Derg regime, as well as to the Organization of African Unity and other international actors. 'We know what we want' was a popular expression used by Garang and other southern politicians prior to the 1991 split in veiled recognition of underlying southern desires for political independence. Nevertheless, Garang's reluctance to give more explicit recognition of these sentiments ultimately undercut budding southern sentiments of national identity. This identity had matured considerably during the first civil war era (1965–72) and during a subsequent period of southern regional autonomy (1972–83). Garang's reticence on this matter created a political rift that began to pull the movement apart from within, even as it succeeded to drive the national army out of much of the South during the 1983–91 period.

At first, the movement extracted recruits and supplies from the civilian population through local chiefs and headman, who were responsible for making their own arrangements with their respective constituencies. This system, however, gradually broke down. And as the war expanded and troop discipline declined, many soldiers took it upon themselves to obtain their material requirements on an individualized, ad-hoc basis. When the war was low key, this looting of civilian resources was limited. However, as the banditry of individual field commanders and warlords gained momentum after 1991, so, too, did the individual commandeering of civilian resources. Following the split, a pattern of tit-for-tat cattle raiding developed between rival Nuer and Dinka military units. The final result was a steady siphoning of civilian livestock into the hands of opposed southern military units.

STRIPPING HOMICIDE OF ITS SPIRITUAL DIMENSIONS

Mustering an effective guerrilla force requires more than a rich cache of arms. Recruits must be taught to kill on command and without remorse. In western Nuer regions of South Sudan, this feat required a temporary suspension of, if not complete dismantling of, former ethical restraints on intra and inter-ethnic warfare. Before this war and indeed up until the 1991 splitting of the SPLA, Nuer and Dinka combatants did not target unarmed women, children or elderly persons in violent confrontations between themselves. Local ethical codes also condemned the burning of houses and the slashing of crops. Any breach of these ethical limits was considered a direct affront against God or Divinity (*kuoth nhial*), as the ultimate guardian of human morality. The expectation was that God would punish the transgressor (or someone closely related to him) through manifestations of sudden death, disease or some other misfortune. Acts of inter-Nuer homicide, moreover, were governed by an even stricter set of ethical norms, which required, among other things, that the slayer be ritually purified of the 'embittered' blood of his victim. Failure to do so left the slayer vulnerable to a highly contagious and lethal form of pollution known as *nueer*.[5]

This set of spiritual beliefs, however, was not shared by neighbouring Baggara (or 'cattle-focused') Arab groups to the north. Consequently, when the central government began arming northern Misseriyya and Rizeiqat Arab militias and encouraging them to raid deep into Nuer and Dinka territories during the mid-1980s, they had few qualms about targeting entire southern communities for annihilation. Indeed, they had been trained in counterinsurgency methods directed at eliminating the civilian support base for the SPLA. At that time, guns were still rare among Dinka and Nuer groups located in the Western Upper Nile and Bahr-el-Ghazal Provinces. It was thus easy for northern Baggara militias, mounted on horseback and wielding government-supplied AK 47s, to raid for Nuer and Dinka slaves and cattle during dry-season incursions. The intensity of these attacks was such that fleeing Nuer and Dinka civilians were often forced to abandon dead and wounded kinsmen to hyenas and birds of prey. One can imagine the psychological distress this created among survivors: terrifying images of birds clawing at wounded human flesh, in fact, subsequently captured the imagination of some converts to Christianity who invoked them as validations of the idea that this war is a form of punishment from God (cf. Hutchinson 2001 and Nikkel 1996).

However, the initial reaction of non-Christian Nuer living in the Western Upper Nile—which constituted the overwhelming majority of the population in the mid-1980s—was to consider this calamity coming directly from God or the 'Divinity of Above' (*kuoth nhial*) as the ultimate source of life and death. In fact, Western Nuer villagers began to equate 'bullet victims' with 'lightning victims' as a special category of spirit—known as *col wic*—which could be potentially transformed, when properly honoured and propitiated, into a guardian spirit and reachable manifestation of Divinity.[6] Lightning victims were not mourned like other deaths. Rather, the spirits of people killed by lightning were said to have been 'chosen' by Divinity, for reasons that surviving kin would not presume to understand. Such 'spirits' were thought to be taken directly by God 'up into the sky', where they blazed a uniquely direct—and hence, potentially beneficial—channel of divine supplication and communication for surviving kin. In times of grave danger, when death appeared imminent, there was no more effective means of prayer than to call upon one's family *col wic* for divine guidance and protection. By thus equating the roar and flash of lightning with those of guns, rural Nuer villagers succeeded in transforming their growing vulnerability to government guns into symbolic assertions of greater individual and collective control over the consequences of homicide. And they did so with a sense of religious optimism. This particular set of spiritual beliefs also gave men added courage in facing the superior arms wielded by Baggara raiders barrelling down from the North. In fact, many Nuer believed that *col wic* were such powerful guardian spirits that they could even protect surviving kin from bullets.

During 1987, however, Dr. Riek Machar, who was then reigning SPLA Zonal Commander of the Western Upper Nile, managed to solidify the region's defences and eventually negotiated a truce with various Baggara militias which supported long-distance trading in place of raiding. A new market centre at Rubnyagia was created and soon became a major Mecca for the export of southern cattle and import of sorghum, seed, cloth, sugar, salt and other consumer goods obtained through black markets in the North. It was during this period of relative stability between 1987 and 1991 that Commander Machar became aware that many western Nuer were classifying 'bullet victims' as *col wic*. Convinced that this would 'cheapen' the notion of *col wic* spirits, which were previously quite rare, Riek Machar embarked on an ideological campaign to rupture this spiritual association and to teach Nuer villagers what amounted to a novel disregard for the dead. He argued that there were actually two kinds of war and hence, two categories of homicide. Homicides carried out as part of a 'government war' (*koor cieng*), he maintained, were completely devoid

of the social and spiritual risks associated with homicides generated by
'homeland wars' (*koor cieng*). Whereas the latter may be subject to
pressing spiritual demands for purification and restitution, homicides
produced by a 'government war' were entirely impersonal, secular and
final. There was no need to purify the slayer of his deed, no possibility of
claiming blood wealth compensation and no need to memorialise the
slain through sacrificial offers or through the posthumous marriage of
'ghost wives'. In essence, the SPLA leadership argued that the overarch-
ing political context of a 'government war' must take precedence over
the personal identities and social relations of the combatants in people's
assessments of the social and spiritual ramifications of homicide.[7]
Because these arguments were introduced at a time when the frequency
of violent deaths was rising and the size of local herds was falling, people's abilities to ensure the 'procreative immorality' of slain relatives
were already severely strained. SPLA assertions of political authority
depended on ordinary people's willingness to accept—however reluc-
tantly—that some slain relatives would be consigned to a form of social
and spiritual oblivion.

Nevertheless, with time and much 'violent coaching' Nuer SPLA recruits came to accept this revolutionary pronouncement. And in the process, they jettisoned any lingering feelings of personal accountability for
slayings carried out under military orders. Consequently, when Garang
and Machar squared off in 1991, the one remaining pillar of local ethical
codes—that prohibiting the purposeful killing of unarmed women and
children of all ages—soon crumbled. Both military factions swung their
guns around on each other's entire civilian populations. God, it seems,
was no longer watching.

Furthermore, as guns burned deeper and deeper into regional patterns
of warfare, many people began to wonder whether the spiritual consequences of intra-ethnic gun slayings were identical to those realized by
spears. Unlike handcrafted spears, the source of a bullet lodged deep in
someone's body often could not be traced with any accuracy. Often a soldier could know for certain whether or not he had killed someone. And,
as a result, a further degree of 'social distance' and 'spiritual ambiguity'
bled into Nuer interpretations of the spiritual ramifications of homicide.

MILITARY GLORIFICATIONS OF THE GUN

These historical developments were reinforced and magnified by military glorifications of the raw power of guns. Indeed, throughout the 1983–
91 period, SPLA military trainers repeatedly told their young recruits that
'the only thing' that prevented earlier generations of South Sudanese

from asserting their rightful claims to the national reigns of power was a lack of guns. On the basis of various reports about SPLA training camps gathered from Nuer recruits, it appears as if the SPLA leadership sincerely valued gun power over manpower during the early phases of this war. As former SPLA soldier explained: 'One gun can kill a thousand men'! In other words, without a gun a soldier meant little.

Consider the following comments made by a high-ranking member of the SPLA political wing during a 1998 interview:

Guns and recruits are intimately related. During the early years of the war many recruits who successfully completed their training received their guns at graduation directly from John Garang himself. And when he handed each person his gun, Garang would tell him: 'This arm is yours forever'! The idea was that there would never be a disarmament campaign again, like there was at the end of the first civil war in 1972. Never again would southerners be reabsorbed into the northern military. Rather, the idea was that: 'This gun will go with you always'. Many recruits took this statement as the truth. Even now, it often happens that, when an SPLA soldier is told to put down his gun temporarily because of some misdeed, he will object, saying: 'I won't give this gun to anyone. It is mine!

Why do we need guns', Garang would continue. 'Because the government in Khartoum won't give us our rights. Every time we try to get our rights, the Arabs resist us. But let us try not to misuse the gun or else everyone in the villages will try to get one as well. If you misuse it, you are telling other people to go and get a gun'. Because almost all the early SPLA recruits [who were trained] in Ethiopia were personally graduated by Garang, this led to their belief that it was John Garang personally who gave them their gun. They were taught to believe that the gun was their strength. The idea was: 'without the gun, you are nothing'! Everyone knows that South Sudan is going to be liberated by the gun, not by politics.

These young men were also taught that only the gun separates you from power. All those people who have come and imposed themselves on southerners—like the Arabs and the British—were able to do so because of the gun. For these reason I think that you are right, Nyarial,[8] to equate the idea of government power with the power of the gun. The problem now is that everybody owns a gun. So does that mean everybody is a government? Disarmament will be a big problem in the future because nearly all villagers are armed now. Armed SPLA guerrilla groups can't go to the cattle camps anymore and just take cows like they used to do. The local people now have guns to protect their cattle.

My impressions of emerging Nuer attitudes in this regard are also based on graphic stories told by SPLA graduates, many of whom witnessed major losses of life during their military training through starvation, abandonment, beatings, drowning, firing squads and other forms of punishment inflicted on disobedient recruits. These memories were especially vivid among Nuer who served in a special youth brigade known as 'the Red Army'. During the latter 1980s the SPLA systematically rounded up tens of thousands of Nuer and Dinka boys between the ages of six and fifteen and marched them to south-western Ethiopia for the avowed purpose of enrolling them in UNHCR-supplied schools. While some of these boys were forcibly collected on a regional quota system, others were voluntarily released by their parents in the hope that they would find a solid education and a safe refuge from the war. The subsequent plight of these 'unaccompanied minors' is well known. Many hundreds died *en route* or during their first months in Ethiopian camps. The vast majority were inducted into the SPLA army as soon as they grew strong enough to bear arms.

The result was a socially-isolated contingent of armed youths who were brutally trained not only to kill on command but also to torture whomever their military superiors designated. When some of these heavily traumatized youths eventually made the long journey back to their home areas following the mass exodus of South Sudanese refugees from Ethiopia after the May 1991 fall of Mengistu, they often experienced great difficulty 'fitting back in'. Some returned only to discover that their parents and siblings were dead or missing. Others bitterly rejected their parents and families once found, much as they felt rejected by their parents in the past. Many of those who eventually reached Kakuma, the main southern Sudanese refugee camp on the northern Kenyan border, eventually turned to Christianity. Those who remained in the South, however, were forced to survive by their wits and are now at risk of becoming a 'lost generation', with little faith in the future or themselves.

One Nuer 'Red Army' recruit, who deserted in 1992 and currently resides in Kakuma, offered the following commentary:

I don't know why we are called the 'Red Army' (*dec in lual*). But the young people are called the Red Army. We were abducted and sent to training camps in Ethiopia. There was no way to escape. I agreed to serve. I had to [agree] because, if not, my father would have felt some disadvantage at home. They transported us to the training camps. We were also enjoying ourselves. We were young. They misled us. We were told: 'You are very good people. Don't go back to your fathers.' What they said made you happy because we were fighting for the independence of our country. And they gave you a gun to chase away your enemy.... I was taught how to kill and how to torture. When I tortured, I felt very good because I was ordered to do it. I have even tortured women. When I did this, I felt nothing. Sometimes [those tortured] died and I would just throw them away.

When I think about it now, I do feel that I made a mistake. God does not command you to kill people. God creates you in his own image. But it was not my mistake. It was the mistake of the people who commanded me. It is the law. If you don't obey, they put you in prison or kill you by firing squad. I have killed people by firing squad. When I came from Ethiopia to South Sudan, I was ordered to do these things. You did it to everybody, even relatives. I can also do that. When I tortured relatives, maybe they thought I was crazy. Maybe they thought that I don't love relatives.

Clearly, this young man aged twenty-six had begun re-examining his earlier military activities in the light of Christian concepts of morality subsequently encountered while living in Kakuma. In this respect, his remarks are less representative of 'Red Army' members who have remained militarily active in the South and who, by and large, have not turned to Christianity (see below).

Nevertheless, his story underscores the degree to which the SPLA leadership sought to convince its young recruits that the life-and-death powers wielded by their military superiors operated entirely independently from those of God. For it was people's acceptance of this ideological premise upon which the secularising thrust of southern militarism ultimately depended.

THE POST-1991 RELIGIOUS TURN OF PROMINENT MEMBERS OF THE SOUTHERN MILITARY ELITE

Political tensions simmering within the SPLA High Command finally exploded in August 1991. At that time the SPLA was still scrambling to regain its footing, following the abrupt loss of its main supply lines and military bases in south-western Ethiopia after Mengistu's fall. The May 1991 collapse of Mengistu's Ethiopian regime also triggered the mass exodus of some 350,000 southern Sudanese refugees from their Ethiopian hiding places. In the ensuing chaos, Riek Machar, who was at that time the SPLA commander responsible for the entire northern front, staged his disastrous coup against Garang.

After months of intensive South-on-South fighting, mostly targeting the civilian population along ethnic lines, a military stalemate was reached. Riek Machar's predominantly Nuer forces controlled most of the countryside in the Upper Nile, and John Garang's predominantly Dinka forces held most of Equatoria and the Bahr-el-Ghazal. By the end of 1992, nearly 70% of the Bor Dinka population, Garang's home area, had been killed or displaced in what became known as 'the Bor Massacre'. Many Nuer communities in the central and western Upper Nile also suffered crippling military blows from 'SPLA-Mainstream' forces.

The dominant reaction of ordinary Nuer and Dinka civilians to this vicious outbreak of South-on-South violence was one of abhorrence. While civilians on both sides realized that this violence served no one's interests but 'the Arabs', they felt powerless to stop it. This sea change in the major focus of political violence has been dubbed by Nuer and Dinka civilians alike as 'the war of the [southern] educated [military elite]' in order to distinguish it from the 'government war' which dominated their lives during the 1983–91 period.

In order to solidify their own positions of power and to ensure a reliable stream of new recruits, rival southern military leaders endeavoured to transform earlier patterns of inter-ethnic conflicts over livestock and other scarce economic resources into a war of ethnicised violence. A system of cross-border cattle raiding developed in which rival southern military units would attack each other's civilian populations for the alleged purpose of 'recovering' cattle lost in earlier raids to the other side. However, since all 'recovered' cattle were immediately declared 'government property' to be distributed as the local field commander saw fit, the end result was a major shift of civilian cattle wealth into military byres. Local military leaders also attempted to suppress all direct channels of communication between Nuer and Dinka civilians and, more generally, to thwart many valiant efforts by local chiefs and religious leaders to restore the peace.

As the military stalemate dragged on, Machar's breakaway 'Nasir' faction became increasingly unstable, owing to internal power struggles and recurrent defections to the sides of both Garang and the national army. In an effort to shore up his dwindling support base, Riek Machar renamed his movement 'SPLA-United' and then, a year or so later in 1994, adopted the politically explicit title of the 'Southern Sudanese Independence Movement' or SSIM.

Ironically Machar also turned to indigenous prophets in the hope of bolstering his political legitimacy. He benefited indirectly from well-known passages of Ngundeng's songs, which predicted that a 'left-handed', 'unscarified' Nuer man would play a decisive role in the military fight against northern domination. The fact that Machar's paternal grandfather had achieved regional prominence as a prophet of the divinity *Teny* strengthened this spiritual association in the eyes of some supporters.

At one point Machar, who is a baptized Presbyterian, attempted to assume the status of a *kuaar muon* or 'earth priest', which is also referred to in the literature as a 'leopard-skin chief'. 'Earth priests' are a class of indigenous spiritual leaders, who are responsible for purifying slayers who have committed acts of inter-Nuer homicide, and more generally for supporting the peaceful resolution of local feuds and fights. The spiritual leaders whom Riek Machar approached with this request, however, rejected it. They respectfully informed Machar that this was primarily an inherited position, which would be inappropriate for him to assume.

Machar also enlisted the personal support of a charismatic Lak Nuer prophet named Wutnyang Gatakek shortly after the coup. Wutnyang, whose spiritual and military activities are described in detail elsewhere, came complete with his own personal army consisting of some 2,000 loyal Nuer recruits.[9] During 1991 and 1992 he travelled throughout the

greater Upper Nile Province, staging elaborate cattle sacrifices and public addresses aimed at uniting southern resistance against the Sudanese
government. He eventually mounted a major attack on the government-
held town of Malakal in October 1992. Although Wutnyang's forces succeeded in overrunning the military barracks in Malakal, he was soon
forced to withdraw, owing in part to Machar's failure to provide adequate and timely reinforcements. After that his reputation for spiritual
inspiration plummeted. This was primarily due to the tremendous losses
of life experienced by his poorly armed troops from attacks by a bevy of
helicopter gunships dispatched from Khartoum. Wutnyang had inspired
courage in his young troops by assuring them that the government's bullets would not pierce their spiritual armour, but after his Malakal defeat,
many Nuer men and women felt that he had misled them and began to
view him as a 'killer prophet', who was personally responsible for the
deaths of hundreds of his followers. Wutnyang later returned to his home
village of Peak in the central Upper Nile. There he built a large pyramid
of ash and dung. In so doing he was imitating the symbolic actions of
Ngundeng Bong, who had constructed a major pyramid one hundred
years earlier in order to 'bury' the smallpox and rinderpest epidemics that
were plaguing his people at that time.[10]

None of Machar's attempts to strengthen his political position, however, could make up for the fact that he lacked access to an international
frontier and hence to a reliable means of resupplying his troops in the
Upper Nile. Cornered and desperate, Machar was gradually drawn deeper
and deeper into the government's camp.

PART TWO: CHRISTIANITY

It was perhaps the secularising thrust of SPLA militarism that fomented
the remarkable religious efflorescence that began among the western
Nuer during the mid-1980s. For many Nuer civilians trapped in the
crossfire of opposed southern military factions, Christianity appeared to
offer a novel source of spiritual inspiration and protection from the war.[11]
On the one hand, it came to symbolize the possibility of political equality,
community development and self-enhancement in the face of the increasingly vicious *jihad* being waged against them from the north. Whereas
the Khartoum regime portrayed indigenous religions of the South as little
more than superstitious fantasies meriting forceful suppression, Christianity, being one of the three 'Religions of the Book' recognized by
Islam, offered a sturdier ideological opponent. Moreover, Christianity
appeared to many Southerners as a 'non-political' and potentially 'pan-
southern' source of identity capable of tempering the 'ethno-national'

impulses of rival SPLA and SSIM military factions. Civilian youth and women of all ages were especially attracted to Christianity's promise of more direct relations with God, unmediated by the rigid age and gender hierarchies characterizing indigenous sacrificial practices. Older men, however, showed greater reluctance to adopt a religion that undercut their privileged position as the sacrificial agents of their dependants' communications with God. For unarmed women and children, in contrast, Christianity encouraged hope in the protective powers of a compassionate and accessible God.

Although Christianity had been previously adopted by many Nuer members of the Southern educated elite, it did not succeed in attracting a massive following within rural regions of the Western Upper Nile until after this war began in 1983. Some early SPLA commanders, including Riek Machar, actively encouraged this civilian turn toward Christian conversion during the latter 1980s, having recognized its potential for galvanizing Southern resistance. Nevertheless, Machar's subsequent withdrawal to Khartoum, following his signing of the 1997 Peace Agreement, effectively removed him from engaging directly in civilian spiritual affairs. He nevertheless retained the counsel of several Nuer pastors living in Khartoum during his active involvement in the national government.

Although parallel religious trends emerging in Dinka regions fall outside the scope of this chapter, it is worth mentioning that John Garang, who was a committed secularist at the start of the war, has reportedly been combing the Bible in recent years in the hope of divining the war's outcome. In a major address delivered to an assembly of Southern Church leaders in Cairo in 1998, Garang reportedly peppered his speech with numerous quotations from the Bible, much to the astonishment of many in the audience.

Whatever their inner spiritual convictions, both Garang and Machar have been fighting against the fusion of political and religious practices advocated by the national Islamicist government in Khartoum. Both men are also intent on undermining, if not destroying, any mediating institutions standing between themselves and the loyalty of their recruits— including, if necessary, bonds of family, kinship, community and religion. Nevertheless, they cannot help but recognize the galvanizing potential of Christianity and, to a lesser extent, indigenous prophetic traditions in countering the Islamic thrust of the national government. Over the years Riek Machar has acted more opportunistically in this respect than Garang. However, if these men continue to play prominent political roles in the future, both will face continuing challenges in striking a dynamic balance between the secularising impact of their military recruitment and training programs on the one hand and the evolving religious impulses and convictions of their rural constituencies on the other.

SHARPENING DENOMINATIONAL DIVISIONS

The lightning pace of the turn to Christian conversion in this civil war among Nuer and Dinka civilians has stimulated considerable concern and debate between expatriate and local church officials over whether it is motivated by a sincere commitment to Christ's message or by sheer panic. The wholesale destruction of the countryside and pillaging of local herds has certainly reduced the faith of both people in and abilities to worship the 'old Nuer gods'. However, this situation has been complicated by the wartime introduction of numerous 'new' denominational distinctions. Before this war most Nuer Christians were self-confessed Presbyterians, a denominational allegiance that dates back to the 'spheres of influence' originally assigned to specific missions by the Anglo-Egyptian Condominium government of Sudan (1898–1955). Although a few Catholic churches were active among the Western Nuer during the early 1980s, the American Presbyterian mission originally founded among the Eastern Jikany Nuer proved much more resilient. It was not until the 1980s and 1990s that other Christian groups such as the Seventh Day Adventists, the Anglican Church and the Lutherans began to win a sizeable number of Nuer followers.

The success of these missions was closely bound up with the relief activities of a UN-led consortium of international humanitarian agencies know as 'Operation Lifeline Sudan' (OLS). The OLS was first established in 1989, after a war-induced famine struck the region in 1988 killing some 250,000 South Sudanese civilians. Operating from its base camp in Lokichokkio on the northern Kenyan border, the OLS coordinated most of the emergency aid flowing into the South over the 1990s, with—at a growing group of critics argues—little lasting impact on the physical well-being of Southern civilians. Over the years, however, an increasing proportion of this aid has been channelled through Christian-affiliated, non-governmental agencies. Increased access to the region by air has also permitted the entrance of expatriate missionaries, some of whom have consciously endeavoured to attract new converts by channelling incoming aid through specific congregations.

This in turn has created considerable confusion among rural Nuer, who are often uncertain about the significance of these new denominational distinctions. It has also resulted in considerable fluidity in people's affiliations with specific congregations—movements which were motivated in part by shifting local perceptions about which church organisations is most generous in the provision of material 'incentives' and individual opportunities for leadership and education. The founding of the first Anglican congregation among the Nuer, for example, was reportedly the consequence of a major rift within the Nuer Presbyterian Church. Two young Nuer pastors were pursuing advanced studies through Presbyterian fellowships in Nairobi, but their fellowships were abruptly cut off by Rev. Matthew Mathiang, who was then head of the Nuer Presbyterian Church, and who apparently sought to force their return to South Sudan. These men refused to accept this situation and promptly approached the head of the Anglican Church, Bishop Nathaniel Garang, who is a Bor Dinka. Bishop Nathaniel welcomed them and encouraged them to break away to establish the first Anglican Church among Nuer, which they did. One of these men was even made an Anglican bishop before his untimely death in 1998.

Consider as well the experiences of a young Nuer man named Goi, who established the first Seventh Day Adventist Church in Duar, a market centre in the Upper Nile. His father was also a Seventh Day Adventist who converted while living in Ethiopia as a refugee during the first civil war. Like his father before him, Goi attended an Adventist College in Ethiopia before returning to the Upper Nile in 1991. Here he discusses the complex politics surrounding the distribution of church-affiliated relief organisations in his home area.

When I opened the first Adventist Church in Duar, there were big problems with the Presbyterians. They would complain: 'You are taking our people away! Why don't you go and preach and get pagans from the villages?' I said, 'The Bible speaks for itself.' Later on, when the Adventist Development Relief Agency gave me 6,000 bales of cloth to distribute to my congregation, I decided that I was not going to give them to my church alone, because this would create conflict. So I gave some to RASS [the humanitarian relief wing of the SSIM] to distribute. The rest I divided into three for the Catholic, Presbyterian and Adventist churches in Duar. And it worked out When the Catholic Relief Services came with aid, some was given to the Adventists. But the problem is that the Adventists haven't had anything now for three years. In Jaibor and Mankien [located in Nuer regions of the central and western Upper Nile, respectively] Commander Matiep Nhial has now dismantled the Adventist churches. The reason he gave was: 'This church is bringing nothing.' Riek Machar has decreed that every church should work [wherever it wants]. But now Matiep has declared Mankien a Catholic area. The Catholics are much richer and now the Seventh Day Adventists are going down. Right now people don't realize this struggle is over religion. But after the war it will become a big problem. People will move from church to church, depending on funds, leadership and education. If the World Council of Churches does not lay its hands off church affairs in Sudan, it is going to increase the problem. If it would just lay off its hands, I am sure that Nuer would come up with a church they liked. They might even call it the 'Ngundeng Church'. But now people fear that if they did this, the aid would be cut off. This aid has really spoiled us—especially church aid.

Fieldwork undertaken among the Eastern Jikany Nuer during December 1999 and January 2000 revealed an even more disturbing aspect of these deepening denominational divides. In that region internal struggles over who was to lead specific church congregations erupted into violent brawls on at least two occasions. With other opportunities for civilian leadership severely constrained by local military personnel, the church has become an increasingly important venue for politically ambitious individuals as well as for the collective expression of local territorial oppositions. In this region it was the ambition of each major *cieng* or local community segment to assert its political independence *vis-à-vis* neighbouring communities either by founding its own denominational division or, when this was impractical, by gaining the most powerful position possible within a shared church hierarchy. This process—which I have dubbed 'segmentary Christianity'—was evolving most rapidly among the Eastern Gaajak Nuer, being motivated in part by increasing competition over church-supplied 'incentives' and in part by longstanding patterns of political opposition and fusion based on the logic of the feud. Unless the New Sudan Council of Churches takes steps to curb this religious fragmentation, Goi's forebodings about the future implications of this process are likely to become a reality.

SOME SOCIAL RAMIFICATIONS OF CONVERSION

Mass conversion by thousands upon thousands of Nuer and Dinka civilians during this war has also driven an ideological wedge between them and many of their seniors. While bearing a powerful message of hope, communal peace, forgiveness and redemption in a life to come, Christianity has also undercut the former religious authority of Nuer and Dinka elders and has splintered, socially and spiritually, numerous families and communities. While there is every reason to believe that 'the Christian call' will continue to attract devout converts in the years ahead, there is considerable uncertainty at present about the position local Christian leaders will adopt with regard to a wide variety of social values and practices, ranging from polygyny and ghost marriage to public dances, animal sacrifices and the prophetic powers of Ngundeng Bong and other indigenous spiritual leaders.

One of the most far-reaching of these issues concerns Christianity's stance toward widows and the levirate. In the eyes of most Nuer converts, leviratic unions are taboo. As Mary Nyaluak, a devout Catholic in her late 30s, who has been struggling to raise her two children since her husband was killed in 1984, explained in 1998: 'It is not Christian for a widow to want to have children [after her husband's death]. If you are given to your late husband's brother, he too might be killed. And if you find children outside [the levirate] as a Christian widow, it could bring problems later on. So it is better just to stay alone and to take care of the children you have'. Another Christian widow, who had only one surviving child, expressed greater ambivalence: 'The problem now is that widows among the Nuer and Dinka do not have any seeds. There is no leviratic marriage any more. Christians have given this up. So, we, widows, don't have children anymore.' Because Nuer do not equate the death of the husband with the termination of the marriage, Nuer Christian widows remain in a kind of social limbo, being free neither to remarry nor to enter into leviratic unions with their late husbands' kin. Christian principles of sexual propriety also preclude their acceptance of unrelated lovers as a means of acquiring additional heirs for their late husbands. So many of them have simply suppressed their desire for additional offspring.

Significantly, Nuer widows were not subject to adultery claims prior to the introduction of these Christian-based principles of immorality. A widow who refused to accept a leviratic union with a close kinsman from her husband's family was free to bear additional children 'in the bush'. In other words, Nuer drew a sharp distinction between a widow's procreative powers and her sexual and domestic services.[12] And this distinction underwrote the personal independence and sexual freedom many Nuer widows enjoyed. The subsequent elimination of this conceptual distinction by the Christian church has thus contributed not only to a wide 'sexual double standard' among Nuer but to a decline in women's abilities to realize their full procreative potential when rates of both widowhood and infant mortality are soaring.

PEACE INITIATIVES SPONSORED BY THE NEW SUDAN COUNCIL OF CHURCHES

Whatever currents of optimism flow through the hearts of Nuer and Dinka civilian populations at present derive from recent steps taken by leading Dinka and Nuer chiefs to end 'this nasty little war that the educated [southern military elite] makes us fight'. With the financial and logistical assistance of the New Sudan Council of Churches (NSCC), two gatherings of Nuer and Dinka chiefs took place during 1998 and 1999. The first was held in Lokichokkio, Kenya, during June 1998 and the second in Wunlit, Bahr-el-Ghazal Province during late February and early March 1999. These two 'peace conferences', both of which I attended, provided the first real opportunities since August 1991 for leading Dinka and Nuer chiefs to air their grievances openly and honestly without fear of military reprisals.

During the first ten-day conference, the chiefs gradually convinced one another of the sincerity of their desire for regional peace and reconciliation. One Nuer chief expressed the dominant mood of those attending by saying: 'There is nothing in the hearts of the Nuer and the Dinka to make this conflict. This conflict was imposed on us from outside.' Nevertheless, were it not for the personal support offered by Commander Salva Kiir, the second highest ranking officer in the SPLA and a Bahr-el-Ghazal Dinka, the Wunlit peace conference would never have taken place. John Garang refused to endorse these meetings in any way. Less than a week before the Wunlit conference was scheduled to begin, several Nuer cattle camps were attacked from the SPLA's side. These raids reportedly resulted in nine deaths, the kidnapping of several women and children, and the loss of some 2,000 Nuer cattle. When those Nuer chiefs most directly affected were asked by the NSCC organizers whether or not they wanted to suspend the peace talks in light of these events, they unanimously affirmed their willingness to continue working for peace. This decision reflected considerable courage since it required these Nuer chiefs to travel deep into SPLA territory without any military escort. It also put pressure on the SPLA leadership—and particularly Commander Salva Kiir—to identify and punish the aggressors, which he did.

In contrast to Garang's resounding silence, Machar—who had long sought to fashion himself as a regional agent of peace—wrote a formal letter to the NSCC organizers in which he voiced unconditional support for this grassroots peace initiative. A delegation of Nuer politicians from Khartoum also attended. Their attendance proved aggravating to some Dinka SPLA representatives, who allegedly worried that the Khartoum delegation would 'hijack' the peace process for its own propaganda purposes.

Despite these lingering suspicions, there is reason to hope that the Wunlit Peace Conference represents a major step forward for rural Nuer and Dinka populations located west of the White Nile. The regional chiefs agreed to return all Nuer and Dinka captives but otherwise to forgive and forget past losses in the interests of 'those of us who are still alive'. It remains to be seen whether or not these Church-sponsored peace initiatives will succeed in transcending the continuing unwillingness of Garang and Machar to resolve their personal and political differences for the greater good of the South. The Government of Sudan has also endeavoured to undermine the accomplishments of the Wunlit Peace Conference in any way it can.

Unfortunately, a third 'People-to-People' peace conference held in Liliir during May 2000 proved unsuccessful in rekindling an atmosphere of intra- and inter-ethnic peace and reconciliation among Nuer, Dinka and other South Sudanese groups living east of the White Nile.

One of the most striking aspects of all three conferences, however, was the willingness of expatriate church leaders to blend prayers and rites of cattle sacrifice offered by indigenous spiritual leaders with Christian theology. Although no prominent Nuer prophets were present at the two conferences I attended, both affairs were more ecumenical and inclusive of indigenous religious traditions than was common, in my experience, in the daily life of rural Nuer villagers. And on these grounds alone, these conferences bode well for the religious future of the South.

INDIGENOUS PROPHETIC TRADITIONS

These noteworthy steps toward increased religious tolerance and inter-ethnic peace were not shared by all segments of the population. Ordinary Nuer soldiers, for example, have by and large shunned Christianity. There is a general perception among Nuer that Christianity and active military service are incompatible. To quote one pastor: 'Christian ways and the ways of the soldiers haven't gotten together. They [the soldiers] didn't learn to treat people well. They were taught to kill and abuse. They are not becoming Christians. The ways of the soldiers and the ways of the politicians go together. There is nothing Christian there'! While it is true that many educated leaders within the local military hierarchy are self-professed Christians, the 'real' soldiers—'those carrying the guns'— I was repeatedly told, are not converting.

On one occasion I asked a prominent Dinka SPLA supporter if he thought rites of Christian conversion could some day be used to help Southern soldiers shed their remorse about military abuses they committed? He immediately countered:

But do they feel remorse? There is no evidence [that they do]. Some soldiers have committed very serious crimes. But when you see them, they are laughing and smiling. There are no signs of remorse. Whether or not they will feel remorseful in the future, we don't know. But, right now, there is no remorse. War adversely affects people's moral values. What Christianity has done is strengthen our resistance to the spread of Islamic fundamentalism.

Although rank-and-file Nuer soldiers are not converting to Christianity, many have continued to turn toward indigenous prophets and other spiritual leaders in their quest for added spiritual protection and direction while carrying out their raids on Dinka cattle camps. This split in religious trends between the civilian population and the military was readily apparent in Nuer regions during 1998 and 1999, where a resurgence of indigenous prophets was fuelled by local military personnel seeking advise about the optimal timing of their cross-border raids. Up until his death in 1998, a Nyuong Nuer prophet named Gatluak Yieh, who was known for his aggressive anti-Dinka sentiments, was routinely consulted by local SSIM military units before staging their raids on the Agar and Ciec Dinka. Similarly, a female Lou Nuer prophet named Nyalam played a pivotal role in orchestrating Nuer 'retaliatory' attacks on the Murle from the early 1990s.

There were, of course, other indigenous Nuer prophets who actively opposed this South-on-South violence, such as Gatluak Paah among the Nyuong Nuer and Gat Dengdit among the Bul Nuer. Gat Dengdit, in particular, has provided an inviolable sanctuary for many Dinka supplicants and war captives in recent years. By so doing, he has allied himself with a tradition of spiritual compassion and inter-ethnic inclusion established during the 19th century by the first and greatest of all Nuer prophets, Ngundeng Bong. What follows is a brief discussion of Dengdit's most recent efforts to quell these Southern rifts.

A PROPHET WITH A TWIST

John Mut Tut Roaa is a third-generation prophet of the divinity Gat Dengdit ('Son of the Great [Divinity] Deng'). Deng is the most powerful divinity in the Nuer spiritual pantheon, being associated with the power of lightning and fertilizing potential of rain. He is a primary channel of communication with *Kuoth Nhial* or the distant creator God or 'Divinity of the Above'. John Mut's grandfather was possessed by Gat Dengdit long before Sudan's present war. His spiritual heritage descended to his son Tut Roaa, who gained spiritual pre-eminence 'when Dinka and Nuer began fighting with pronged spears'. During one such battle Tut Roaa lost most of his cattle to Dinka raiders and allegedly slipped into a depression and died. Not long after that, Dengdit fell upon his son, John Mut. The year was 1985.

At that time northern Baggara Arab militias, wielding government-supplied AK-47 rifles and mounted on horseback, were raiding deeply into Nuer and Dinka regions of the Western Upper Nile and northern Bahr-el-Ghazal. Entrusted with the task of clearing the oil-rich lands of the Western Upper Nile of their troublesome Nilotic inhabitants, these avid slave and cattle raiders created havoc among a civilian population armed primarily with spears. The western Bul and Leek Nuer suffered terribly, losing much of their cattle wealth and many of their women and children to these dry-season attacks. Between 1987 and 1990 Riek Machar, who was reigning SPLA zonal commander of the Western Upper Nile during this period, succeeded in establishing a working truce with these marauding militias which encouraged long-distance trading over raiding.

During this period of relative peace, Dengdit's reputation as the spiritual leader of the Bul Nuer solidified. Like his father and grandfather, he became a renowned 'rain maker', who also used his spiritual powers to cure the sick and the infertile. His ability to curse with words, like that of other leading Nuer prophets, was widely respected and feared. Indeed, he became a spiritual magnet for many neighbouring Dinka communities as well, especially during periods of drought.

This SPLA-negotiated truce with various Baggara militias dissolved in 1991 with the collapse of southern military unity. Relations with neighbouring Dinka groups soon became extremely tense, as SSIM and SPLA cattle raiders stormed back and forth across this ethnic divide. Dengdit, however, opposed this explosion of violence. He opened his homestead to some fifty Dinka boys, who had been caught 'off-side' or kidnapped by SSIM raiders. He treated them as his own sons until they could return to their home areas several years later. Indeed, anyone who reached his homestead, whether Nuer or Dinka, was assured of finding physical and spiritual protection. But Dengdit could not control the actions of local SSIM officers—who remained deeply suspicious of any Nuer/Dinka contacts up until the time of the Wunlit Peace Conference in 1999.

By the mid-1990s drought-stricken Baggara cattle herders were once again seeking seasonal peace agreements with Bul Nuer chiefs in order to gain access to critical dry-season grazing lands in the Western Upper Nile. But when the season changed, some of these Baggara groups would break the truce, attacking Nuer villages and carrying off many women, children and cattle on their return north. During the early dry-season of 1998/9, Gat Dengdit called a meeting of Bul Nuer chiefs and religious leaders in which he urged them to refuse all grazing agreements with the Baggara over the coming season. As one attending Bul chief later explained: 'They will stay on their lands and we on ours! Gat Deng said "Even if their cattle have no pasturage, let them die!" [We will do this] so that they [the Arabs] know that this year we, in the South, want our country.'

Gat Dengdit also played a prominent role in helping to reunite the Twic Dinka and Bul Nuer during October 1998. He was considered a pioneer in Nuer/Dinka peace and reconciliation, successfully supporting a re-unification of many Nuer soldiers, who formerly served under Commander Paulino Matiep Nhial, with Garang's SPLA-Mainstream forces. This inter-ethnic alliance was accomplished before the 1999 Wunlit Peace Conference.

Where Gat Dengdit's spiritual leadership contrasts most sharply with that of his forefathers was with respect to Christianity. Like the prophet Wutnyang Gatakek before him,[13] he has actively encouraged his family and followers to accept Christian conversion. As William Ruei Diu, a leading Bul chief, remarked in a 1999 interview:

> Gat Deng rejects the idea of Southerners killing one another. He wants all the people to become Christians because he doesn't want them to adopt Islam—that is what he rejects! All of his children have been baptized and two of his sons are now Catholic Catechists. Gat Deng is the only person in his family who has not been baptized.

One wonders whether Gat Dengdit's preference for Roman Catholicism influenced Commander Matiep's recent declaration of Mankien, the district capital of the Bul Nuer, as a 'Catholic zone'. Be that as it may, Gat Dengdit's ecumenical embrace of Christianity represents an extension of longstanding traditions of religious tolerance advocated by indigenous Nuer prophets as well as an implicit recognition that Christianity currently offers a more sturdy bulwark against northern attitudes of religious and racial superiority. It remains to be seen whether or not Bul Nuer soldiers will follow Gat Dengdit's advice and convert to Christianity. As things stand, however, most Nuer soldiers have either drifted to contemporary Nuer prophets or retained a secularist viewpoint. In the eyes of the latter, the only power of real value remains that of the gun.

THE ENDURING FORCES OF SECULARISM

'Although these soldiers were our children yesterday and should understand the primacy of spiritual life, they act as if they are from a different world. They are the same on both sides.'

These words were uttered by an Apuk Dinka chief, who witnessed at first hand the tragic consequences of this disregard for spiritual matters demonstrated by some Southern military personnel. In 1997 he and other community leaders from the Apuk and Twic Dinka embarked on a religious pilgrimage to the home of Deng Loth, another renowned western Nuer prophet, in quest of rain. Their mission demanded considerable courage. After all, opposed Southern military factions had ruthlessly suppressed all direct contact and communication between Nuer and Dinka civilians since 1991. Nevertheless, these Dinka leaders were hopeful that their peaceful motives and traditional status as spiritual suppliants, who were considered immune from attack, would be respected. When they reached Deng Loth's homestead, however, the prophet was nowhere to be found. Nor did he return to receive his guests. Instead

Deng Loth, who feared being accused of 'harbouring spies', took the pre-caution of informing the local military commander of the Dinka chiefs' arrival. Although Deng Loth expected the military to understand the usual protocol regarding spiritual exchanges of this sort, the command-ing officer proceeded to arrest all of the Dinka leaders on charges of spy-ing for the SPLA. Four Dinka leaders were killed and the others were imprisoned for five months before being allowed to return home. This event sent a wave of pessimism throughout the Apuk and Twic Dinka, who began to lose hope of ever restoring peaceful border relations.

Although these feelings of despair have been tempered by the success of the 1999 Wunlit Peace Conference and other grassroots peace initia-tives, the deep-rooted secularism of many Southern troops and warlords remains profoundly dangerous and disturbing in the eyes of many Nuer and Dinka—Christians and 'traditionalists' alike.

We have seen how the secularising thrust of southern militarism was motivated in large part by SPLA leaders seeking to convince their rank-and-file recruits that the life-and-death powers they wielded operated entirely independently from those of God. Homicides carried out under the orders of a military superior were proclaimed impersonal, final and pollution-free. Note that this revolutionary proclamation did not require Nuer and Dinka fighters to deny the essential humanity of their military targets. Many SPLA soldiers were, in fact, forced to participate in disci-plinary firing squads aimed at fellow recruits. All that was required was their acceptance of a situational withdrawal of divine interest and con-cern—a withdrawal that was subsequently elaborated by many South Sudanese, as we have seen, in terms of the justified anger of God. In this perspective, what might otherwise appear to be parallel processes of reli-gious intensification and of military secularism converge in an image of eroding ethical constraints and values.

'War adversely affects people's moral values' is a statement which few, if any, contemporary Nuer would challenge. Moreover, when the world appears shattered and cursed, one of the few things people can do to maintain their faith in the future and in themselves is to band together to reaffirm their collective commitment to God's will—however that may be defined. At present, these reaffirmations remain fragmented by deep-ening denominational divisions and by a multiplicity of indigenous pro-phets. Additional evidence suggests that they are further subdivided by the divergent religious leanings of a largely Christianised civilian popula-tion, a secularised military hierarchy and a more prophet-oriented coterie of rank-and-file soldiers. Nevertheless, there are ample possibilities for future religious fusion. Although rank-and-file Nuer soldiers have thus far tended to resist Christianity's pull in the interest of receiving more immediate and definitive answers to their security questions through indigenous prophets, there is nothing to preclude the emergence of more Christian-oriented prophets in the future, as the ecumenical leanings of both Gat Dengdit and Wutnyang Gatakek bear witness. Looking toward comparative examples among the Nilotic Acholi in Uganda, the spiritual movements of Alice Lakwena and Joseph Kony—though hardly positive in their impact on regional peace and harmony—reveal, nevertheless, the possibility of creative fusions of Christian doctrine with indigenous prophetic traditions.[14] Manifestations of the Holy Ghost or the spirits of Jesus or Mary are by no means precluded by the ecumenical openness of Nuer religious practice. In fact, possession is becoming an increasingly accepted and desired aspect of religious worship among some Nuer congregations, particularly within the Anglican Church. The Nuer Presbyterian leadership, in contrast, has tended to stigmatise such spiritual manifestations as the work of the devil.

At present, there are two major factors inhibiting the possibility of Nuer Christian congregations evolving in this direction—first, people's deepening dependence on church-sponsored, humanitarian aid distributed by expatriate church officials in Nairobi and beyond and, second, the continuing reluctance of Nuer evangelists and local church leaders to return the ecumenical embrace extended by Nuer prophets. Unless expatriate church officials refrain from reinforcing denominational differences or otherwise interfering in the spontaneous development of local religious practice, the progressive religious and social fragmentation of Nuer communities will create, as Goi remarked, 'a big problem' when this war ends.

NOTES

1. Andrew Wheeler's excellent contribution to this volume provides historical overviews of Sudan's first civil war (1955–72) and the early phases of the current war (1983–present). This chapter concentrates on historical developments associated with the post-1991 collapse of Southern political and military unity. Much of the ethnographic material presented here was gathered during a total of four months of field research conducted between May 1998 and January 2000. This information is supplemented by more than two years of field research carried out between 1980 and 1996. My most recent field trips were funded by fellowships from the Harry F. Guggenheim Foundation, for which I am profoundly grateful. I also wish to thank the PEW Evangelical Scholars Program for having awarded me a Senior Fellowship during the 1998–9 academic year, which allowed me to develop many of the themes incorporated here.

2. Significant recent publications on processes of political fragmentation in the South include: Daly and Sikainga 1993; Fukui and Markakis 1994; Johnson 1998; Human Rights Watch 1999 and 2000; Nyaba 1997; Jok and Hutchinson 1999, and Hutchinson 2000 and 2001.
3. See especially Human Rights Watch 2000 and Amnesty International 2000.
4. Jok and Hutchinson 1999; Human Rights Watch 2000.
5. See Hutchinson 1992, 1996 and 1998, for details.
6. See also Evans-Pritchard 1949 and 1956.
7. Hutchinson 1996 and 1998.
8. Nyarial ('daughter of the black and white splashed cow') is the author's Nuer name.
9. See Hutchinson 1996, pp. 338–45.
10. See also Johnson 1994.
11. For comparative discussions of this wartime turn to Christianity among South Sudanese see Wheeler 1997.
12. See Gough 1971.
13. Hutchinson 1996, pp. 339–40.
14. Behrend 1999.

BIBLIOGRAPHY

Amnesty International 2000, *Sudan: The Human Price of Oil*, London: Amnesty International Press.

Behrend, Heike 1999, *Alice Lakwena and the Holy Spirits: War in Northern Uganda, 1986–97*, Oxford: James Currey.

Daly, M. W. and Ahmed A. Sikainga (eds) 1993, *Civil War in the Sudan*, London: British Academic Press.

Evans-Pritchard, E. E. 1949, 'The Nuer *Col Wic*', *Man*, vol. 49, pp. 7–9.

———— 1956, *Nuer Religion*, Oxford: Clarendon Press.

Fukui, K. and J. Markakis (eds) 1994, *Ethnicity and Conflict in the Horn of Africa*, Oxford: James Currey.

Gough, K. 1971, 'Nuer Kinship: A Re-examination', in T. Beidelman (ed.), *The Translation of Culture: Essays to E. E. Evans-Pritchard*, London: Tavistock, pp. 79–121.

Human Rights Watch 1999, *Famine in Sudan, 1998: The Human Rights Causes*, New York, Human Rights Watch.

Human Rights Watch 2000, *Sudan, Oil and Human Rights*, New York: Human Rights Watch.

Hutchinson, Sharon E. 1992, 'Dangerous to Eat: Rethinking Pollution States among the Nuer', *Africa*, vol. 62, pp. 490–504.

———— 1996, *Nuer Dilemmas: Coping with Money, War and the State*, Berkeley: University of California Press.

———— 1998, 'Death, Memory and the Politics of Legitimation: Nuer Experiences of the Continuing Second Sudanese Civil War', in Richard Werbner (ed.), *Memory and the Postcolony: African Anthropology and the Critique of Power*, London: Zed Books, pp. 58–70.

—— 2000, 'Nuer Ethnicity Militarized', *Anthropology Today*, vol. 16 (2), pp. 6–13.

—— 2001, 'A Curse From God?: Religious and Political Dimensions of the Post-1991 Rise of Ethnic Violence in South Sudan', *The Journal of Modern African Studies* vol. 39, 2 pp. 307–31.

Johnson, Douglas 1985, 'Foretelling Peace and War: Modern Interpretations of Ngundeng's Prophecies in Southern Sudan', in M. W. Daly (ed.), *Modernization in the Sudan*, New York: Lilian Barber Press, pp. 121–34.

—— 1994, *Nuer Prophets*, Oxford: Clarendon Press.

—— 1998, 'The Sudan People's Liberation Army and the Problem of Factionalism', in C. Clapham (ed.), *African Guerrillas*, Oxford: James Currey, pp. 53–72.

Jok, Jok Madut and Sharon Hutchinson 1999, 'Sudan's Prolonged Second Civil War and the Militarization of Nuer and Dinka Ethnic Identities', *African Studies Review*, vol. 42 (2), pp. 125–45.

Nyaba, P. A. 1997, *The Politics of Liberation in South Sudan: An Insider's View*, Kampala: Fountain Publishers.

Nikkel, Marc 1997, "Children of Our Fathers' Divinities' or 'Children of Red Foreigners'? Themes in Missionary History and the Rise of an Indigenous Church among the Jieng Bor of Southern Sudan', in Andrew Wheeler (ed.), *Land of Promise: Church Growth in a Sudan at War*, Nairobi: Paulines Publications Africa, pp. 61–78.

Wheeler, Andrew (ed.) 1997, *Land of Promise: Church Growth in a Sudan at War*, Nairobi: Paulines Publications Africa.

FINDING MEANING AMID THE CHAOS
NARRATIVES OF SIGNIFICANCE
IN THE SUDANESE CHURCH

Andrew C. Wheeler

CHAOS

Sudan has been at war with itself, apart from a brief and uneasy respite from 1972 until 1983, for more than 40 years. Decades of war, centred in the South, have ensured the thorough destruction of economic and social infrastructure, the collapse of educational and medical services, repeated displacement internally or into neighbouring countries, and the death, in all, of perhaps 3 million people;[1] this from a Southern population in the 1980s and 1990s of between 6 and 8 million.[2] Several generations of Southern Sudanese children have gone without education. Women and children especially have suffered all the trauma of repeated displacement, abuse, multiple bereavement, violence and grinding impoverishment. Africa's longest and most destructive conflict shows no sign of resolution as it becomes ever more complex, with a kaleidoscope of shifting alliances and loyalties as governments, factions and warlords jockey for position, power and survival. The struggle for control of the oilfields in the South only intensified the conflict in the late 1990s. Successful exploitation of the fields by the government has assisted in the funding of the war effort. The core reality for the vast majority of Southern people is an endless chaos that they have no power to control or shape, characterizing their inner world as well as their outer experience.

Yet during this period one of the dominant features of Southern society, both civil and military, is the immense growth of the Christian Church, both in numbers and as a significant social institution—a development still largely unrecognised in the outside world. This dramatic transformation has taken place in two main phases, the first from 1964 to 1972, and the second since the late 1980s.

The Anyanya civil war, 1964–72. 1964 is a key date in the evolution of the Sudanese Church. In that year, following several years of increasing

54

constraint and harassment, all missionaries in Southern Sudan were expelled. This compelled the Sudanese Churches to assume full responsibility for the leadership, administration, pastoral care and witness of their communities. Because of the war full national hierarchies were not inaugurated until the mid 1970s, but the reality had existed for a decade before that. Sheltered from the eyes of the outside world, the forces of General Abboud's military government launched a ferocious attack throughout the South on towns and villages, killing and looting without restraint.[3] The civilian population of Southern Sudan took refuge, either deep in the forests of the South, or in exile in Congo, Uganda and other neighbouring countries. This was the period in which the Church in the Equatoria area of Southern Sudan was transformed from a small community of those brought up on mission stations and in mission schools into a mass movement affecting almost every rural community. Similar dramatic changes took place amongst those thrust into exile in East Africa or in Khartoum. In the forests of Equatoria close relations existed between the settlements of the displaced and the camps of the Anyanya guerrilla forces, and Christian faith began to be the framework for an emerging Southern identity. The judgement of Lilian Sanderson, historian of Southern Sudanese education, was that, after independence in 1956 and through this period, Christian faith inevitably came to fill the 'disastrous void' in Southern identity and political expression created by the barrenness of colonial policy in the South. Faced by ruthless policies of Arabization and Islamization that sought to compel the South into submission, she writes that '… the Churches embodied doctrines and values which enabled Southerners to challenge the Northern Sudanese claim to total superiority.'[4] Certainly from the late 1950s, the movement towards the Christian faith in the South began to assume the proportions of a mass movement with a close sense of identity with the liberation movement.

By 1972 the association between the churches and the Southern Sudan Liberation Movement (SSLM) had become very close. Father Saturnino Lohure[5] was one of the founder members of SANU (Sudan African National Union), the first and most significant organisation of Southern exiles, in 1962 and remained in close consultation with the expelled Comboni[6] missionary bishop, Sisto Mazzoldi. Episcopal Church Bishop Elinana Ngalamu, exiled in Uganda, was warmly supportive of the Anyanya, the guerrilla forces fighting in Southern Sudan. Joseph Lagu, who reorganised the Anyanya into the more professionally run SSLM, was a deeply committed Christian, strongly influenced by his father who had been a close companion of the pioneer CMS[7] missionary, Archibald Shaw. Nonetheless, we cannot speak of any Christian ideology of resistance or liberation at this period. Christian faith was supportive of a deep-seated African cultural objection to religious and cultural domination

from the North. Through the provision of vernacular scriptures, vernacular education and worship expressed in the vernacular, the Christian
missionary enterprise had revitalized African culture and re-equipped it
for participation in a changing and widening world and given it tools to
resist Northern attempts at cultural and religious assimilation. But the
Christian faith provided little theological or ideological underpinning for
the resistance movement. There was little that could be called a 'liberation theology'.

1983–99: The SPLA and the return to civil war. The Addis Ababa Agreement (1972) ushered in a period of calm and consolidation for the Churches. For some years they were warmly supportive of Jaafer Numeiri
whose military coup in 1969 had paved the way for the peace agreement.
However, his increasingly Islamic agenda led to the alienation of the
South. 1983 saw the abrogation of the 1972 Addis Ababa Agreement, the
breaking up of the Southern region into three smaller regions, the imposi-
tion of Islamic *sharia* law, and the birth of the Sudan People's Liberation
Army (SPLA). This development caught the Churches unprepared. They
found themselves bewildered and confused, caught between an aggressive and Islamizing government and a violent liberation movement, dominated by the Dinka, and using a strongly Marxist rhetoric imbibed from
their Ethiopian backers. Until 1991 the Churches in the South, though
mainly under SPLA control, felt themselves marginalized and victimized
by military forces with alien ideologies. This changed with some rapidity
from 1991 when, following the fall of Mengistu, Sudanese refugees and
the SPLA were forced to flee from Ethiopia back to Sudan. This caused
the SPLA to attune itself much more closely to the values and commit-
ments of the people for whom it claimed to act, and meant, slowly and
with considerable awkwardness, beginning to listen to the Christian element in its support base, to its ecumenical expression in the New Sudan
Council of Churches, and to the increasing number of Christians within
the ranks of its army. This was the period in which the pastoral Nilotic
people (largely Dinka and Nuer) of the vast grasslands of Upper Nile and
Bahr el Ghazal turned to the Christian faith as the people of Equatoria
had done during the 1960s. Only towards the end of the 1990s, as the
SPLA became more responsive to Church concerns over human rights
and destructive inter-factional fighting, can it be said that the Church was
beginning to use the language of 'liberation' about the struggle in Sudan
with any sincerity.

It was, rather, the Islamicist regime brought in by the military coup
of 30 June 1989 that injected a strident religious tone into the conflict.
A significant step was taken in 1992 when the governor of Kordofan
declared the struggle against rebels in the Nuba mountains to be a *jihad.*

Funds and recruits were raised all over government-controlled areas of the Sudan to prosecute this *jihad*, which was notable for targeting Muslims in rebellion as well as Christians and traditionalists. Although a *jihad* has not been formally declared in the South as it was in the Nuba mountains, since 1992 the language of *jihad* and of religious war has been consistently used there as well. The militia soldiers of the Popular Defence Force (PDF) are now termed *mujahadiin*, and those slain in battle are regarded as Islamic martyrs. Grieving families are compelled to have mock weddings to celebrate their martyrdom and the joyous marriages they are enjoying in paradise. It is striking that Southern resistance has not adopted a similar stance. Whilst there is much bitter feeling against 'Arabs', rooted in the distorted racial attitudes created by slavery, and by half a century of oppression, there is relatively little anti-Islamic rhetoric. The SPLA continues, in public, to press for a secular and non-religious political system that pays proper regard to Sudan's plural identity.

The place of Christian faith in the emerging identity and political awareness of Southerners is a complex and varied relationship that would need a much more thorough analysis. The purpose of this chapter lies elsewhere, in an area so far little explored. This concerns the specifically *religious* function of Christianity during the long years of war. Christian faith has not been a decisive factor in forging the political and military ideology of resistance in the South. It has, though, been of the greatest possible importance in enabling countless thousands of ordinary people to survive, to gain a sense of purpose and meaning, and sustain hope during interminable and unspeakable suffering. It is the capacity of the Christian faith to give structure and meaning to life—to reveal the 'purpose of God'—which has been its richest contribution to Southern Sudanese during these last 40 years. These 'structures' and 'meanings' are varied, depending on the specific shape of people's experience. They are given definition in 'narratives'—in stories, accounts and events that capture in parable and symbol the meaning of the cascade of chaotic events that constantly threatens to overwhelm. From the multitude of such narratives, seven are presented here that are representative of the range of responses to the bewildering chaos of present day Sudan. They are 'narratives of significance' that indicate how Southern Sudanese Christians find meaning in the heart of confusion.

FINDING MEANING AMID THE CHAOS

1. *Spiritual Warriors: 'Jiec Amar', a Christian Red Army?*[8]

The trek from Bahr el Ghazal. One of the most powerful Christian narratives to come out of the war has been that of the young men of the *Jiec*

Amar (from the Arabic, *jesh ahmar*, meaning 'Red Army'). In 1987–8 most of Bahr el Ghazal was caught in the most appalling warinduced famine that led eventually to the death of approximately 250,000 people. Many thousands fled northwards to towns in Kordofan and even further to Khartoum. SPLA commanders, guided by the Marxist thinking the movement was absorbing from its Ethiopian mentors, saw the opportunity to mould the many thousands of displaced youth from Bahr el Ghazal and elsewhere into a 'Red Army'—an elite force of educated and ideologically sound young people, cut off from their roots, to build the 'New Sudan'. About 30,000 young boys were recruited amidst the appalling confusion prevalent in Bahr el Ghazal and taken, mostly on foot, across desolate terrain to the huge refugee camps in Ethiopia, lured by the promise of education. Many thousands died of starvation on the way.

In the camps of Ethiopia. The boys arrived in Ethiopia exhausted, sick and starving, traumatized by their experiences on the trek. Church people cared for them, struggling to keep them alive and to provide a gentler environment alongside the military discipline of the SPLA. Many came hoping to join the army and fight for liberation. Many too had been promised education, and the SPLA, which was entrusted with the administration of the camps, and the Churches combined to care for and educate the boys. An estimated 12,000 boys were in schools jointly run by the churches and the SPLA and were formed, individually and as a group, by two powerful influences—the vision of the military liberation of their country, and a daily immersion at school and in church in the narrative and the images of the Bible.[9] The values of these two processes of formation presented both compatibilities and profound dissonances. The boys were bound together by their desire for education and for participation in the liberation of their country, also by shared experience and, to a large degree, by ethnic solidarity.[10] However, the ruthless military ideology of the SPLA contrasted with the spiritual and Biblical formation provided by the Churches. It was the purpose of the military training to sever the boys from the social restraints and moral sensitivities of their traditional background and to weld them together as a tightly disciplined, politically trustworthy and ruthless youth army on a Marxist model.

These values were in tension with those the boys experienced in the Churches. Here the exclusively male environment of the military training was exchanged for the warmth of a spiritual community, predominantly composed of women, many of whom were of the age and assumed the roles of the boys' mothers. In new songs, often accompanied by dance and movement, the boys used Biblical images to describe their journey and to wrestle with its meaning. Many thousands of them were drawn into youth groups in the Churches. Large baptismal services were held, especially in the Episcopal and Presbyterian churches. The shared sufferings of the trek to Ethiopia, the shared calling to Christian faith and to the liberation struggle experienced in the camps, created strong bonds between the boys that have lasted through the subsequent years. The vision of a youthful, politically committed and revolutionary 'Red Army' was overtaken for many by the reality of a vibrant Christian youth movement, bound together by shared experience, by shared education, Bible study and spiritual songs. Here in Ethiopia many came to understand themselves to be a 'chosen generation' selected by God as his shock troops to overthrow evil spiritual powers and usher in the reign of *Nhialic*, the Creator God, revealed in Jesus Christ. This sense of being specially chosen sustained them through the many hardships ahead, and energized them for aggressive evangelism wherever they went.

The expulsion from Ethiopia, May–June 1991. The conditions of life, the provision of education and basic health care, and the building of community in the camps in Ethiopia continued to improve until May 1991 when it was abruptly terminated. The Sudan government had been backing several rebel groups in Ethiopia and in May a coalition of these groups succeeded in driving Mengistu from power. The new regime moved quickly to expel the SPLA and the Sudanese refugees. In June 1991 perhaps 300,000 refugees streamed back over the border to Sudan. They fled through heavy rains and swollen rivers as Sudan government planes bombed them from the air. Many drowned in the rivers, others died of malaria and other diseases, or of starvation and malnutrition on the way. By their thousands people made their way back to their homes in Southern Sudan, whether those areas were safe or not. People returned from Ethiopia to almost every area of the South. However, the greatest numbers made their way to Bor on the east bank of the Nile (mainly Dinka), to Upper Nile (mainly Nuer and Shilluk people) and to northern and western Bahr el Ghazal (again, mainly Dinka, who had been driven out by the Baggara militia raids of 1987–8). Some of the 'unaccompanied minors', the *jiec amar*, made their way to their home areas, though in the chaos of war it was often difficult for them to find their families.

Not all of the Red Army boys had absorbed Christian faith in Ethiopia and not all sustained it during the harsh experiences of 1991. The anthropologist Sharon Hutchinson,[11] visiting subsequently, observed large numbers of bitterly alienated young men roaming in Upper Nile. Their military socialization in Ethiopia had inured them against the emotional impact of violence and cruelty and had alienated them from the values and structures of local rural life. Cut off from the camaraderie of the camps of Ethiopia, they had become dangerous misfits, a lost, rather than a chosen, generation.

However, many thousands of the young boys knew nothing of the whereabouts of their families, and preferred to stay together. The story of their march through remote and dangerous areas of the South, from Pachalla on the Ethiopian border to Kakuma refugee camp in Northern Kenya, became internationally known.[12]

On the long march to safety in Kenya, the boys demonstrated a remarkable care and support for each other. Each contributed according to his skill and strength. Reading and writing lessons continued even as they marched. Some boys had medical knowledge as others took responsibility for cooking. The strong carried their few belongings, or even those who were sick. And when in July 1992 they eventually reached Kakuma refugee camp, specially constructed to receive them, the first items to be brought out from their scarce possessions were their red choir vests, their long wooden crosses, and any Bible or hymn book they might possess. The young 'Red Army', the *jiec amar*, had become a Christian army—though armed with cross and Bible rather than Kalashnikov. 12,000 of them settled in Kakuma and became the foundation of a vibrant Christian community there. As many were orphaned, their faith, their comradeship and the faithfulness of a Father God gave them a new sense of family, of belonging and of purpose.

Soldiers of the Cross. With the fall of Mengistu and the flight from Ethiopia, the Marxist rhetoric of the SPLA began to fade, to be replaced by greater openness to the Christian faith now ardently embraced by so many of the young men coming into its ranks. From Kakuma many of the young *jiec amar* were recruited into the SPLA, passionately committed to both political and spiritual liberation. Others returned to their home areas—notably to Bor and Northern Bahr el Ghazal—to engage in the spiritual struggle there against the spiritual divinities and powers that through their deception of the people had brought the judgement of *Nhialic*[13] upon the land.

Widely scattered across Southern Sudan's war-ravaged landscape, those members of the *jiec amar* who still sustain the faith they had learned in Ethiopia, now mostly in their 20s and 30s, continue to hold a sense of being bound together by a shared story and to see themselves as radical Christian soldiers committed to confrontation with traditional spirit powers and the spiritual liberation of their people. This fraternity and this calling have sustained them through unimaginable sufferings and loss.

2. *Building Zion here: the prophetic ministry of Paul Kon Ajith*[14]

Many of the young spiritual warriors of the *jiec amar* had originally fled to Ethiopia from the Bor area on the East Bank of the Nile, and there they returned to find themselves at the heart of a spiritual confrontation such as they relished. This confrontation between the old powers and the new had been provoked by the ministry of Paul Kon Ajith, an uncomfortable and unconventional figure reminiscent in many ways of John the Baptist.

Paul Kon Ajith: a Christian prophet? Paul Kon was one of the earliest and certainly one of the most significant figures to challenge Bor people about the spiritual meaning of the war. This traditional and illiterate pastoralist was baptized by Bishop Nathaniel Garang[15] in 1986 following a series of powerful dreams and took the name of Paul. These dreams intensified after baptism and drove him out on an extensive three-year preaching tour throughout the Bor and Kongor areas, through Upper Nile and far to the west to Bahr el Ghazal. He walked naked,[16] wearing only a belt, and carried a cross, a bell and a drum.

His message had two main thrusts. First all the shrines of the traditional spirits (the *jak*) should be destroyed together with all the objects associated with them (spears, posts, stools and drums). Secondly a huge central place of worship should be built, to be known as Zion. The location and design of this place were revealed to Paul in dreams. It was to be shaped like a cross and would be a focus of unity and reconciliation. The four traditional enemies of the area—the Dinka, the Nuer, the Murle and the Shilluk—would enter through the four arms of the building and be reconciled. Paul asserted publicly that the present war was a judgment on the people for their godlessness. If they repented and destroyed the shrines of the *jak*, peace and prosperity would return. If not, God's judgment would intensify and the land would be totally devastated. At first few in the Church or the SPLA heeded Paul's message.

The great Nuer raids, October–November 1991. Paul Kon's message suddenly gained authority and relevance during the great Nuer raids of late 1991. In August 1991 most Nuer and Shilluk forces left the main body of the SPLA, following the defection of two senior commanders, Riek Machar and Lam Akol. Following this, between September and November, armed bands of Nuer, both military and civilian, swept into Bor territory, slaughtering and destroying everything they found. An estimated million head of cattle were slaughtered or looted. Tens of thousands of people were killed, many with great brutality, and others were abducted. An estimated 250,000 people fled the area, fleeing westwards across the Nile or southwards, eventually becoming settled in three huge camps north of Nimule on the Uganda border. Here they were joined by many more thousands still seeking a home after leaving Ethiopia. It is not fully clear what lay behind this assault. The break-away commanders Riek Machar and Lam Akol only lent their support to the attack after it had begun. However, it was on a scale and possessed a ferocity that indicate that the intention was to wipe out the Dinka Bor economy, destroy the social structure of the people and with it their will to survive. Many months later, no cattle could be found any-where between Malek in the south and the borders with Nuerland in the north. Indeed it was the most devastating and desolating blow suffered by the Bor people, or probably any people in Southern Sudan, throughout the whole course of the war. It is the defining event for all that has happened amongst the Bor Dinka in the subsequent years.

The assault shook the pillars of Bor society to their foundations. The priests and guardians of the shrines of the *jak* sacrificed countless bulls in a fruitless attempt to turn back the enemy. Nuer raiders instead swept into the shrines, burning them to the ground and slitting the throats of the priests. The raids destroyed the credibility of the traditional cults. Many shrines and cult objects were destroyed, either by the Nuer or subsequently by disillusioned devotees. Some of the most famous, like the spear *Lirpiou*, were carried across the Nile to safety. The new pastors were vindicated in their assertions that the *jak* were deceptive, greedy and selfish, manipulating and controlling people for their own ends. And, most significantly, Paul Kon was vindicated. The judgement he had foretold had indeed fallen on the land. The very powers that the Bor had relied on for generations for protection were abandoned in a few brief months.

The raids of 1991 created a radical break with the past—a new framework was desperately needed. Military and civilian leaders began to implement Paul Kon's remedies. Grass, bamboo and poles in vast quantities were collected by the remnants left in south Bor for the construction of the great church of Zion at Pakeo, just north of Bor Town. This church may be the largest building of traditional construction ever built in Southern Sudan. Simultaneously, a widespread assault began on the traditional shrines of the area. Sometimes voluntarily, sometimes forcibly, the shrines were destroyed and all the artefacts used for the cult were assembled at Zion for a great holocaust. In these first months after the raids countless thousands were baptized—overwhelmed by the realization that the powers that had controlled their lives for generations had been forcibly overthrown by *Nhialic*, the true creator God, acting in judgment through the raids. There was nowhere else to hide except in Him. By the late 1990s it could well be that 90% of the Bor Dinka identified themselves as Christians, the great majority having been baptized during these months following the raids. Amongst them were many of the priests and diviners whose whole world had been overthrown, and who now sought a new spiritual home.

Very soon government military authorities in Bor Town heard of the dramatic events occurring throughout Bor area, probably from those angry with Paul Kon's leadership of the assault on the shrines. Fearful that this could develop into a military threat, soldiers were sent to Zion. On 26 December 1992 Paul Kon was captured and shot and his body hacked into pieces. His followers buried it besides the church at Zion—which strangely was not touched by the soldiers. Nevertheless, the movement he started maintained its momentum. The great church was completed and from all over the Bor area the artefacts of shrines and traditional worship were brought and stockpiled. It is said that these months were a time of intense spiritual awareness throughout the area, with dreams and visions and a powerful sense of divine presence. Finally in February 1994, an estimated 30,000 people gathered at Zion to witness the destruction through burning of the vast pile of religious artefacts that had been gathered.[17] For the Christian people of Bor it marked the final and total destruction of the old spiritual powers and demonstrated the triumph of Christ over all evil forces.

The Christian revolution in Bor has continued since these overwhelming events. However, there has been a tendency on the part of church leadership to play down Paul Kon's significance and to absorb his followers back into the mainstream of the church.

3. *Evolution or revolution? Rival visions in Bahr-el-Ghazal*[18]

The spiritual warriors of the Red Army had an important impact on one further area—northern Bahr el Ghazal, the area from which many of them had fled in 1987–8. Fortified by their confident sense that they were the 'chosen generation', they returned expecting to engage in spiritual combat for the soul of their people.

The Catholic Church: pastoral care stretched thin. Traditionally, this whole area, north and west from Tonj, had been in the Catholic sphere.[19] The expulsion of the missionaries in 1964 hit this area particularly hard, as there had been little development of an indigenous priesthood, or of an adequate body of catechists. In the following years, from the mid 1960s up to the present day, the Catholic Church in northern Bahr el-Ghazal has been very vulnerable. In 1992 Fr. Rudolf Deng[20] estimated that, at most, one quarter of the population in the old Catholic sphere would call themselves Catholic. There were few priests to administer the parishes and chapels and bring the sacraments to the people. The catechists became discouraged at the lack of support. Since the return of war in 1983 and the prevalence of raiding, displacement and famine, it has remained difficult to maintain pastoral care in the area. Many Dinka Catholics in the area continued to be Catholic in name only.

The 'chosen generation' goes to war. However, the most significant religious event of the 1990s was the abrasive intrusion into the Aweil and Gogrial area of the Episcopal Church. The aggressive young evangelists who returned to the area in 1992–3 were the very same who had made their way to Ethiopia during the great exodus of 1987–8. Some were from Catholic backgrounds, most were from traditional homes. There, as we have seen, they were moulded into the *jiec amar*, the 'Red Army' of the SPLA, but also, through the schools and the churches, experienced Christian conversion, and were integrated into the highly committed and evangelising youth groups of the Episcopal Church. Church and movement taught them to struggle for liberation both spiritual and political— and impatience with traditional custom that might inhibit the birth of the 'New Sudan.'

Wilson Garang, Santino Manut and a handful of colleagues were the first evangelists to reach the Aweil-Gogrial area in May 1992. They preached the radical message they had learned in Ethiopia—that the God of Jesus Christ, who was drawing near within the tumult of the war, required a sweeping away of all the old ancestral powers, with their shrines and sacrifices. A complete and total dependence on Christ was needed if the blessing of God and the experience of salvation were to be enjoyed. Some of the young evangelists destroyed traditional shrines—an act which earned the anger of traditional religious leaders and catechists as well as the SPLA. Some spent periods in jail for their violent disregard of local feeling and custom.

Gradually the evangelists' fire and intolerance was moderated by local stubbornness. Tolerance developed on both sides and it became possible to establish ECS churches in this formerly exclusively Catholic area. In February 1993, despite a complete absence of formal training, Wilson Garang was ordained by Nathaniel Garang and sent back to start planting churches. The first was opened at Adwor in June 1993. Whereas the emphasis of the Catholic Church at this time was on humanitarian response to human suffering, mainly through the provision of relief and education, the emphasis of the new evangelists of the ECS was on spiritual confrontation and conflict. The real problems of Bahr el-Ghazal in the perception of the young ECS evangelists were spiritual. The reliance of the people on their ancestral spirits, their shrines and sacrifices, was what separated them from God and brought all manner of troubles upon them. A radical break with the past was necessary. In response, since 1993, ECS congregations have sprung up in many centres in northern Bahr el-Ghazal.

Rival visions? Since the arrival of the *jiec amar* evangelists and the development of ECS congregations after 1992, relations with the Catholic Church have been uneasy. Particularly at first there was some feeling among catechists, local chiefs and SPLA commanders alike that this was an unwanted intrusion on the part of the ECS.[21]

However, the Catholic community in northern Bahr el-Ghazal was not greatly affected by the ECS intrusion. Under firm and effective leadership during the 1990s, the Catholic Church has recovered something of its strength and morale. Catechists have been trained, and priests, both Sudanese and expatriate, have been deployed through the region. The people have received considerable humanitarian assistance through the Catholic Church and its international partner agencies. In terms of evangelisation and engagement with the spiritual needs of the people at a time of immense turmoil, the approach of the Catholic Church has been non-confrontational. Early Verona missionaries, like their Protestant counterparts, had been hostile to traditional Dinka religious practice. Church leadership in the 1980s and '90s, influenced by the Second Vatican Council (Vatican II), has been more open—seeing the Christian revelation as a fulfilment and completion of traditional spiritual perception and insight. These various features of Catholic presence and witness have led to a consolidation of the position of the Church as an institution of service in Bahr el-Ghazal.

The young Episcopal pastors and evangelists, by contrast, have a deep sense that spiritual conflict rages over the Southern Sudan. This conflict which has several dimensions. It is between the military forces of the SPLA and those whose purpose is to eliminate the Dinka as a people. But this conflict is a reflection of a larger struggle between *Nhialic*, the Creator God who is now drawing close in judgment and salvation, and the deceiving spirits of the shrines. Only the overthrow of these spirits and the rooting out of their influence and power will avert divine judgment and bring God's peace. The vision of the 'Red Army evangelists' of Northern Bahr el-Ghazal is very similar to that of Paul Kon and the evangelists of Bor. Their impact in Bahr el-Ghazal has been among the most devastated and destitute of the people—those whose lives had been shattered by government and militia raids in the late 1980s and again in the late 1990s, and for whom the traditional framework of life—homes, cattle, family and shrines—was destroyed.[22] In this situation of widespread trauma the ECS has been gathering together a church of the destitute, providing an assurance and a demonstration of divine protection among the threatening and uncontrollable forces of war, famine, disease, spiritual assault and death.

4. *A universal vision: the apostolic journeys of Joseph Pal Mut*[23]

In a few brief months between 1990 and 1992, the Catholic Church was planted in many centres all across eastern Nuerland, in areas that had traditionally been considered Presbyterian. Although the ground had been prepared by a number of catechists and by Fr. Zachary Bol, an energetic Catholic priest who worked in the area in the 1970s and '80s, the reaping was the achievement of one man—a catechist named Joseph Pal Mut.

Joseph Pal was born in Adok in 1964, and in 1981 went to Khartoum in search of schooling. Very soon after his arrival he underwent training as a catechist in the Catholic Church and served in that capacity in Omdurman until 1983. In that year he left Omdurman and returned to the South where he joined the SPLA. He left the SPLA in 1987 and went to the refugee camps in Ethiopia. At first he worked with the Presbyterian Church, but after a while he returned to his previous calling as a catechist, opening a Catholic chapel and establishing a catechumenate class in Itang. Whilst in Itang he had repeated conflict with the two Catholic priests in the camps, Benjamin Madhol and his colleague in Panyido Fr. Dominic Matong, and also with the Protestants. From a consideration of his whole career, it appears that he was frustrated by his lack of educational opportunity to become a Catholic priest himself, and as a result was resentful of priestly direction. He was at his most effective when working on his own, and had chosen a celibate life-style as being in keeping with his life as an itinerant evangelist and his aspirations to the priesthood.

It may have been this conflict over leadership that led Joseph Pal to leave Ethiopia, probably in early 1990, to seek out Bishop Paride Taban in Torit. Under Paride's oversight he gained further training there, 'a time of formation' in the phrase of Fr. La Braca.[24] From Torit, Pal set out on an extensive series of missionary journeys through the eastern part of Upper Nile during 1990 and 1991. He is reported to have preached and to have established Catholic communities in Ayod, Nasir, Akobo, Maiwut and Waat, and doubtless many other smaller communities. In each major centre he appointed catechists, sending them out to other villages to teach, build chapels and establish prayer and worship in the Catholic tradition. In this way, in a period of about eighteen months, a network of 200 catechists and a similar number of chapels and growing congregations were established all over eastern Nuerland.

Pal's itinerant ministry came to an abrupt halt in early 1992. In January he met Bishop Paride in Nasir. This moment represented the drawing of this huge new Christian movement into the orbit of the institutional Catholic Church. Maybe Pal sensed that his contribution was drawing to an end. In March he moved on across the Nile to Ler, his home area, where he became head catechist. He died on 29 March 1996 in a motor accident in Nairobi where he was undertaking further studies as a catechist.

Pal was unconventional and difficult to work with, and appears to have been resentful of authority. Nonetheless, it was a deep commitment to the Catholic faith that drove him. Asked what motivated him, he said, 'Can you announce the darkness after you have seen the light?' A community of expatriate priests and nuns is now established in Ler, but the Catholic Church throughout Upper Nile is still, of necessity, essentially non-sacramental and lay-led. Its origin in the apostolic journeys of Joseph Pal is still vividly remembered. Pal is remembered specifically as having introduced the *Catholic* faith—linking rural and isolated Nuer to a large international community, presided over by a renowned leader in the Pope, and introducing more colourful and elaborate prayer and liturgy than was characteristic of the more prosaic Presbyterian Church. A Catholic identity in Upper Nile is about being integrated into this wider, more powerful and more exotic world—and about the dignity, significance and purpose that devolve from it.

5. *Exile and exodus: the people of Yei in pilgrimage*[25]

The striking feature of the Sudanese Church during these years is its determination to find meaning within the unutterable confusion and horror of its experience. The Bible constantly provides images, narratives, symbols, assurances and promises that enable a Church on pilgrimage through a frightening landscape to find meaning and purpose. This wrestling for meaning and significance enables the Sudanese Church continually to renew its life and vision. The story of the pilgrimage of the people of Yei between 1990 and 1997 provides a particularly striking example of this Biblical wrestling for meaning at work. In the telling of the story, elements of the Biblical stories of the Exodus and the Exile come to the fore.

A pilgrim people. Early in 1990 Bishop Seme Solomona (ECS Bishop of Yei) and Fr. Peter Dada (Vicar-General of the Catholic Diocese of Yei) led their people out of Yei town. The evacuation was ordered by the SPLA who expected shortly to attack the town. Under SPLA guidance a convoy of more than a hundred vehicles, with about 10,000 people on foot, made its way to the small deserted border town of Kaya. Travelling by night for fear of government attack, the journey took three days. In Kaya the SPLA abandoned them to their own resources. There in the deserted town the two church leaders set up a new community in displacement. The two churches worked closely together on all aspects of the life of the community, most notably in the obtaining and distribution of relief food and emergency aid. Kaya became in many senses the town that the Church built. The ecumenical partnership of the two men became legendary, and the model on which later inter-church committees and other forms of ecumenical cooperation throughout Southern Sudan were based. Eventually about 30,000 people came to live in Kaya.

Then in mid-1993, the SPLA began to face setbacks. Government troops pushed its forces out of Yei and began to threaten the border town. In the judgement of the church leaders it was time to leave again. Bishop Seme and Fr. Peter Dada stood firm against the attempts of the military authorities to keep them in Sudan. At 8 a.m. on 3 August 1993, the border barrier was lifted and in the subsequent daylight hours 30,000 people crossed over into Uganda as refugees. Bishop Seme, viewing the sight from his hill-top church in Kaya, compared it to the Exodus of the Children of Israel from Egypt. Perceived as a sign of divine protection, not a life was lost that day—indeed more than one baby was born on the road from Kaya to Koboko. The re-establishment of the community in camps around Koboko at the height of the rainy season did, however, bring many hardships and deaths from exposure, hunger and sickness. The churches were built first, followed by the homes of the people. A new community, centred around the new church buildings, came into being. A saga in Biblical style was created—a story of God's leading, protection and provision. It was a story which upheld the people, made meaning out of their sufferings and gave energy to live positively and hopefully. Catholics and Protestants were bound together in this shared pilgrimage—though the instinct to structure and interpret their experience Biblically arose primarily from the rootedness of many Episcopal Christians in the East African Revival. The establishment of Bishop Allison Bible School in Koboko gave physical expression to the story—dreamed of in Yei, planned in Kaya and realised in Koboko.

The return from exile. In 1996 and 1997 the position of Sudanese refugees in West Nile became increasingly insecure—they were a soft target for local Ugandan rebel groups, especially the West Nile Bank Front. In October 1996 Bishop Allison Bible School was burned down, and attacks on Sudanese refugees in the camps increased. It appeared that the refugees had nowhere to turn. They were caught between government troops in Sudan and rebel bands in Uganda. A sense of despair began to creep in. Then, in what appeared to be a miraculous transformation of the situation, within a few weeks the SPLA was able to reverse the military situation. Yei was captured and government troops were thrown back to within

30 miles of Juba. In a situation that many compared to the predicament of the Israelites at the Red Sea, a miraculous deliverance was provided, enabling the people to return home. Bishop Seme was able to return to his cathedral in Yei in time to celebrate communion on Easter Day 1997. The significance of the day was not lost on Christians in Yei. Within weeks it was reported that 80,000 refugees were moving back to the Yei area from Uganda.

Biblical parallels were endlessly invoked to demonstrate the faithfulness of God amidst the tumult and chaos of war. Biblical stories of Exodus, Exile and Return nourished the communal story-telling of the Yei people. The saga had come full circle with the return to their homeland of a 'faithful people', vindicated in their confidence in a 'faithful God'. Such experiences, allied with a capacity to understand them in the light of Biblical parallels, has given the Kakwa Church,[26] Protestant and Catholic, a resilience born of a confidence that God guides, protects and blesses his people. Whilst the story of the people of Yei is particularly striking, it is this openness to the possibility that God can be known in the midst of suffering and war, that has sustained the Sudanese Church through these many years of war, and attracted to its ranks thousands bewildered and battered by loss and pain.

6. *Recovering meaning from the past: the Zande Church*

The Azande have a distinguished history. Their dynamic and expanding military empire were only halted in their sweep westwards to the Nile by the advent of British and Belgian colonialism.[27] With the arrival of Christian missionaries—first the CMS and later the Verona Fathers—they set themselves to master the skills and tools of the new rulers. Of all the peoples of the South, the Azande were outstanding in the enthusiasm and the success with which they took to missionary education.[28] And for CMS and Verona missionaries alike, the Azande Church was the showpiece of their success.

The expulsion of the missionaries (1964) left both the Catholic and the Episcopal Churches quite well equipped with skilled and devoted lay leadership. It was during the Anyanya war (1964–72) that the Christian faith spread beyond the boundaries of school and church and began to gain the allegiance of many thousands of rural people displaced into the forests along the Congo and Central African borders. The Church that emerged from the forests in 1972 was transformed—countless congregations were scattered through the villages, led by evangelists and catechists trained in practical ministry in the bush. The return to war in 1983 bewildered and alienated the Azande. They possessed an historic hostility towards the Dinka. In 1983, during the public debate about government plans to divide the South into three regions, their leading politician, Joseph James Tambura, had been a leading proponent of *kokora* (re-division), a policy which, for Equatorians, was aimed at removing Nilotic influence from their territories. The rise of a resistance movement dominated by Dinka held little attraction for them. When Yambio and Maridi fell to the SPLA in 1990, many felt simply that one occupying army had been replaced by another. Many thousands went into exile in Zaire (Congo) or the Central African Republic. Both Bishop Joseph Gasi Abangite of the Catholic Church and Bishop Daniel Zindo of the Episcopal Church were then themselves in exile and away from their people until 1993. For several years the SPLA behaved like an occupying army—there were many reports of looting and harassment of the civilian population.

The strongly hierarchical and institutional traditions of the Azande had enabled them to adjust to colonial rule with great success. But they were ill-equipped to cope with the turmoil, the chaos, and the lack of political purpose that characterised this new era. The Anyanya war had united the people around a shared political vision for which they were prepared to fight, and a Christian commitment that associated them with the spiritual and material powers of the outside world. Such a combination was energizing and unifying. The renewed war found the Azande without shared commitment and purpose; somehow renewed war, with all its attendant griefs and losses, its visions and aspirations, was unable to energize the Azande soul. Whereas for Dinka and Nuer the extreme sufferings of the war were purging and renewing society, for the Azande the war was undermining society, destroying the pillars on which it was built. For illustrations of this, constant reference was made to the disappearance of many aspects of Zande culture, to poor standards of behaviour amongst the young—especially the lack of respect for elders—and to the decline in sexual standards. Deprived of its traditional social structures and authorities, Azande society was being overwhelmed by the tumult of war.

Just as the Nilotic Churches have wrestled with the meaning of their experience, so the Zande Church has endeavoured to grapple with the crisis in its midst. The cultural crisis is one which affects society in its entirety, but it is interesting that the major forum in which it has been debated is the Church, and in particular the Episcopal Church. In 1994 the Diocese of Yambio held its diocesan synod. Many critical issues were on the agenda (not least the ordination of women). However, the issue which dominated the synod and spilled over into many conversations and debates was the perceived disintegration of Zande culture. The young no longer knew or were willing to listen to the stories and wisdom of the elders. Marital and sexual relations were everywhere in disarray. Traditional knowledge of medicinal herbs, traditional rites and dances was fading away.

In a striking decision the Episcopal Church made itself the guardian of traditional Zande culture, dedicated to rescuing it from further decay. The synod established a committee whose responsibilities included gathering traditional artefacts in danger of being lost (such as Zande war axes), establishing a museum to preserve them, promoting traditional manufacturing skills such as iron-making, reviving traditional dancing, gathering and spreading knowledge of medicinal herbs and promoting the telling of traditional wisdom to young people by the elders. This has been the most decisive action of the Church in recent years and the one that has evoked most response in the Christian community and beyond. Subsequently vigorous steps were taken to implement this decision and such activities have become a conspicuous feature of the life of the ECS in and around Yambio.[29] Although the Episcopal Church took these steps, in 1999 it was reported that the Catholic Church in Yambio was also opening a museum for the preservation of traditional artefacts, indicating that the anxiety about the decay of the traditional heritage is widespread.

It is interesting to compare these developments in Yambio with simultaneous developments in Bor Diocese. Almost simultaneously with the diocesan synod in Yambio, in February 1994, countless thousands of artefacts from traditional shrines were being consigned to the flames at Zion. There the comprehensive destruction brought by the war had totally undermined confidence in the traditional spirit powers and driven the people in their thousands towards the Christian faith in total rejection of their traditional spiritual heritage. In Yambio, in apparent contrast, the bewildering circumstances of the early 1990s drove Episcopal Christians, at least, to attempt a new synthesis between Christian faith and traditional resources and values. Here the gap may not be quite as wide as first appears, for Bor Dinka Christians understood that in moving forward towards Christian faith they were also moving back to a more original and authentic encounter with Nhialic, the Creator God. What is important about these two stories (and about other similar stories around the South) is the living and dynamic dialogue that is taking place between traditional spiritual understanding and values on the one hand and Christian faith on the other. The first was perceived as being somehow the bearer of the identity of the people, and the latter as providing more comprehensive answers in a threatening world, and a stronger bulwark against Islamization and Arabization.

However, a question remains. The Zande Church is responding to the turmoil and radical upheaval of the present by presenting itself as the defender of the old ways, perhaps turning inwards, and offering a vision of a past world where authority, tradition and order provided security and assurance. How adequate is this vision for a future which is sure to contain further rapid and confusing change?

7. *The marginalized find meaning: the Jur*[30]

The examples related so far of the development of 'narratives' by which people give structure and meaning to tumultuous and bewildering experiences have come from the larger and more dominant peoples of Southern Sudan, which is a patchwork quilt of countless different ethnic groups with a multitude of languages.[31] Many of these groups are quite small, and because of colonial educational policy had only restricted access to education. As a result they have been politically, economically and socially isolated. Marginalization is not only the condition of the South with regard to the power centres of the North, it is also the condition of many Southern groups in relation to their more powerful neighbours, such as the Dinka, Nuer, Azande, the Bari-speakers and the Moru. One of the striking features of the dramatic church growth, first in the 1960s and later in the 1990s, is that it not only took place amongst groups with some political awareness and some stake in the conflict. It also took place amongst isolated and marginalized groups with no stake in the war—groups who are only aware that violent turmoil that they cannot control and which they do not understand threatens their very existence. They too have turned to the Christian faith in large numbers, and their stories show a process in which faith and the Biblical story are enabling people to forge structure and meaning out of a chaotic and threatening war. Here we consider briefly the story of one such group, representative of many others.

The Jur Church. Despite the proximity of the Jur country to the Moru area, where evangelisation had commenced in 1920 and there was an established Church, there was no Christian movement among the Jur until 1960, when a young schoolboy, Jontana Mamuru, returned from the mission centre in Lui and began to share his new faith. An early movement into the Church in the 1960s stagnated during the years of peace between 1972 and 1983. When war returned in 1983, the Jur country was one of the first to be seriously disturbed. It lay on the frontier between the Dinka areas of Lakes Province, where SPLA bands roamed freely, and Equatoria, which the government still held securely. Mundri was like a frontier town, and Yeri, the only significant town in the Jur area, was a vulnerable government military outpost. The Jur were liable to be raided and looted by armed gangs from further north, and then punished by government troops for helping rebels. The people who had previously lived in settlements along the road, retreated deep into the bush. By 1985 there were large settlements of displaced Jur in and around Mundri town. Here they initially experienced the kind of discrimination that had inhibited church growth during the 1970s. ECS church authorities in Mundri would not at first allow Jur Christians to hold their own services in their camps—any service in a Jur language had to be held in the town church, more than five miles from the camps. This situation was not rectified until 1986.

Revival and the 'Third Growth'.[32] Further north, those still living in the Jur homelands between Yeri, Domeri and Mvolo experienced the unpredictable terrors of being trapped between opposing forces in a civil war. In the midst of repeated lootings and reprisals a remarkable thing happened. 'God poured out his Holy Spirit on the people starting from Domeri to Mvolo. Both young and old went out to preach the Gospel of Christ to others,' writes Sapana Abuyi. In the midst of great danger and deep uncertainty, a profound experience of God's presence was received, together with an assurance that the Gospel was a sufficient resource for terrible times. The experience of God and the conviction of the power and relevance of the Gospel drove people out to preach and share the Gospel. A prominent feature was the public burning of traditional spirit shrines and the artefacts associated with them. It is a movement that has continued to the present day and has spread through all sections of the Jur people, resulting in the fact that today the great majority of the Jur consider themselves to be Christians.

When the government garrison heard of these events they supposed it to be yet another anti-government movement. Troops were sent out to Domeri to arrest Frederick Amba, a lay reader who was the leader of the new revival. The homesteads and granaries of Domeri were all burned down. Amba was detained in Yeri for about a year. A story is told of his miraculous delivery when he was eventually released from detention, and government soldiers attempted to murder him and his family.[33] But the new spiritual movement found itself under pressure too from the SPLA, who were suspicious of it, and feared it would take young men away from its own units. The commander attempted to stifle the movement by forbidding the preaching of the Gospel from village to village. When Frederick and the evangelists persevered, arrests were made. At Minikolome a forty-five-year-old woman church leader, Mama Zeripa Mogo, was subjected to fifty lashes. Following her beating she stood up, praised God and preached the Gospel to the very soldiers who had lashed her. A soldier tried to cripple Frederick Amba by shooting him in the leg. The bullet passed through his trouser leg without injuring him. Such events impressed the SPLA commanders and the Christians were eventually released to preach the Gospel without any hindrance. Stories of this kind are repeatedly told to demonstrate that God has been with the Jur people through their terrible ordeals, and to indicate a triumph of the Gospel which is of profounder consequence than the ideologies of warring armies. The 1989 revival began a remarkable process by which the Gospel was preached throughout the Jur country and churches and preaching centres were built in almost every community.

The Jur are not a numerous people, and have little political or military importance. It might appear, consequently, that their story is of limited importance. However, they are representative of many other small and politically unimportant peoples caught up in Sudan's civil war who have also had to struggle to survive and to make some kind of sense of a war of endless destruction and brutality.[34] Issues of liberation matter to few. Islamization and Arabization are remote concerns. What matters is family survival—how to stay alive, how to feed your children, how to remain a community and not fragment, how to maintain hope and meaning when the suffering seems endless.

MEANINGS

Most analyses of the Sudanese problem and exploration towards a resolution have focused on the political and economic issues that underlie the war. These issues must be addressed if the conflict is to be resolved. However, what the foregoing narratives make clear is that below the level of political, military and church leadership a profound spiritual transformation is taking place as countless local communities appropriate elements of the Christian faith in their struggle to survive the upheaval and horror of war with integrity. Through this process, only partially described here, an indigenous form of Christianity—or rather, a mosaic of differing but complementary forms of Christianity—is taking shape. And this indigenous and highly contextualized form of Christianity has become the major means by which many Sudanese societies are recreating themselves, redefining their identity and equipping themselves to face the future. In many places the Church has already become the major civil institution, central to all questions of local social and economic development as well as political policy.

What are the main factors that have brought about this transformation? The catalyst for this dramatic shift in personal and communal commitment, this transformation in world view, has undoubtedly been the intense, prolonged and desolating suffering and destruction which almost all Southern Sudanese have experienced over a period of 40 years. The impoverishment that has resulted, the desolation, the grievous loss and the isolation from all outside succour for many years, has resulted in a desperate need and hunger, both physical and spiritual. Body and soul in anguish cry out to God for help. The fragile communities left behind by the missionaries proved, with all their limitations, to be the bearers of a message of potent relevance to the needs of a people in almost limitless distress. The distinctive features of the Christian faith have spoken deeply to communities and individuals *in extremis*—the central message of Cross and Resurrection, the presence of God with his people through the Holy Spirit, deliverance from the powers of evil, the invitation to forgive and be forgiven, the solidarity experienced in Christian community, the healing and protection received through prayer, divine judgment on evil, injustice and unbelief and the hope of heaven where suffering and pain will have no place.

An important effect of the war has been to thrust people who live in one of the most remote parts of Africa into close contact with many aspects of the wider modern world. Those whose lives had previously been lived in almost entirely traditional ways are now familiar with many kinds of modern weaponry, with cars and planes, with relief food from many far places, with expatriate workers who administer the aid. They have been displaced into strange and alienating places—cattle-keepers into agricultural areas, or into desolate refugee camps and lonely cities. Compact and complex socio-economic and religious worlds have been blown apart, exposing a need for a new and more comprehensive framework. In cities as far flung as Khartoum, Nairobi, Cairo, London, Nashville and Toronto, in refugee camps, cattle camps and hidden deep in the forest, frameworks of belief, access to spiritual power, personal and communal hope are being reconstructed through the strands of Christian belief that are conveyed by lay men and women, equipped sometimes with a New Testament, a Prayer Book or a hymn book, but often only with their memory and personal experience. Alienated from forceful government programmes of Islamization and Arabization, Christianity has provided an alternative and contrasting structure for life, belief and conduct—comprehensive in its understanding of the world, and more humanizing in its impact on both individual and community. Alongside these renewing forces, however, exist all the features that one would expect in fragmented and broken communities, cut off from their roots, traditions and authorities—struggles for power, greed, moral confusion, loneliness, despair. But amongst these broken shards a new cohesion can be seen emerging.

As our narratives illustrate, however, there is considerable variety in the way that Christian perspectives and teachings address different Southern societies. These differences relate to the specific ways in which the war has been experienced. Only amongst some of the Nilotic peoples—notably the Bor Dinka and some Nuer sections—has Christian understanding developed in dialogue with the ideology of the SPLA or another rebel military faction. But even here the wrestling of the Christian community for understanding has a vitality all its own and the Church a dynamic that does not allow it to be reduced to 'the spiritual arm of the Movement'. Elsewhere, ideological connections with the liberation movement are much harder to detect. Amongst the Azande the central concern is with constructing a new synthesis of the Christian and the traditional that will consolidate the foundations of Zande life and enable it to withstand the batterings of the war. Elsewhere—we looked at the Jur, but we could equally have looked at the Uduk, the Murle or a host of other small ethnic groups—the turning to Christian faith has been centrally about finding a new and more comprehensive spiritual framework to withstand the threatening and uncontrollable intrusions from outside. Widely throughout Southern Sudan, with the possible exception of the Azande, the circumstances of the war have led to a profound disillusionment with traditional spiritual powers and authorities[35] and a willingness to jettison them for a faith perceived to know the mysteries of the modern world.

There can be no doubt that a colossal transformation in the faith commitment of a great number of Southern Sudanese has taken place. It is impossible to produce reliable figures—estimates can only be based on fragmentary calculations and impressions gained through widespread travel. Estimates in 1980, when figures had somewhat greater reliability, suggested that maybe 20% of Southerners were Christians, i.e. about 1.5 million people, of whom about 1 million were Catholics and half a million Protestants. Today, with huge growth among the Protestant Churches, especially the Episcopal Church, we must suppose that at least 60%, and maybe 70%, of Southerners claim a Christian allegiance. The most dramatic transformation has probably been among the Bor Dinka. Whereas before the current war less than 15% would have claimed to be Christian, today the evidence suggests that 90% would make that claim. This indicates a Christian population among Southerners (in the South, in exile, and displaced in Northern Sudan) of between 4 and 5 million, approximately half of whom are Catholics. This represents approximately 16% of the national population, and constitutes a social and political reality of great consequence for the future of Sudan.

However, it must be recognised that having come into being in these circumstances and with such rapidity, this new and highly dynamic Christian movement is likely to exhibit instability. Untrained clergy and lay leaders lead churches filled with untaught converts. Two questions hang over the future of the Church in Southern Sudan. First, what if the war does not end? Much of the church growth is premised on the understanding that the war and its attendant sufferings are in some way, in God's mysterious purposes, intended to bring the Sudanese people to faith. And as the Sudanese people raise their hands to God in prayer (Psalm 68:31) and come in worship to Zion (Isaiah 18:7), so an age of peace and blessing will dawn. But what if peace does not come?

Secondly, what if the war does come to an end? Much of the energy of this mass Christian movement comes from the intense experience of the war, and the questions and challenges it poses. Christian faith has become the indispensable tool for understanding, confronting and overcoming the multiple challenges of the war. Christianity has become structural to survival in wartime. How would it address the questions of peace?

NOTES

1. It is estimated that 1 million people died in the most violent phase of the first war between 1964 and 1972. The most recent estimates for casualties in the phase of the war since 1983 put the death toll close to 2 million.
2. The 1957 census indicated a national population at that time of 10,200,000. Current estimates are around 28 million. About one quarter of Sudan's population live in the historic Southern Region.
3. For an account of this period see chapter 12, 'Behind the Grass Curtain' in Werner, Anderson and Wheeler 2000.
4. Sanderson and Sanderson 1981, p. 421.
5. See the account of Lohure in Contran 1998. It should be said that, apart from his friendship with Bishop Mazzoldi, Lohure did not stay in close contact with Catholic Church leaders.
6. Bishop Daniel Comboni (1831–81) was the dominant figure in 19th-century Catholic missions in the Sudan, and the inspiration of all subsequent Catholic endeavour. The Verona Fathers (together with associated congregations of Sisters and Brothers) descended from congregations that Comboni founded. Often known as 'Combonis', in modern times they have taken the name 'Comboni Missionaries.'
7. The Church Missionary Society, a voluntary society within the Church of England. Llewellyn Gwynne, pioneer missionary of the Gordon Memorial Sudan Mission of CMS, arrived in Omdurman at the end of 1899. Gwynne and Shaw and five others made up the pioneer missionary group to Southern Sudan, establishing a new station at Malek amongst the Bor Dinka in 1906. See the short biography of Shaw in Nikkel 1998.
8. This section and the following ones on Paul Kon and the evangelists of Bahr el Ghazal are based on a number of my own personal interviews, on Marc Nikkel's PhD thesis (Nikkel 2001), and on various writings by Sharon Hutchinson (notably Hutchinson 1996).

9. Chris Patten, as British Minister for Overseas Development, visited the Ethiopian camps in 1988 and was moved to tears as Sudanese schoolboys sang a song they had composed themselves based on Isaiah 9:2. 'The people who walked in darkness have seen a great light. Those who lived in the land of the shadow of death, on them has the light shined.'

10. The great majority were Dinka young men.

11. Personal communication, cf. Hutchinson's contribution to this volume.

12. Two booklets give a graphic description of the journey and experience of the unaccompanied minors: Oostland and Berkvens 1998 and Zutt, n.d...

13. *Nhialic*, the Dinka term for the high Creator God.

14. The material on Paul Kuon in this section is largely drawn from Nikkel 1993, 1997a and 1997b, as well as from other personal interviews.

15. Nathaniel Garang, Episcopal Church of Sudan Bishop of Bor. Consecrated in 1984 and cut off from the outside world by the war until 1990, Bishop Garang had laid the foundations of the Episcopal Church amongst the Bor Dinka. It became in the early 1990s the most rapidly growing and dynamic section of the Episcopal Church.

16. People later associated this with Isaiah 20, in which Isaiah walks naked as a sign of impending judgment on Egypt and Sudan (Isaiah 20:3).

17. The only significant *jok* to escape the holocaust was the most famous of all—the great spear of *Lirpiou*. Bishop Nathaniel Garang himself was related to the family of the custodians. It was finally brought to 'trial' by secular and church authorities in 1995 and its *jok* publicly abused. It was then smashed into pieces and thrown down a well.

18. This section is based on personal experience whilst on the staff of the New Sudan Council of Churches (1992–6), conversations with pastors and evangelists from the area, and the continuinng enquiries of Marc Nikkel and interviews with a number of participants in these events, including Rev. Wilson Garang.

19. The main Catholic missions amongst the Dinka of Bahr el-Ghazal were Kwajok (1923), Nyamlell (1933), Mayen (1948), Thiet (1949), Warap (1952), Rumbek (1953), Tonj (1953) and Aweil (1954).

20. Rudolph Majak Deng. Dinka Rek, born 1946, and baptized by Fr. Ireneo Dud in 1955. Ordained priest in Wau 1970. He has served as Rector of the Major Seminary in Bussere (1975), and in pastoral work in Kwajok, Wau, and Aweil. Vicar-General of Wau (1987) and consecrated Bishop of Wau in 1996.

21. There was little real ground for complaint as the Catholic missions had always resisted the old 'spheres system' and had initiated work in Protestant areas whenever the opportunity arose.

22. An observation of Marc Nikkel.

23. For a full account of the career of Joseph Pal, see Wheeler 1998.

24. Comboni missionary in Ler from the mid-'90s.

25. This section is based on personal experience—I have myself shared in parts of the story—and on interviews conducted with a number of people involved, including Bishop Seme Solomona.

26. Kakwa: the dominant ethnic group around Yei. Numerous communities also live in northwest Uganda and northeast Congo. Kakwa speak a dialect of the Bari language, and in Sudan use the Bari Bible.

27. Gbudwe (also known as Yambio), the last great warrior prince of the Azande, was killed by the British in Yambio in 1905. His tomb may still be seen there.

28. It may be that, like the Baganda in Uganda, the Azande adjusted quickly and enthusiastically to missionary boarding schools because of their similarity to the traditional practice of training the sons of leading families at the court of the king.

29. By 1995, for example, the museum already existed, and at the 1995 NSCC General Assembly, held in Yambio, I witnessed a display of traditional dances put on by ECS pastors and lay leaders. This performance included a 'demonstration' of divination conducted by two pastors dressed as witch-doctors. An uneasy atmosphere, somewhere between amusement and trepidation, prevailed. By 1995 also, a substantial record of traditional herbal remedies had already been compiled.

30. This section is based on my own research and interviews and on the substantial work of Sapana Abuyi. See Abuyi 1998.

31. An account by the Summer Institute of Linguistics lists 118 Sudanese languages, in addition to which there are a great number of related dialects.

32. So called by Abuyi as there had been two distinct phases of growth during the 1960s.

33. See Abuyi 1998, pp. 142–5.

34. Another striking example is provided by the story of the Uduk who live on the eastern borders of Sudan with Ethiopia. A summary account is provided by Arensen 1997. This is based on several works of Wendy James, which are listed in the bibliography.

35. There have been some reports from Equatoria of a renewal of traditional religious practice in predominantly Christian areas (e.g. amongst the Kakwa). This needs further research, but would appear to be of much smaller social significance than the major developments in the Christian community.

BIBLIOGRAPHY

This chapter is the fruit of a major research project on Sudanese Church History conducted by William B. Anderson and Andrew C. Wheeler since 1996. It culminated in 2000 in the publication in Nairobi of a major textbook on the subject entitled *Day of Devastation, Day of Contentment: The History of the Sudanese Church across 2000 Years*. This book provides not only more field research on church growth in Sudan, but general background on this whole phase of Sudan's history. Otherwise very little is commonly available on Sudan's Christian history. The bibliography indicates some of the literature that is available, together with some major anthropological and political studies.

Abuyi, Sapana A. 1998, 'From the Margins to the Centre: Jonathan Mamuru and the Evangelists of the Jur', in A. C. Wheeler (ed.), *Announcing the Light:*

Sudanese Witnesses to the Gospel, Faith in Sudan No. 6, Nairobi: Paulines Publications Africa, pp. 122–47.

Arensen, Jonathan E. 1997, 'Conversion among the Uduk. Continuity versus Discontinuity', in A. C. Wheeler (ed.), *Land of Promise: Church Growth in a Sudan at War*, Faith in Sudan No. 1, Nairobi: Paulines Publications Africa, pp. 79–85.

Contran, Neno 1998, 'A Priest—a Leader—a Rebel: Contributions of Father Saturnino Lohure', in A. C. Wheeler (ed.), *Announcing the Light: Sudanese Witnesses to the Gospel*, Faith in Sudan No. 6, Nairobi: Paulines Publications Africa, pp. 253–63.

Dellagiacoma, V. 1996, *History of the Catholic Church in Southern Sudan 1900–1995*, Khartoum, privately published.

Deng, Francis M. 1995, *War of Visions: Conflict of Identities in Sudan*, Washington, DC: Brookings Institution Press.

Hutchinson, S. H. 1996, *Nuer Dilemmas: Coping with Money, War and the State*, Berkeley: University of California Press.

James, Wendy 1979, *Kwanim Pa: The Making of the Uduk People*, Oxford: Clarendon Press.

——— 1988, *The Listening Ebony: Moral Knowledge, Religion and Power among the Uduk of Sudan*, Oxford: Clarendon Press.

Kayanga, S. E. and A. C. Wheeler 1999, *'But God Is Not Defeated!' Celebrating the Centenary of the Episcopal Church of the Sudan 1899–1999*, Nairobi: Paulines Publications Africa.

Nikkel, Marc 1997a, 'Children of our Fathers Divinities or Children of Red Foreigners? Themes in Missionary History and the Rise of an Indigenous Church among the Jieng Bor of Southern Sudan', in A. C. Wheeler (ed.), *Land of Promise: Church Growth in a Sudan at War*, Faith in Sudan No. 1, Nairobi: Paulines Publications Africa, pp. 61–78.

——— 1997b, 'The Cross as a Symbol of Regeneration in Jieng Bor Society', in A. C. Wheeler (ed.), *Land of Promise: Church Growth in a Sudan at War*, Faith in Sudan No. 1, Nairobi: Paulines Publications Africa, pp. 86–114.

——— 1998, 'Archibald Shaw "Machuor". The Only White Man With the Heart of the Jieng' in F. Pierli, M. T. Ratti and A. C. Wheeler (eds), *Gateway to the Heart of Africa. Missionary Pioneers in Sudan*, Faith in Sudan No. 5, Nairobi: Paulines Publications Africa, pp. 102–25.

——— 2001, *Dinka Christianity. The Origins and Development of Christianity among the Dinka of Sudan with Special Reference to Songs of Dinka Christians*, Faith in Sudan No. 11, Nairobi: Paulines Publications Africa.

Oostland, Rolanda and Ronald Berkvens 1998, *Sudanese Life Stories: Voices from Kakuma Refugee Camp*, Utrecht: Churches in Action and Pax Christi.

Persson, J. 1997, *In Our Own Languages: The Story of Bible Translation in Sudan*, Faith in Sudan No. 3, Nairobi: Paulines Publications Africa.

Pierli, F., M. T. Ratti and A. C. Wheeler 1998, *Gateway to the Heart of Africa: Missionary Pioneers in Sudan*, Faith in Sudan No. 5, Nairobi: Paulines Publications Africa.

Sanderson, Lillian Passmore, and Neville Sanderson 1981, *Education, Religion and Politics in Southern Sudan 1899–1964*, London: Ithaca Press.

Werner, R. S., W. B. Anderson and A. C. Wheeler 2000, *Day of Devastation, Day of Contentment: The History of the Sudanese Church across 2000 Years*, Faith in Sudan No. 10, Nairobi: Paulines Publications Africa.

Wheeler, A. C. 1998, 'Can You Announce the Darkness after You have Announced the Light?' Catholic Catechists' Achievement in Upper Nile 1970–1996, Reflecting the Life and Work of Zachary Bol Chatim, James Duol Kai, George Gatguec, Jerome Yac and Joseph Pal Mut', in A. C. Wheeler (ed.), *Announcing the Light: Sudanese Witnesses to the Gospel*, Faith in Sudan No. 6, Nairobi: Paulines Publications Africa, pp. 161–79.

Zutt, Johannes n.d., *Children of War: Wandering alone in southern Sudan*, n.p., UNICEF.

CHURCHES AND SOCIAL UPHEAVAL IN RWANDA AND BURUNDI

EXPLAINING FAILURES TO OPPOSE ETHNIC VIOLENCE

Timothy Longman

Two distinctive images of the social engagement of Christian churches in Africa have emerged in the past several decades. One image regards churches as instruments of imperialism and allies of authoritarian rule. Christian churches have been denounced as the cultural wing of the colonial project and, in independent Africa, as conservative strongholds that ally themselves with political leaders to preserve the *status quo*. The other image regards churches as the masthead of civil society, the only effective institutions outside state control, playing the role of human rights observer, peasant organizer, and advocate for democracy. As authoritarian regimes were shaken in the 1990s, churches were portrayed as leading the charge in many countries.

On the surface Rwanda and Burundi would seem to exemplify perfectly these two contrasting images. In the wake of the Rwandan genocide of 1994 many observers criticized Rwanda's Christian churches for supporting the massacres, both through the historic role that missionaries played in promoting ethnic conflict and for the alliance that existed between the leaders of church and state which was manifested in the participation of some pastors and priests in the massacres of Tutsi. In contrast, Burundi has been treated as a classic case of church-state conflict, where churches were heavily regulated by a state that feared their power; the churches seemed to be the only voice of opposition to an authoritarian, ethnically based military regime, and church leaders were therefore targeted for violence.[1]

In reality the contrast is not so stark, and the situation in each country is considerably more complex than a simple reduction to church-state alliance or conflict can suggest. Churches have taken a variety of roles in Rwandan and Burundian societies, some of which are contradictory. The relationship of churches to the state in each country has been mixed, sometimes supporting, sometimes challenging, and often living in peaceful coexistence. This chapter contend, that in neither country has church social engagement been driven primarily by a higher vision of the church's purpose in society. Instead, the two primary guiding principles have been gaining popular support and avoiding conflict with political authorities. Varieties in church social engagement arises out of the contradictions between these two goals and competing ideas of how best to realize them. Six major roles that churches have played in Rwanda and Burundi are reviewed here: as allies of the state, kingmakers, social engineers, civil society, havens for the oppressed, and arbiters. In each case recent social engagement is linked to historic precedents.

CHURCHES AS ALLIES OF THE STATE

From their arrival in Rwanda and Burundi, Christian missionaries determined to make themselves and their churches important political players, a decision that has profoundly affected the nature of the Christianity subsequently practised in the two countries. Cardinal Charles Lavigerie, founder of the Missionaries of Africa (called White Fathers because of their long white robes), believed that efforts at conversion should focus first on the political leaders of a territory, because their acceptance of Christianity would create an accommodating environment for the conversion of the masses. Where civil authorities resisted Christianity, Lavigerie argued, the church would never develop a strong presence. After meeting with little success in the initial mission grounds in North Africa, Lavigerie received a grant in 1878 from Pope Leo XIII to begin working in East Africa. Although he died before mission work expanded into Rwanda and Burundi, his successors embraced his principles of mission, and it was in these two kingdoms that the principles developed most fully.[2]

White Fathers first entered Burundi in 1879, but two missionaries were killed two years later under orders of a minor chief, and another attempt at evangelising the region was not made until 1896, a year after the first German military post was established at Bujumbura. These missionaries fled within a few months, but in 1898, as the German military presence expanded, the White Fathers established their first two permanent missions in Burundi. In 1900 they established two stations in Rwanda.[3] These earliest mission efforts affirmed the need for missionaries to gain the cooperation of both the colonial state and indigenous authorities. Following the flight of the missionaries from Burundi in 1896, a German military expedition in 1897 punished those chiefs believed responsible for creating the threat and opened the possibility for missionaries to return in 1898.[4] While conflicts between missionaries and the colonial regime sometimes arose, their relationship was on the whole cooperative. The colonial administration provided protection to the missionaries, while the missionaries—who substantially outnumbered colonial officials under German occupation—helped extend colonial authority, creating a European presence in regions otherwise untouched by the colonial state.

The early failures in Burundi also confirmed Lavigerie's argument for the necessity of the acquiescence of local authorities for mission to succeed, since the alternative could have deadly consequences. The White Fathers thus sought the permission of the Rwandan king to establish missions there, and they worked with the Burundian king on expanding mission work in his territory. The leaders of the order repeatedly exhorted the missionaries in the field to develop a cooperative relationship with both the royal court and the local chiefs, and they reprimanded or removed those missionaries who resisted this charge. They called on missionaries to ally themselves with the authorities against the population, even when the behaviour of officials was immoral or abusive. As one regional church official wrote,

Regarding the injustices ... that are committed around you in a revolting fashion, you see and note that we cannot remedy them. All that we can do, we can do by our patience, by acceptance, and by love of the humiliations that come from our absolute abstention.[5]

As the royal courts in Rwanda and Burundi sought to centralize their rule under colonial tutelage, gradually simplifying the political system and taking away the autonomous power of the local chiefs, the superiors of the White Fathers urged their missionaries to support the royal court whenever conflicts arose between the court and the local authorities and local population. A 1904 entry in the diary of Rwaza mission in Rwanda reflects the official attitude: 'We want only to raise and affirm the authority of the king ... we want to be always his friends ... we will have people pay tribute.'[6]

Despite the missionaries' open support of their authority, the indigenous leaders were slow to accept the White Fathers and their religion, but eventually the strategy of allying with the state paid off. By the 1920s chiefs and other members of the ruling elite began to convert in large numbers, and by the end of the 1930s membership in the Catholic Church was a virtual prerequisite for holding public office. The Rwandan king who took power in 1931, Rudahigwa Mutara IV, was a Catholic catechism student who eventually not only became a baptized church member but in 1946 dedicated Rwanda to Christ the King.[7] While the Burundian monarch Mwambutsa, who reigned from 1915 to 1966, was never baptized, he married a Catholic and eliminated 'pagan' rituals from the court.[8] The conversion of the chiefs did in fact prepare the way for a more general conversion. As one missionary in Burundi wrote in 1936, 'The example of the Chiefs stimulates the subjects ... [There are] 29 primary chiefs who are Christian or on the way to becoming so, against 4 pagans; 535 sub-chiefs Christian or close to baptism, against 124 pagans'.[9] As church membership became a means of seeking social advancement, thousands of people converted. While in 1930 fewer than 100,000 people in Rwanda had converted to Catholicism, by 1940 the church counted over 300,000.[10] Church officials claimed 'The Holy Spirit blows a tornado!'[11]

The remarkable success of the White Fathers in winning the conversion of the population of Rwanda and Burundi convinced them and other missionaries of the efficacy of Lavigerie's principle of seeking alliance with political authorities. Protestant missionaries who worked in the countries, rather than appealing to the population excluded by the Catholic-ruling class alliance, sought to emulate Catholic success, seeking their own alliances with political officials. The earliest Protestant missionaries, the Lutherans, sought to gain access to the royal courts, and subsequent Protestant groups, including the Seventh Day Adventist Church and the Reformed Church, also curried favour with the monarchs and chiefs.[12]

The idea that a close alliance with state authorities would facilitate church operations profoundly shaped Christian social engagement in Burundi and Rwanda. In addition to the personal cooperation between church and state leadership, churches worked closely with the administration in the colonial period to provide education and health-care, which gave material incentives for people to come to the churches. These practices continued after independence, with churches providing over half of medical care and over half of education.[13] When leadership changes took place, as when Micombero took power in 1966 in Burundi and when Habyarimana came to power in Rwanda in 1973, both by coups, church leaders quickly sought to show their support for the new regime. In seeking to maintain their privileged relationship with the state, churches avoided open conflict. Just as the early White Fathers were cautioned to remain silent even in the face of injustices committed by the state, churches in the independence period remained silent in the face of ethnic massacres of Hutu in Burundi in 1965 and of Tutsi in Rwanda in the early 1960s and 1973.

The ultimate result of this policy of state alliance was that people in Rwanda could participate in the 1994 genocide believing that they were acting in a fashion consistent with Christian teachings. Evidence gathered in Butare, Gikongoro and Kibuye prefectures in 1995–6 implicated pastors and priests directly in the killings. In Kaduha parish, of Gikongoro, for example, the priest used his knowledge of the local population to identify Tutsi and ensure that they were gathered in the church before death squads attacked it. Witnesses reported seeing him later sporting a gun and helping to direct the killing. In one Butare parish people went to mass to pray before going out to kill each day. In some cases people paused during the slaughter in a church building to pray at the altar. Even when the genocide was a well-known fact, church leaders refused to condemn it, choosing instead to defend the regime and urge the population to help restore order. For the Hutu population of Rwanda, being Christian meant supporting the government, and in 1994 supporting the government meant wiping out the Tutsi population.[14]

CHURCHES AS KINGMAKERS

While the principles promoted by Cardinal Lavigerie and early church leaders in Rwanda and Burundi like Hirth and Classe urged appeasing political authorities, they did not call for unquestioned obedience to the state. Where leaders were hostile to Christianity, church leaders were quite willing to use their power to influence the selection of new leadership. The Catholic missionaries had a major influence on administrative reforms in the 1920s and 1930s, advising the colonial administration in designing reforms and promoting candidates for new chieftaincies who were Catholic or at least sympathetic to the churches. Protestant missionaries also promoted Protestant candidates for chieftaincies in order to advance their own interests. By the late 1920s baptism had become a clear aid to gaining political power.[15]

The practice of playing king-maker reached its apogee when the White Fathers played a major role in the deposition of the Rwandan King Musinga in 1931. While the missionaries had worked closely with Musinga in the first decades of the 20th century, they found him increasingly recalcitrant. Finding his power challenged by both colonial authorities and the ruling class, he sought increasingly to assert his independence, resisting Catholic demands and even seeking support from Protestant missionaries. The Catholic missionaries began a campaign in the late 1920s to convince the colonial administration that Musinga stood in the way of Rwanda's development, accusing him of sexual immorality in addition to his political intransigence. The White Fathers then hand-picked Musinga's pro-Catholic son, Rudahigwa, to succeed his father.[16]

The Catholic missionaries again played an important part in promoting new leaders in Rwanda a few decades later. Following the Second World War, after several decades of a close church-state relationship, tensions between Catholic missionaries and the ruling elite in Rwanda again emerged. As nationalist sentiments began to spread in Africa, certain Tutsi intellectuals began to regard the Catholic Church critically as an instrument of colonial power that meddled too much in Rwandan affairs. Meanwhile younger missionaries influenced by social democratic ideas arrived in Rwanda and were disturbed by the serious inequalities that existed in Rwandan society. They began to create opportunities for Hutu in church schools and church employment, and cultivated a Hutu counter-elite. White Fathers even participated in drafting the 'Bahutu Manifesto' in 1957, a document that expressed demands for greater rights for the Hutu masses of Rwanda. After Hutu peasants attacked Tutsi chiefs in 1959, the missionaries urged colonial authorities to replace Tutsi chiefs with Hutu, and within only two years Rwanda's political leadership was transformed from entirely Tutsi to almost entirely Hutu. The first president of Rwanda at independence, Grégoire Kayibanda, had been editor of the Catholic newspaper *Kinyamateka*, head of a Catholic consumers' cooperative, and personal secretary to the archbishop.[17]

Despite these examples, the practice of promoting particular candidates for political leadership was exceptional. In general, church leaders have been willing to work with whomever was in office, and they have instead taken a position in favour of the *status quo*, whatever that might be. Hence, in the democracy movements that emerged in both Burundi and Rwanda in the 1990s, while church leaders in both countries gave mild support to some of the basic principles of democracy, they did not promote particular opposition candidates. The only church leaders who openly supported candidates were those supporting the existing regime.

CHURCHES AS SOCIAL ENGINEERS

As René Lemarchand notes, 'As an instrument of socialisation, nowhere else in Africa did the Church play a more critically important role than in Rwanda.' In both Rwanda and Burundi, the churches, both Catholic and Protestant, did not simply conform to the existing societies but actively shaped them according to their visions. Both through intentional social and political engineering and through attempts to reinforce what they believed already to be Burundian and Rwandan social reality, the missionaries profoundly reconfigured social identities, relationships of power, and other social facts in the two countries.

The most obvious area where the churches had a major influence was on the construction of ethnicity. The exact meaning of the labels Hutu, Tutsi and Twa in pre-colonial Rwanda is widely debated, but several facts are clear. They were not ethnicities in the modern sense, since members of the groups shared a common language, religious practices, and territory. These labels were only significant in certain parts of the region,

since in other areas family, clan, and regional identities were more significant. Even where the terms were most used, as in the central kingdom of
Rwanda, where they referred to a status distinction, the label applied to a
particular family could change if its fortunes changed. Hutu families that
gained wealth (counted mostly in cattle) and became patrons to others
would eventually be considered Tutsi, while Tutsi who lost wealth and
clients would become Hutu.[18]

The missionaries brought to Rwanda and Burundi ideas about race and
identity then current in Europe that shaped their understanding of local
society. Believing that all people on Earth fit neatly into distinct racial
and national categories, the missionaries regarded Tutsi, Hutu and Twa
as three separate groups representing three racial categories—Hamitic,
Bantu (or Negroid) and Pygmoid respectively—who came to live on the
same territory through successive waves of immigration. The missionaries attributed to each group both a physical and psychological stereo-
type—the Tutsi as tall, thin, light-skinned, regal, and intelligent, the Hutu
as short, stocky, hard working, and unsophisticated, and the Twa as short,
dark, and dishonest. As the White Fathers sought to ally themselves with
the ruling powers, their prejudices caused them to overlook the complexi-
ties of local political systems and to interpret the power arrangements in
Rwanda and Burundi in straightforward ethnic terms. Considering Tutsi
more like Europeans, they regarded them as the natural rulers of the two
countries. This ignored the fact that the ruling elite in Burundi was
known as Ganwa, considered neither Hutu nor Tutsi, and that in both
countries there were Hutu chiefs.[19]

Despite the lack of historical basis for the belief that Tutsi had come to
Rwanda and Burundi and dominated the Hutu and Twa through their military might and superior intelligence, the missionaries' belief in the natural superiority of the Tutsi became a basis for public policy. The Catholic
Church reserved for Tutsi positions in their higher schools and other
opportunities. As the colonial administration centralized power, independent Hutu kingdoms were eliminated, and the missionaries consistently
sided with the Tutsi kings against the minor monarchs. Missionaries also
influenced administrative reforms in the 1920s that replaced Hutu chiefs
with Tutsi. When the colonial administration considered naming Hutu as
chiefs, Monsignor Classe counselled against it, claiming that the Tutsi
were better suited to rule.[20] In Burundi church interpretations took no
account of Ganwa as a separate category, helping to bring about its demise as a distinctive identity, even as Ganwa consolidated political power
in the royal court.[21] Ethnicity became an important reality in the lived
experience of Rwandans and, to a lesser extent, Burundians, helping to
determine their life prospects. While historically the groups may not have

been deeply divided, colonial policies—promoted largely by churches— created fixed and distinct groups.

The missionaries played an important part in other fundamental social transformations in Burundi and Rwanda as well. The schools they established were essential for creating a French-speaking, europeanised elite, initially Tutsi but later including Hutu as well. After its creation in 1932, Groupe Scolaire of Astrida (now Butare) became the primary source for chiefs, administrators, teachers, medical personnel, and other professionals in both Rwanda and Burundi.[22]

Another major social change instituted largely by the missionaries was the elimination of the quasi-feudal system in which wealthy patrons (mostly Tutsi) lent cattle to poorer clients (mostly Hutu) in exchange for loyalty and occasional labour. While in pre-colonial Rwanda and Burundi this patron-client system had substantial regional variations and was often a relatively balanced exchange, one impact of colonial policies was to exaggerate the inequalities of the system, so that by World War II the system was impoverishing Hutu and requiring them to participate in forced labour while enriching Tutsi. In the post-war era reformist priests, anthropologists, and administrators, entirely lacking historical perspective, assumed this unequal situation was deeply rooted in indigenous society and set about eliminating the system. Catholic priests helped influence the administration and the monarchy to phase out *ubuhake* in Rwanda in the 1950s.[23]

Thus churches did have a major impact on the shape of modern Rwandan and Burundian societies. Contrary to analysts who have considered ethnic violence in the countries as a reflection of Christianity's limited influence,[24] Christianity actually played a major role in shaping the very ethnic identities that later became a basis for conflict. The missionaries and, later, Burundian and Rwandan church personnel helped reshape fundamental social relationships, like the clientele systems. Since independence, churches have continued their attempts at social engineering, most notably in the realm of economic life, where churches have supported massive development projects, seeking to change the behaviour of farmers and create new cooperative structures in rural society. Other major social reforms have attacked polygamy, sexual promiscuity, and alcohol consumption. In short, if churches failed to challenge the conflictual nature of ethnic identities in Rwanda and Burundi in the 1980s and 1990s, it was not because they lacked the capacity to change society nor because they were reluctant to engage in social engineering, but rather because challenging the ethnic structure that they had themselves helped establish could undermine the church relationship with the state and possibly alienate important portions of the population.

CHURCHES AS HAVENS FOR THE OPPRESSED

Despite the supreme value given by church leaders to maintaining cordial relations with state officials, conflicts with the state have sometimes arisen. Only rarely have these conflicts resulted from principled disagreements over moral issues. Instead, have mostly resulted from church interest in maintaining good connections to the population. Churches are voluntary organisations, and as such they must be concerned about maintaining membership. Typical for African countries, in Rwanda and Burundi church leaders have been very conscious to find means to maintain the interest, participation, and financial support of the population, since numerous religious options exist—not only because of competition between Catholics and established Protestant churches, but also because of the endurance of indigenous religions and the growing popularity of newly imported religions, such as Islam (which has seen a substantial growth in recent years) and new Protestant sects. Particularly when the political regime has lost public support, church leaders may become concerned that too close an association with state officials may alienate them from the population, which may then turn towards other religious movements for their spiritual needs As social and political transformations have taken place, religious leaders have wanted to remain relevant, and have therefore tried to express their support for change—generally in terms intended not to enrage existing state officials.

The first people in Burundi and Rwanda to be drawn to the Christian message were marginal individuals who saw the missions as a potential source of power or protection. Most were poor people hoping the missionaries could provide assistance in the face of drought and famine, but some were once-powerful individuals who had fallen out with the regime and turned to the missionaries for support. Not surprisingly this situation annoyed the established chiefs who in some instances viewed the missionaries as rivals for political power. The superiors of the White Fathers, thus, repeatedly urged their missionaries to seek above all the support of the local chiefs and the kings and to avoid taking a side against them with the common people or with rivals for power. These directives were strongly reinforced in 1906 when the order sent back to Europe Father Brard, the most outspoken critic of the pro-regime strategy, and named as head of the important Save mission Father Classe, a priest distinguished by his obedience to the directives of his superiors.[25] The directive to support temporal authorities was reaffirmed periodically in the Catholic Church and also became a principle in most Protestant churches.

Despite the intentions of their leaders, however, churches did become havens for the socially marginalized in a number of cases. In highly unequal and authoritarian societies, as both Rwanda and Burundi have long been, religious institutions may be the only social institutions outside the state allowed to operate with a degree of autonomy. As a result, those who are excluded from access to the state and its benefits and opportunities may turn to religious institutions as an alternative, or they may seek protection from religious groups if they feel threatened. Indeed, in colonial Rwanda, even though Tutsi dominated both church and state, many Hutu were drawn to the churches because of the access they offered to health care, primary education, and spiritual power. After the revolution and the assumption of power by Hutu, the churches became a haven for Tutsi, many of whom sought employment in the churches because government positions were closed to them. Into the 1990s, Tutsi comprised the majority of clergy in the Catholic and most Protestant churches.

In Burundi the role that churches played as havens for the Hutu became a major source of church-state conflict. While the churches, particularly the Catholic Church, remained openly supportive of the state, the vast majority of church members in all churches were Hutu. In the 1970s, while the state was dominated by Tutsi military personnel who feared the possibility of Hutu revolt and therefore took little interest in using the state to improve the conditions of the Hutu population, the churches continued to provide health and education to Hutu and to offer opportunities for them to meet and organize. In 1976 the Catholic bishops initiated a program of Basic Christian Communities (BCCs), church groups that gathered together families in an area for periodic prayer meetings and Bible study. While these groups had no overt political intent, the government feared that they could become a source of Hutu dissent. In 1979 the Bagaza regime placed restrictions on the activities of the BCCs, limiting group meetings to recognized church buildings and only on weekends. When the bishops objected, Bagaza expelled several missionaries. As tensions mounted, the number of missionaries expelled grew and spread to include Protestants. In 1984 the government banned weekday church services. Church officials responded with public criticisms of the regime, and the state responded again with even harsher measures, banning church youth groups and catechism classes and nationalizing high schools. Eventually, this conflict seriously undermined public support for the state and was a factor in the 1987 coup in which Bagaza was overthrown by Pierre Buyoya. Among the first actions Buyoya took was to normalise relations with the churches.[26]

Although the conflict between the churches and the state in Burundi under Bagaza was serious, leading to severe restrictions on church activities and the expulsion of over 300 missionaries from the Catholic Church alone, the conflict did not arise because the churches intentionally sought to challenge or undermine the state. Rather, the conflict arose inadvertently out of the position of churches as alternatives for the Hutu masses, which the state saw as a threat to its hegemony. The government regarded the ostensibly apolitical acts of providing education and other services to the population as potentially providing the skills and the self-awareness that could translate into empowerment, and they saw the formation of small church groups like the BCCs as a possible location for fomenting rebellion. The churches only openly challenged the state in order to defend their rights to function.

CHURCHES AS CIVIL SOCIETY

Despite the general reluctance of churches to challenge the state, they have occasionally spoken out on issues of principle, but they have generally sought to do so in ways that did not compromise their close connections to state power. In Rwanda, for example, the Catholic Church openly opposed government family planning programs initiated in the early 1980s. The bishops issued a letter condemning the practice of encouraging artificial contraception and forbade Catholic hospitals and health centres from cooperating with the government family planning agency. The scope of this conflict was, however, limited to these specific issues and did not affect the overall good rapport between the Catholic Church and the Rwandan state, and a compromise position was worked out fairly quickly.[27]

In recent decades, however, a variety of factors have pushed churches to take a somewhat more critical stance in relationship to the state. First, some people within the churches have questioned their close relationship with the state. Influenced by Liberation Theology and other new religious ideas, some Christian individuals and groups have called on the churches actively to stand up for the rights of the poor and oppressed. Going further even than the post-World War II missionaries in Rwanda, they have sought to address the broader structures of inequality in both Rwanda and Burundi. They have played a leading role not only in encouraging economic development and empowerment for the poorest members of society, but also in demanding increased respect for civil liberties and human rights. For example, under the leadership of Father André Sibomana, the Catholic newspaper *Kinyamateka* played a major role in promoting press freedom in Rwanda by bravely exposing government corruption and incompetence. Sibomana and other church personnel were instrumental in the foundation of Rwandan human rights groups in the early 1990s. Similarly, in Burundi at least two of the Catholic bishops were founding members of the major human rights group, ITEKA. Archbishop

Joachim Rumania, a progressive Tutsi, was murdered by government supporters in September 1995 for his outspoken defence of human rights. These progressive church people have challenged the churches as institutions to distance themselves from the state and openly take the side of the population in general and the marginalized in particular. In Rwanda the bishop of Kabgayi, Thaddée Nsengiyumva, published a letter in 1992 criticizing the Rwandan church for its failure to exercise political independence.

International church institutions have also encouraged greater social and political engagement by the churches. With decolonization, the relationship between mainline Protestant churches in Africa with the European and American churches that founded them has changed drastically. Northern churches continue to provide substantial funding to the African churches, but they have changed their focus from evangelism to issues of economic development and equality and have attempted to pressure local churches to take more independent and progressive positions. The Dutch Reformed Church, for example, questioned certain patrimonial practices in the Presbyterian Church in Rwanda during the 1990s and threatened to cut off funding. Ecumenical bodies like the World Council of Churches and the All Africa Conference of Churches have also pushed member churches to take more prophetic positions in society.

In the wake of the Second Vatican Council, Catholic churches around the world have been encouraged to adapt themselves to their local environment by engaging in issues of national significance. In both Rwanda and Burundi, as in most other countries around the world, Catholic bishops' conferences have been formed, and they have taken up the practice of issuing pastoral letters. In addition, the Vatican has intervened periodically. In 1985 the Vatican ordered the Archbishop of Kigali to resign from the central committee of the ruling party. The papal nuncios have also instructed the bishops to take positions on certain issues, as when the nuncio in Rwanda in the early 1990s encouraged the bishops to speak out in support of democratic reform. The concern of the Vatican seemed to be, however, not so much taking a prophetic stand as in remaining relevant to the population, and the Vatican retains a concern for the position of the church *vis-à-vis* the state. After the Rwandan genocide the new Tutsi-dominated Rwandan government openly accused the Catholic church of complicity. The church responded by denying any institutional responsibility for the genocide, instead accusing church personnel who were involved of personal moral failings. At the same time, the church sought to appease the new government and win its support. Sibomana, when named acting bishop of Kabgayi, was told by the Vatican to temper his criticisms of government human rights abuses because of the need to gain the favour of the state,[28] and the bishops the Vatican ultimately named to replace those killed in the war were remarkable only for their moderation.

A final important factor driving churches to take a more critical stance in relationship to the state has been the need to retain popular support. As voluntary agencies, churches have to worry about retaining the participation of their membership, who supply much of their funding and provide their *raison d'être*. If a church loses legitimacy, members may leave to attend a competing church or other religious institution. Many church leaders in Rwanda and Burundi have worried that challenging the state could endanger their privileged relationship, but they also worry that being perceived as too closely linked to an unpopular regime could damage their public appeal. During the 1980s and 1990s Evangelical Protestant churches experienced impressive growth in Rwanda and Burundi at the expense of established churches, in part because the population saw the older missionary churches as corrupt and tied to unpopular political regimes.

Responding to these pressures, the Catholic bishops in Rwanda in the 1990s felt compelled to issue pastoral letters addressing the key issues of the day—democratisation, war, and growing insecurity. But the bishops were only willing to sign pastoral letters that called for respect for civil and human rights in general terms without ever directly criticizing the government. In fact, the letters generally praised the President for his interest in protecting the public good, even as they called for certain reforms.[29] Furthermore, the bishops failed to defend church personnel, as when they remained silent when Sibomana and other writers for *Kinyamateka*, published by the bishops themselves, were put on trial or when Tutsi priests were among those arrested in the aftermath of the 1990 invasion of the Rwandan Patriotic Front.

In Burundi the experience of persecution under Bagaza drove church leaders to be somewhat more outspoken, but even here church leaders were reluctant to challenge the government overtly. In the midst of ethnic violence in northern Burundi in 1988, the bishops stated in no uncertain terms that ethnic-based violence is unacceptable:

> We energetically denounce all those who have killed their fellow citizens for the sole reason that they belong to a different ethnicity than their own. We recall once again the fundamental respect for all human life, created in the image and the resemblance of God.[30]

In a more detailed follow up letter, after the violence had subsided and the facts of the events were better known, the bishops specifically addressed the killings and their implications for the country, directly questioning the implication of the church in the violence:

In the majority of cases, those who planned and executed these massacres are Christians. Those who allowed the blind repression are Christians. Those who managed the secret campaign of hate are Christians. Those who encouraged suspicion and spread false news, those who continue to do so, are Christians. ... The fifth commandment of God is direct: 'YOU SHALL NOT KILL'. ... The extermination of brothers can never in any case be proposed as a means of resolving a problem or a conflict of any sort whatsoever. And the Faith that does not live under this law is not Faith.[31]

The language in these two letters is more forthright than anything that appeared in letters by the Rwandan bishops, who never discussed specific instances of violence or unequivocally denounced ethnic attacks. At the same time, the letters do not mention the specific responsibility of government officials and the military for killing unarmed civilians, and thus they fall far short of pastoral letters from bishops in Kenya or Zaire that challenge the government more directly.

The role of the churches as institutions of civil society has thus been important yet limited. While some church groups have been key participants in civil society and some individuals have used their positions within the churches to support democratic reform, human rights and ethnic reconciliation, the principle of remaining closely linked to state power has prevented churches as institutions from presenting a more profound political critique. Progressive voices have been unable to push the broader church structures beyond superficial social analysis and platitudinous exhortations to respect the sanctity of human life. Brave voices like those of Archbishop Ruhana and Bishop Thaddée Nsengiyumva have remained isolated.

CHURCHES AS POLITICAL ARBITERS

A final social role that churches have played in Rwanda and Burundi is as arbiters in conflicts. This function of referee settling disputes between divided parties is one that church people across the ideological spectrum can support. Those linked to the regime do not feel their relationship with political authorities threatened by such a role, while it makes the church relevant to the population. Those urging the churches to a more prophetic role cannot object to efforts to bring peace and end conflicts.

In Rwanda church leaders founded a Contact Committee in January 1992, after government resistance to pressures for a multiparty government had created a crisis situation. Meeting with members of the opposition parties and the ruling party, church leaders were able to hammer out a compromise that led to a transitional multiparty government. Similarly, Rwanda's churches, represented by the All Africa Conference of Churches, helped to initiate negotiations between the Rwandan Patriotic Front and the Government of Rwanda in 1992 and again after the breaking of a cease-fire in February 1993. In Burundi the Rome-based Catholic lay Community of Sant'Egidio arranged secret peace talks between the government and Hutu rebel groups in 1996 which led to the open peace negotiations that have been ongoing since 1997 in Arusha.[32]

It is surprising, perhaps, that churches have not taken the role of arbiter more often, but there are distinct problems to this type of political engagement. First, churches are not, in fact, neutral observers on the sidelines of political conflicts. They have vested interests and have generally been tied to the established regime, making them suspect to other parties. When the state is itself a major instigator of conflict, churches tied to it may share an interest in avoiding resolution. Second, churches do not really have the capacity to act as effective negotiators. They can get a process of discussion started, but they must ultimately turn it over to those better suited, like the UN or the OAU. Third, churches may fear the repercussions of the failure of negotiations. They may not wish to be linked with unpopular settlements, like the Arusha Accords for Rwanda, and they may not wish to face the consequences of contacting ostracized groups, like the Hutu rebels in Burundi.

It is the contention of this chapter that the churches in Rwanda and Burundi have been driven by two basic imperatives: to retain the good graces of the government and to retain the popular support of the population. Voices calling for the churches to act out of principle as advocates for the marginalized or as champions of democracy have had only limited impact on the churches. The decision to issue pastoral letters on democratisation or human rights or otherwise to engage in potentially controversial political initiatives has been inspired by a desire to remain socially relevant while being tempered by the desire also to avoid offending political authorities. As a result, the churches in both Rwanda and Burundi have failed to present a meaningful obstacle to the ever-expanding social and political violence gripping the two countries. To do so they would have to rethink their motivations, the principles undergirding their social engagement, and the ways in which they engage their societies.

These principles can be seen in the response of churches to waves of ethnic violence that swept both countries in the 1990s. In Burundi ethnic violence exploded in October 1993 after a group of Tutsi military officers killed the first popularly elected Hutu President, Melchior Ndadaye, in a coup attempt only four months after his inauguration. Hutu civilians responded by massacring thousands of unarmed Tutsi, and the predominantly Tutsi military then sought vengeance on the Hutu population. In all, as many as 50,000 people were killed, roughly equally divided between Hutu and Tutsi.[33]

Over the next several years, a multi-ethnic civilian regime was able to retain nominal control of the country, but the Tutsi-dominated military gradually expanded its control, as Hutu rebel groups launched attacks on the country. In July 1996 a military coup brought former President Pierre Buyoya back to power.[34] Not surprisingly, the churches responded to these developments inconsistently. Catholic bishops expressed their condemnation of the attempted coup in October 1993, but their support for the subsequent civilian governments wavered, and they offered no condemnation of Buyoya's coup in 1996. The hierarchy seems to have been concerned with the state of the country but did not wish to compromise its relationship with the military by taking too strong a position in support of civilian rule. Nevertheless, individual clergy continued to take brave stands in favour of human rights. The bravery of Archbishop Ruhana, a Tutsi who openly criticized the military for violations against civilians even after threats on his life, is well known, but many local priests also sought to defend their parishioners from threats from both the military and Hutu rebel groups. Often, however, church personnel have remained silent in the face of atrocities. The churches have generally been less comfortable confronting the causes of ethnic conflict and division than in encouraging conversation across ethnic lines, whether at the national level through peace talks or in the local parish reconciliation programs. Such actions allow the churches to appear socially engaged without compromising their position with either the state or the population.[35] Looking at the situation of the churches in Burundi, one commentator wrote in a Catholic journal that even in the church:

The truth becomes ethnic and no longer human or divine. What results from this, in a polluted context, is a progressive loss of confidence even in church institutions, to the point of doubting its pertinence and apostolic efficacy. The consequence is clear for the Church: a crisis of identity and a loss of reference, even for the educators in the faith.[36]

In Rwanda the churches' response to ethnic violence was even less commendable. Church leaders fell almost entirely silent as Rwandan society became increasingly polarised and militarised in late 1993 and early 1994. The bishop of Nyundo publicly warned that arms were being distributed to civilians following the death of Ndadaye, but other church leaders failed to condemn the growing scapegoating of Tutsi and progressive Hutu or to respond to the growing signs of an impending genocide. When the genocide did break out in April 1994, both Protestant and Catholic leaders called on the population to support the new government, even as government-sponsored groups were gathering Tutsi in church buildings and systematically slaughtering them. Since church leaders failed to condemn clearly the ethnic violence that took place periodically from October 1990 through February 1993 and since the anti-Tutsi sentiments of some church officials were well known, many Rwandans assumed, in the absence of any condemnation, that church leaders supported the genocide. In fact, as research in Rwanda reveals,[37] church leaders accepted the claim of those who organized genocide that the Tutsi posed a threat to national security and needed to be eliminated. To this day, some church leaders have refused to acknowledge that a genocide took place. Their close alliance with the state and popular support for genocide seem to have blinded many church officials to the moral implications of slaughtering unarmed civilians, mostly women, children and the elderly. Some church personnel did speak out bravely against the violence, but their voices were few, and without the support of the church hierarchy they were easily stifled.

In short, in both Burundi and Rwanda Christian churches have failed to provide the moral leadership that might have slowed or even stopped the spread of violence. While their role as an element of civil society has increased in recent decades, this concern to maintain political influence through alliance with the state has hampered efforts to challenge injustice. Progressive forces in the churches have focused instead on social engineering at the grassroots, but even these efforts have been hampered when they become controversial. For example, a highly successful Catholic empowerment program in Butare diocese has been gradually gutted by church officials because its success in bringing Hutu and Tutsi together had gained too much attention. Church leaders have instead sought to gain popular support by portraying themselves as arbiters in the ongoing conflict, but without real neutrality and without a demonstrated commitment to reconciliation (such as serious grassroots reconciliation programs) such efforts have had few results. Rather than seeking to confront the sources of social division and to begin a process of national self-evaluation, churches in both Rwanda and Burundi have sought to regain a favoured political position by appeasing new governments and making as few waves as possible. As ethnic violence recurs periodically in both countries the churches remain ill placed to discourage it.

NOTES

1. On the conflicts in these two countries, see Reyntjens 1994; Guichaoua 1995; Lemarchand 1994; Prunier 1995; Des Forges 1999.
2. Kalibwami 1991, pp. 116–17, 174–81.
3. Linden and Linden 1977, pp. 29–34.

4. Chrétien 1993a, pp. 347–71.
5. Letter from Father Leonard to the superior of Rwaza mission, March 16, 1911, quoted in Rutayisire 1987, p. 52, All translations from French by the author.
6. Quoted in Rutayisire 1987, p. 3.
7. Linden and Linden 1977, pp. 198–201; Prunier 1995, pp. 31–4.
8. Chrétien 1987, pp. 63–8.
9. Father Leloir, quoted in Chamay 1987, pp. 159–70.
10. Kalibwami 1991, p. 153.
11. Chamay 1987, p. 160.
12. Twagirayesu and van Butselaar 1982; Gatwa and Karamaga 1990.
13. Chrétien 1987, pp. 63–4.
14. See Longman forthcoming.
15. Linden and Linden 1977, pp. 186–192; Lemarchand 1970, pp. 75–6.
16. Des Forges 1972; Linden and Linden 1977, pp. 167–74.
17. Lemarchand 1970, pp. 133–45; Linden and Linden 1977, pp. 220–39.
18. Newbury 1988, argues that Hutu and Tutsi as status terms spread into the Kinyaga region in southern Rwanda on the border with Burundi only shortly before the colonial period.
19. Lemarchand 1994, pp. 6–30; Jean–Pierre Chrétien 1993b, pp. 335–41; Rennie 1972, pp. 11–54.
20. Kalibwami 1991, pp. 195–202.
21. Lemarchand 1994, pp. 34–44.
22. Mbonimana 1978, pp. 125–63; Lemarchand 1970, pp. 74–5, 134–9.
23. Newbury 1988, pp. 144–7; Linden and Linden 1977, pp. 186–219; Maquet 1961.
24. Cf. Aguilar 1998. In the introduction Sister Agatha Radoli, looking at the 1994 genocide, declares, 'In spite of a century of evangelization, Christianity has not taken root in Rwanda and many other parts of Africa' (p. viii).
25. Linden and Linden 1977, pp. 38–67; Rutayisire 1987, pp. 36–45.
26. Chamay 1987; Chrétien 1987; Lemarchand 1994, pp. 107–17.
27. Funga 1984; Rwabukwisi 1988, pp. 17–20.
28. Sibomana told me with dismay about his silencing by the Vatican in an interview in his office in Kigali in April 1996. He told me that he asked the Vatican representative, 'How can I remain silent when God's children are suffering?' but was told not to upset the government.
29. The letters are collected in *Conférence des Evêques Catholiques du Rwanda* 1995.
30. 'Message des Evêques Catholiques du Burundi' 1988, pp. 342–4.
31. *Les Evêques du Burundi* 1988, pp. 345–50.
32. Weissman 1998, p. 24.
33. For details on the 1993 violence, see the evidence presented in Commission Internationale 1995. Both Hutu and Tutsi officials were clearly implicated in the violence.
34. Longman 1998.
35. Rutayisire 1994, pp. 552–67; Nyberg 1995.

36. Ntabona 1994, p. 351.
37. See Longman forthcoming. See also Des Forges 1999, pp. 245–6; African
    Rights 1995, pp. 896–8.

BIBLIOGRAPHY

African Rights 1995, *Rwanda: Death, Despair, and Defiance*, London: African
Rights.

Aguilar, Mario I. 1998, *The Rwanda Genocide and the Call to Deepen Christianity in Africa*, Nairobi: AMECEA Gaba Publications.

Chamay, Philippe 1987, 'L'Eglise au Burundi. Un conflit peut en cacher un autre,'
Etudes, February.

Chrétien, Jean-Pierre 1987, 'Eglise et Etat au Burundi. Les enjeux politiques,'
Afrique Contemporaine (April–May–June), no. 142, pp. 63–8.

———— 1993a, 'Conversions et crise de légitimité politique. Muyaga, poste
missionaire catholique, et la société de l'est du Burundi (1896–1916),' in Jean-
Pierre Chrétien (ed.), *L'invention religieuse en Afrique. Histoire et religion en
Afrique noire*, Paris: Karthala, pp. 347–71.

———— 1993b, ''Vrais' et 'faux' Nègres: L'idéologie hamitique,' in Chrétien,
Burundi: L'histoire retrouvée 25 ans de métier d'historien en Afrique , Paris:
Karthala, pp. 335–41.

Commission Internationale d'Enquête sur les Violations des Droits de l'Homme
depuis le 21 Octobre 1993, 1995, *Rapport Final*, Paris: FIDH, July.

Conférence des Evêques Catholiques du Rwanda 1995, *Recueil des Lettres et Messages de la Conférence des Evêques Catholiques du Rwanda publiés pendant la
period de Guerre (1990–1994)*, Kigali: Episcopal Conference of Rwanda.

Des Forges, Alison 1972, 'Defeat is the Only Bad News: Rwanda under Musinga
(1896–1931)', PhD dissertation, Yale University.

———— 1999, *Leave None to Tell the Story: Genocide in Rwanda*, New York:
Human Rights Watch.

Evêques du Burundi, Les 1988, 'Lignes de force pour des réflexions sacerdotales
sur la situation actuelle du pays', *Au Coeur de l'Afrique* , vol. 52, no. 5 (September–October), pp. 345–50.

Funga, François 1984, 'Espacement des naissance … et après?', *Dialogue*,
no. 104 (May–June), pp. 56–64.

Gatwa, Tharcisse and André Karamaga 1990, *La présence protestante. Les autres
Chrétiens rwandais*, Kigali: Editions URWEGO.

Guichaoua, André (ed.) 1995, *Les crises politiques au Rwanda et au Burundi
(1993–1994)*, Lille: Université des Sciences et Technologies.

Kalibwami, Justin 1991, *Le catholicisme et la société rwandaise, 1900–1962*,
Paris: Présence Africaine.

Lemarchand, René 1970, *Rwanda and Burundi*, New York: Praeger.

———— 1994, *Burundi: Ethnocide as discourse and practice*, Cambridge University Press.

Linden, Ian with Jane Linden 1977, *Church and Revolution in Rwanda*, New York: Africana Publishing Company.

Longman, Timothy 1998, *Proxy Targets: Civilians and the Civil Wars in Burundi*, New York: Human Rights Watch.

—— forthcoming, *Commanded by the Devil: Christianity and Genocide in Rwanda*, Cambridge University Press.

Maquet, Jacques 1961, *The Premise of Inequality in Rwanda: A Study of Political Relations in a Central African Kingdom*, London: Oxford University Press.

Mbonimana 1978, 'Christianisation indirecte et cristallisation des clivages ethniques au Rwanda (1925–1931)', *Enquêtes et Documents d'Histoire Africaine*, vol. 3, pp. 125–63.

'Message des Evêques Catholiques du Burundi' 1988, *Au Coeur de l'Afrique*, vol. 53, no. 5 (September–October), pp. 342–4.

Newbury, Catharine 1988, *The Cohesion of Oppression: Clientship and Ethnicity in Rwanda, 1860–1960*, New York: Columbia University Press.

Ntabona, Adrien 1994, 'Au coeur du drame burundais. Le totalitarisme ethnocentriste, ses soubassements et ses consequences', *Au Coeur de l'Afrique*, vol. 57, nos. 3–4 (July–December), pp. 333–58.

Nyberg, Richard 1995, 'Protestants at Forefront of Tribal Reconciliation', *Christianity Today* (December 11), pp. 72–3.

Prunier, Gérard 1995, *The Rwanda Crisis: History of a Genocide*, London: Hurst.

Rennie, J. K. 1972, 'The precolonial kingdom of Rwanda: a reinterpretation', *Transafrican Journal of History*, vol. 2, no. 2, pp. 11–54.

Reyntjens, Filip 1994, *L'Afrique des Grand Lacs en Crise. Rwanda, Burund, 1988–1994*, Paris: Karthala.

Rutayisire, Paul 1987, *La Christianisation du Rwanda (1900–1945). Méthode missionnaire et politique selon Mgr. Léon Classe*, Fribourg: Editions Universitaires Fribourg.

Rutayisire, Paul 1994, 'Une année de crise. L'Eglise dans la tourmente', *Au Coeur de l'Afrique*, vol. 57, nos. 3–4 (July–December), pp. 485–567.

Rwabukwisi, Viateur 1988, 'Relations juridiques entre l'Etat rwandais et les confessions religieuses en matière socio-sanitaire', *Imbonezamuryango*, no. 12 (August), pp. 17–20.

Twagirayesu, Michel and Jan van Butselaar 1982, *Ce don que nous avons reçu. Histoire de l'Eglise Presbytérienne au Rwanda (1907–1982)*, Kigali: Eglise Presbytérienne au Rwanda.

Weissman, Stephen R. 1998, *Preventing Genocide in Burundi: Lessons from International Diplomacy*, Washington: United States Institute of Peace, July.

THE VILLAGISATION OF KINSHASA AS PEOPLE'S MEANS TO DOMESTICATE RAMPANT VIOLENCE

René Devisch

At the risk of aesthetisation, but in tune with most influential healers and Christian healing communes in Kinshasa (the capital of Congo, former Zaire), this chapter deals with people's 'oiko-logical' settling of rampant violence. Its focus is on the cultural means which neighbourhood communes in Kinshasa develop to come to terms with the moral ruin of the postcolonial modernisation scenarios, the collapse of the state order and formal market economy, in a nation-state exhausted by the war in its eastern territory. Healers as well as the matricentric neighbourhood support networks, such as the lay-therapy management groups and grassroots healing communes in suburban Kinshasa, engage in their vicinity in care for the ill and excluded, as well as for the settling of violent conflict. The community support networks in the neighbourhoods, mobilised by the independent Christian healing communes or by healers and matrons, strengthen the inhabitants' sense of belonging and locality. These hundreds of communes re-enact, localise and domesticate the sequels in people's sense of self, community and agency, in as much as these traumas have been caused by the authoritarian colonial state or more recently by both the destabilised and abusive postcolonial state, and the frustrating chimeras of hedonist consumerism's global realm, out of reach as it is for most of Kinshasa.

FIELD

The empirical data used here are based on anthropological research conducted in Kinshasa from 1987 onwards. For an average period of three weeks annually, I have worked with families and in healing communes in these suburbs and similar settings in the vicinity, participating in hundreds of family meetings, liturgical celebrations and healing sessions. Lengthy interviews with numerous health seekers, healers and resource

102

persons in lay-therapy management groups were directed at eliciting bio-graphical-vocational and socio-historical information on the many aspects of people's relations with missionaries, the school, the village family, the white(ned)[1] models of self, scientific truth and Western humanism, Christian faith, male subject, devout wife, local and national community, emancipation, evil, the country's history, the most important factors regulating daily urban life.

The data used here cover Kinshasa's disillusioning experience of a bankrupt state, and people's mimicking of Western-style modernity during the ruthless regimes of Presidents Mobutu and Laurent Kabila in the 1980s and 1990s. At a first encounter, Kinshasa stands as a vast and bustling city, home to some 6 million inhabitants. With less than 500,000 in 1960, it expanded in the 1970s and 1980s by approximately 10 per cent annually. Massive immigration and high birthrates among a young population, for whom having many children constitutes a mark of wealth and a social security strategy, have deepened the division that the Belgian settlers initially created between the European sections of the city (called *la ville*, the city), and the ever-expanding slums (known as *la cité*, town) growing around it. The former includes the downtown areas, containing government offices, business premises, shopping malls, and large residences for the privileged few. The latter covers more than three-quarters of the total area of the capital, where most Kinois (as Kinshasa's inhabitants are called) live in conditions of abject poverty. Here are the older, somewhat planned suburbs and the newer and obviously much poorer zones or shantytowns where successive waves of immigration have occupied the urban terrain. Many of the shantytowns in the expansion zone are inhabited by members of the same ethno-cultural group sharing a common language, thus making Kinshasa a microcosm of Congo. Since the 1970s there has been such pressure on every aspect of the city's infrastructure, along with lack of maintenance and mismanagement, that public schools, medical and administrative services, transport, roads and telephone communications have deteriorated considerably, if not broken down altogether. The failure of the suburban dwellers to gain access to the benefits of the privileged has turned their earlier expectation of the good life in the city into a forlorn hope, which waits to be compensated through prayer and communitarian initiatives in the healing communes.

The focus in this study is primarily on two densely-populated and large districts of Kinshasa, namely the Camp Luka shantytown in the Ngaliema suburb and Quartier XII in Ndjili suburb. The living conditions in Camp Luka are in a state which has led many observers to regard them as among the most disadvantaged of Kinshasa. Many residents of these districts are from the neighbouring Bandundu and Lower Congo provinces and are linked to each other by kinship, mutual help or neighbourhood association.

Camp Luka, a slum quarter with crowded households, is on the fringes of the city occupying the hillsides of the opulent Ngaliema residential quarter. A squatter zone of recent origin in a marshy area, it developed rapidly over the 1970s and '80s with no formal urban planning. Its inhabitants thus enjoy few of the public services and infrastructural amenities available in the older suburbs and the city centre. Education levels are exceptionally low. Less than 5 per cent of Camp Luka's inhabitants earn regular wages. Houses are rudimentary shelters with two or three rooms with breeze-block walls and tin roofs. Hillside construction leaves homes vulnerable to the effects of erosion: heavy rains often wash away whole plots and the dwellings on them. For many of the inhabitants kerosene lamps are the only source of lighting; cooking is done on charcoal fires and water is drawn from shallow wells dug near dwellings. Although the major streets were connected to electric and water lines around 1986, only a few homes along these streets have electricity. No paved roads, sewerage or sanitary systems exist. Camp Luka has the appearance of an immense village with its numerous unfenced lots, unfinished homes, and lanes inaccessible to motor vehicles. Most households keep some poultry and have a small garden with a fruit tree.

Ndjili suburb—of which only the old and impoverished Quartier XII in the vicinity of the international airport is the focus of this study—was built in the 1950s as a 'modern' township. It represented an attempt at what the colonial authority defined as a 'harmonious association' among members of the upcoming generation of white-collar workers and urban middle-class families, both European and Congolese. It aimed to house the new citizen, in line with the utopian reformist preoccupations that in the former decades had inspired the architectural, hygienic and educational modernisation of suburbs in Belgian towns such as Ghent and Liège. The spacious suburb of Ndjili originally enjoyed a well-equipped infrastructure with a diversity of community services such as schools, health care, markets, entertainment, sports and sanitation. Its development was administered with the aim of raising a Congolese elite to European standards of rationality, work, family, marriage, hygiene and health care, in contrast with underdeveloped and illiterate villagers.

Compared with Kinshasa as a whole, Ndjili XII shows high indices of educational qualification. However, an apparent increase in single female heads of family over the last years reflects both men's loss of status and their reluctance to engage in equal marriage relations. As in many other parts of Kinshasa, most parents in this suburb are no longer able to provide for their children the levels of education and health care they themselves enjoyed in their youth. This deterioration reinforces awareness of their destitution. They are increasingly confronted by their exclusion from the social privileges and material comforts enjoyed by the leisured class living in the downtown areas and propagated by modernisation discourses and transnational television programmes.

THE TRAP OF THE MASTER SCENARIOS OF MODERNISATION

In the last (post-war) years of the colonial period, the models offered as mirrors to the (urban) people for evaluating their status rested on optimistic theories of development inspired by Western evolutionist visions of High Modernity. These visions were expected to be tailored by the political economy and bureaucratic colonial state or the independent nation-state. Through these mirrors the modernising Congolese in the colonial settlements (called extracustomary centres) and the suburban ghettos first assimilated new ideals of education, health care, mobility, civic responsibility, employment and consumption habits. Beginning in the late 1940s reformist modernisation discourse described the village as a negative space to be converted or abandoned. The battle was largely focused on the dismantling of such 'pagan' practices as polygyny, 'magical healing', sorcery and the conservative authoritarianism of the elderly.

Development rhetoric has given way to the denunciation of precarious living conditions and shelter, inadequate food, polluted water and poor hygiene, which left villagers defenceless in the face of natural disasters and disease. The indices that accompanied this development discourse included mortality, fertility and vaccination statistics. The colonial administration reports presented hygiene, obstetrics and other medical action as if they added new frontiers to High Modernity's monopoly of progress. In this vision of reality, village life was reduced to the imaginary[2] realm of untamed and unsafe nature. Life 'in the bush', as colonial discourse would define it, was considered to have little social or cultural existence and was crudely viewed as devoid of any of the civilising function of literacy, capitalist economy and universal conversion to Christian religion.

In the context of the so-called extra-customary settlements of the townships and suburbs, scenarios of so-called 'acculturation' were part of the passage towards civilisation as an upward movement leading to a higher space promising access to the new areas of instruction, information and civil belonging. The acculturated suburb-dweller had moved from the peasantry to the urban lifestyle, from tradition to modernity, offering an alternative to the otherwise debasing living conditions. The move to the city was thus conceived of as gaining access to the benefits of modern hygiene and biomedicine. It also meant quitting the routine of barter economy for efficient productivity and commodities created by modern technology. Moving from suburban to urban space (from *la cité* to *la ville*) was similarly understood as a vertical progression: the more one's life involved *going up* to the town (*monter en ville*), the closer one would get to the best schools, business offices, central hospitals or churches. Moving to well-urbanised areas meant climbing one step further up the ladder of civilisation. One of the most notorious legacies of the colonial area has been the rise of the so-called *évolués* or new petty bourgeoisie. This was a class of white-collar workers, clerks and teachers who behaved and dressed like their white counterparts and were allowed limited access to areas inhabited by colonial settlers. They depended for their living on salaries and wages provided by the capitalist economy. The Congolese *évolués* fostered the view that migrant families should renounce their village lifestyle if they wanted to be up to the task of fitting into urban society. In their view it was a matter for Congolese migrants to the urban areas to decide whether to return eventually to the village and maintain outmoded 'village customs' or to embrace modern urban life with all its requirements.

It is ironical that in their collective imagination migrants to Kinshasa from the rural hinterland since before independence have associated their move to the capital—pre-eminently the place of the coloniser—with the sub-social magical domain of the 'forest'. Unlike the colonial image of the forest realm as one of total lack of civilisation, the migrants from south-west Congo in their folklore depict the forest as a realm both of fabulous imagination and passionate acts out of sight of law and judgement. As seen in fairy tales, the enchanted wanderer's or hunter's exploits in the forest thus bring into play imaginary force-fields that seek to tap and harness the manipulable energies in the living world, while activating a sense of fusion, connectedness and plenitude.[3] These force-fields are entrenched in the pre-symbolic domain of dream and fabulation, prior to evoking the urge for a hermeneutic or even an ethical framework in the quest for the meaning of good and ill luck. Seen in that perspective, the hunter's wandering around in the forest realm, at least at the level of the collective imagination, disarms the evils of daily life, and in particular the threat of death. The fairy-tale spectacle of the hunter's wanderings evokes a mood of lust and frenzy very similar to that of the Kinois discos and 'dancing' and the collective trances and glossolalia (speaking in tongues) in the healing communes.

In particular in Kinshasa, where the missionary ethics have never succeeded in exerting a collective grip on the migrants' sexual mores, the mass entertainment culture invented in the discos steadily develops into a 'new moral economy of individual pleasures'[4] and a most appealing scene of innovative personal display and ostentation yet also one of cultural-ethical enfranchisement. Staging unrestrained sensuality and verbal extravagance, parody and mockery, artists recast and 'unwhiten' the colonial imageries of self-discipline and work ethos bestowed on the petty bourgeois *évolués*. From the 1970s on, a pervasive dandy cult spread in the bars and nightclubs, with adepts all over town, in particular among the young people eager to join the parody breed of *évolués*: it is popularly called *Sape*, an acronym for *Société des Ambianceurs et des Personnes Élégantes*.[5] The pervasive mood of contempt for authority as well as the erotic ambience and sexual exploits of the *Sapes* recreates in town the dream-world of fabulous hunting exploits, which village youths evoke with liberal amounts of palm wine and smoking of narcotic hemp. The euphoria and fellow-feeling of nightlife in the discos mocked the white colonial dictates of 'work, discipline and progress' which were meant to redeem people from underdevelopment and marginalisation on the world scene.

And yet the frenzy of *Sape* in Kinshasa as in Brazzaville (two capital cities facing one another across the Congo river) may easily spill into subcultures of violence. Here the heroes' violence in western or Japanese—such as the Ninja—action films seems increasingly to legitimise the sexual and physical violence perpetrated by gangs of youngsters and private militias.[6]

During his heyday, that is between 1965 and the 1990s in view of leading the Zairian nation back to authenticity, President Mobutu undertook the messianic endeavour of debunking the Eurocentric rhetoric of modernisation (as defined in line with models from the West). Through his policy of authenticity he achieved a situation where no Congolese could be at the same time Christian, like a white man, and Zairian. Politically the battle against Western modernisation and for the, and 'Return to Authenticity' was fought within the party-state made synonymous with the MPR (People's Movement of the Revolution). The battle was presented as a way of regaining lost roots and advancing the nationalist cause. This rhetoric reached its climax when President Mobutu proclaimed his faith in the primacy of the state and ordered an abrupt 'Zairianisation', i.e. nationalisation of private property and enterprises owned by foreigners. Failure to adapt to the new nationalist scene, which such a Return to Authenticity orchestrated, was considered a fault or failure to adapt on the part of 'villagers' to the pattern of true Afro-modernity. It became a byword for taking the village back to outdated traditional customs.

It is noteworthy that under President Mobutu's rule the underprivileged immigrant villager (*villageois*) in the city was now being defined as a *citoyen* (a citizen), a typical member of the new nation-state. However, the new characterisation continued to be trapped in the contrast between the *citoyen* with the *villageois*. The latter evoked the colonial image of the 'indigenous' person, bound to lead a farming life and espouse parochial traditional worldviews. The individual who persisted in being attuned to both local and so-called modern urban lifeways remained sidelined from the party-state politics. Until the 1980s public discourse condemned village lifestyles—chiefly authority, initiatory rites, divination and ancestral cults—symbolising witchcraft and sorcery. However, from the point of view of most Kinois adults, it was and still is important to establish the link between a person and his ancestral lineage in order to secure a sense of ethno-cultural identity.

VIOLENCE AND RUPTURES IN THE LAST DECADES

From the 1980s Kinois people have become increasingly aware that their faith in the liberating Westernising modernity has paradoxically led to proletarisation and beggary. With extensive pillaging and uncontrollable rioting the Kinois population have stifled the mirroring process and false hopes generated by the post-colonial legacy of 'modern' social state institutions.[7] The mirrors of progress and improvement helped the state to conceal the extent to which it has contributed to the decline. In fact, the adaptation to the ideals of the authenticity project consisted in merely recycling the westernisation endeavour, which in the 1990s proved a dead end. This is forcefully illustrated by a song made popular in 1994 by pop star Pepe Kale: '*Bakendeki na Poto, bakweyi na désert*' roughly meaning 'Those who went to *Poto* (i.e. the outside developed world) have entered a desert'.[8]

By the late 1980s many Kinois felt that they were the victims of an enormous deception, particularly those who had failed in the 1960s as *évolués* (also called 'black whites', a vernacular expression depicting their cultural hybridity) to gain access to the material goods and benefits of the dreamed-of modernisation. The party-state generated unanimous enthusiasm among the Zairian population, particularly in the cities, by placing itself in the African vanguard of modernisation and authentic nationalism to break the colonial mirror of identification and overcome the contradictions of an alienating colonial past. Yet by the late 1980s in the bankrupt party-state, they felt they had completely lost out on the reward of emancipation promised them by literacy, Christian conversion, paid jobs, urbanisation, Zairianisation. Their self-victimising reaction has been to distrust any discourse, pledge or project put before them by the state.

Today many Kinois find themselves in the thick of the struggle for survival, human dignity and decent housing. Living standards continue to decline as the labour market shrinks. Since 1990 the average salary for a civil servant has covered less than one-fifth of a family's basic necessities. Above all, people understand that life in the city amounts to a form of global imperialism, which exacerbates class differences. Their everyday consumption is influenced by the capitalist economic competition in the neo-liberal global market; people have coined the term 'dollarisation' to designate this economic imperialism. On the domestic scene hyperinflation and the breakdown of political leadership, public services, and the health and school systems have imposed an ambience of persistent crisis.[9] An enormous number of jobs[10] are thought to have been lost because of the looting and rioting that occurred in September 1991 and January 1993.[11] The divide between the wealthy few and the poverty-stricken majority was widening due to an annual inflation rate of 8,000 per cent in the early 1990s and a decline of at least 30 per cent in salaried jobs in Kinshasa following the mass riots of 1991 and 1993. Today it is estimated that less than 5 per cent of Kinois earn a regular salary.

For a growing number of young people living in the city, the 'street economy' has become the only means of survival. The whole move has a fictitious legal analogy, called Article 15, which in the popular imagination stipulates that in the face of crisis 'you will just have to manage for yourself'. In the popular view the state has failed its own people, who have no choice but to take the notorious Article 15 literally. Ironically this means breaking the laws against theft, robbery and unjust enrichment. We suggest that the 'street economy' is an urban version of the rural subsistence economy based on barter, hunting and gathering. Much as in the subsistence economy, people in the urban areas adopt a sort of predatory behaviour which need not be violent. For the oppressed petty crime is a mode of survival. Men and boys refer to this Article 15 with great pride and humour especially when confronting an external observer. With the collapse of formal job opportunities, Article 15 simply allows a man to preserve his honour and procure benefits comparable to those of regular employment.

From the end of 1990 to May 1991 a series of lotteries, popular games of chance, and pyramidal money schemes or 'millennial capitalism'[12] called *promotions* profoundly destabilised the urban economy. Yet paradoxically these games and money schemes brought venture capital, and more generally the capitalist financial endeavour, to the centre of all attention.[13] By promising and initially delivering spectacular profits for minimal investment within a few weeks, they attract the whole of the Kinshasa population, causing one observer to comment: 'The demagogy of the sensational drowns out the responsibility of effort.'[14] But in May 1991 came the crash. The agencies cannot maintain payments after reim-

bursing several investors, who obtain considerable profit; it was ru-
moured that the first to be paid were military personnel, which only
increased the tension. With such a large part of the population of Kinshasa caught up in these financial schemes, the effects of the collapse on
the economy, and especially the informal sector replete with unremuner-
ative occupations, were disastrous.

In August 1991 the fury of the masses reached a peak following the
collapse of the saving schemes, a 48 per cent devaluation of the currency,
and the authoritarian closure of the negotiations held under the auspices
of the National Conference, which left the people without a voice. These
failures not only stoke people's frustration but deprive them of hope and
any trust in the public moral order and rule of law. The globalised mass
media inflame the ever-larger public of the suburbs with hedonist fantasies, thereby sharpening the Kinois' growing sense of exclusion. Indeed,
the bitter frustration of the people is largely about the incapacity of both
themselves and their own networks, such as the communes, to bring an
end to the evils of perverted state institutions, the many brutalities against
civilians committed by police and the army, and the economic mirage
caused by rampant inflation. People's frustration exploded on 3 December 1990. Luxury motor vehicles, symbols of a rapacious state and an
opulent, ostentatiously self-indulgent privileged minority, became the
target of the violence of the underprivileged youth. In their own fashion
the sub-proletariat of the shantytowns replayed the violence they had
internalised: their acts were symbolic assassinations of the life of ease by
those whom its grip has defeated. More and more people are prepared to
destroy anything that recalls the failure of the Return to Authenticity
endeavour, or what is complicit in the 'cycle of the serpent'—an expression invented by the people after the formal dissolution of the People's
Movement for the Revolution as the single party and its subsequent
denial. The phrase signifies the contradictions of state politics, the pervasive anarchy and disregard for the public good, as well as the resigned
mentality of the populace.

At the end of September 1991 (and again in January 1993) a form of
military mutiny ignited a mass uprising and looting that spread to all the
residential, commercial and industrial areas of Kinshasa and set off similar disorder in other major urban centres.[15] In a kind of *Jacqueries* or
Luddite eruption, yet without the kind of leaders such movements produced in industrialising Europe, many thousands of men and women of
all ages and origins attacked factories, businesses, industrial complexes,
warehouses and dispensaries as well as the homes of expatriates and several Congolese *dinosaures* (as the richest Congolese are called), and carried off equipment, furniture, cars, machines and articles of all sorts

without, however, physically harming the owners. By destroying in the space of two or three days both business and private property on a large scale, Kinois seemed to be seeking to exorcise false hopes awakened by the myth of Eurocentric modernity and by the imperialist technology of the north. The Belgian School of Kinshasa, an almost private lycée staffed largely by Belgian teachers and offering the Belgian curriculum, and a Belgian 'GB' (*Grand Bazar*) luxury supermarket were among the first targets, and by destroying these institutions the population rid themselves of a significant but frustrating mirror of identification.

Dreams of progress and the hedonism of the city, which for decades have fascinated Kinois, have never so disappointed them as at the end of the Second Republic just before the May 1997 takeover of state power by President Kabila's Alliance of Democratic Forces for the Liberation of Congo (AFDL). The Second Republic was characterised by disastrous inflation, violence, extortion and arbitrary arrests during the last months. Yet it had once set itself at the head of the African states on their march towards full integration into the world of global capitalism and mass consumption. It seemed as if through these paroxysms of physical violence the populace was attempting to thwart and dispel the ill-fate of exclusion and general misfortune constantly threatening them. These revolts, given the complicity in them between the army and the poor, appear to have been an acting-out, through euphoric and perverse lawlessness, of the inert violence internalised by people under the pressure of galloping inflation and a bankrupt labour market. The uprisings gave rein to both the law of 'might is right' and individual resourcefulness, however questionable the means, which had already become widespread through institutional failure at all levels.

THE VILLAGISATION OF TOWN: A COUNTER-HEGEMONIC FORCE

Mothers, healers, the matricentric lay-therapy management groups and neighbourhood healing communes[16] share some responsibility for the care of the sick and community support, all tending towards creating a home for erring youngsters and dispersed kin to return to. In ritual practice and in their care for the people, which explicitly shuns a political discourse concerned with claiming rights, diviners and healers as well as prophets in healing communes take up an androgynous identity.[17] They act as as agents who transform the unspeakable, the unbearable, the ruptures. Unlike possessors of rights and the rhetorical and institutional means for social redress, healers are involved with the world. They approach a client's misfortune as an occasion not for moralising but to remake or re-awaken the life-world, to restore balance to its constituents.

Healing in both rural and urban settings proves to be a 'gynaecological' endeavour, remobilising the life-bearing functions of the mother, the home and the inhabited world.[18]

Today many Kinois are de-whitening themselves and remobilising a collective memory—separate from any exemplary, redemptive Christian or modernising horizon, or heroic position—as a strategy to rehabilitate themselves. To expel the foreignness of the state and imported commodities, the healing communes first associate cash with *sataani*, then exorcise the money collected during the celebrations to purify cash for future use. Are they thereby creating, in tune with the urban logic, an unprecedented moral incentive toward individual entrepreneurship? Today youngsters in particular increasingly seem to claim citizenship beyond any direct white(ned) references, i.e. no longer in terms of strivings for material gain or in hedonistic terms (associated in the 1970s and 1980s with the ambience of the city, and now with western consumer society), but with hope and a sense of community.

From 1993 the formation of new communes out of urban social networks has been called the villagisation of the town; it involves no less than a moral revaluation of one's place in the *cité*, as mediated through a new sense of neighbourhood or communalism. Although it does not actually entail a physical return to rural village life, this socio-cultural rooting in the (sub)urban space draws on ancient habits quiescent in the collective unconscious and fantasy world, as well as on an ethic of matricentric solidarity. Villagisation concerns a small neighbourhood with a few matricentric households; there will be between ten or twenty houses along a road with interconnected streets. It is a place for nesting, homecoming, re-territorialisation and social solidarity in the daily struggle for survival and protection against the whims of monetary devaluation, abusive state institutions, street violence and witchcraft due to envy.

Paraphrasing Bourdieu (1980), villagisation addresses the alienating post-colonial modernity that the *évolué* has adopted often as an alien garment to assert a distinctive social position. It seeks to transform this position into a community-oriented disposition more in line with his or her inner predispositions. Villagisation is about people's domestication of urban and capitalist modernity, attuning it to their collective unconscious and habitus which remain rooted to some extent in the 'socio-logic' of the extended family structure in the village realm and the overall concern with regeneration associated with it. It gives the migrant, the mother and the poor individual in particular—all outcasts of the predatory state or at the margins of the liberal-capitalist urban economy—access to a communitarian economy of barter and, by extension, recognition in the public suburban space.[19]

The trend of communalisation embraces a wide range of local or loosely-structured voluntary or non-governmental associations. There are also women's associations and co-operatives, and unions of petty traders (Li: *likelemba; moziki; moziki cent kilos*). The inspiration for communalism at the grassroots clearly derives from traditional patterns, as in the Koongo-related areas of matricentric authority, women's roles and the ethics of food production and sharing (largely the domain of women). These movements are increasingly vocal about people's wish to live with dignity to reinforce their own local, communitarian values and about their hope for a better future; a striking example is the massive popular support for the 1990 Sovereign National Conference. The conference was convened by president Mobutu in Kinshasa and brought together some 3,500 representatives from all over the country in order to discuss the ills of the nation. A coalition of local Christian communes and movements launched a series of Hope Marches in early 1992, but these were brought to a halt by the army.[20] Since then the same people have practised passive resistance by way of general strikes popularly known as Dead-Town Days (*journées villemorte*). All these phenomena express the gradual dismemberment of national political power and the disintegration of the state's normative arenas in a move towards a decentralised society. People's reaction to rampant informality, anarchy and abandonment stimulates their search for new forces—communitarian and also occult—of communal sentiment, mutual self-help, and a re-enchantment of modern life and its concern with money.

In retrospect one can argue that today the healing communes, in their own terms and on a voluntary basis and in the name of the people, are taking over the programme of cultural decolonisation set out in the 1970s by the now defunct party-state, meanwhile softening people's response to their utter disappointment with modernisation's millenarian expectations. The communes help to revise in a communitarian mode the desire of a destitute population for the material goods imported or otherwise vaunted by the capitalist economy around them. They incite people to 'more critical speech [however that fosters solidarity]', labelled in liNgala (Li) as *solola bien*.

Healing communes, local communities and associations alike situate the destitution of modern urban life within a cultural or moral framework of empathy, and hence solidarity. Coping with endless suffering and deprivation in the current chaos (Li: *sangisa sangisa*) puts everyone on the same level and encourages people to build links, while recognition of mutual suffering testifies in the general public domain to a person's dignity and social stature. The independent communes and associative movements are indeed proposing a new communitarian ethic. In particular matrons 'share courage and solidarity in a group' (Li *basi bakomi batsiamutu bakata*), thereby confronting the materialist, hierarchical, discriminatory tenets introduced by a colonial and Christian civilisation, and the predatory state. The new communes do not derive mainly either from consanguinity or from mere clientelism; in particular, the healing communes draw on a common vital force (Yi: *mooyi*) and a hope originating in the ancestral, namely white, source of life (Yi: *mpeemba*) and the saving power of the holy spirit: while associating the holy spirit with the ancestor, they broaden brother-and-sisterhood beyond ethnic and class divides. Since all members of the commune draw from this common source, there is a profound levelling of relationships throughout the group: in church celebrations adepts consider each other as brothers and sisters, thus putting husband and wife, elder and junior, cadre and worker all on an equal footing. It is most remarkable that in this way the healing communes are helping to challenge patriarchal and hierarchical authority structures typical of both the post-colonial government and the established Catholic, Protestant and even Kimbanguist churches. Correspondingly, the charismatic communes are impervious to any notion of evolutionary (i.e. potentially racist) time-space. They expose the emptiness, (literally 'the barrenness'-Li: *ba botaka te*) of the state and its *Objectif 80* which was heralded as making the country a vanguard on the African continent by 1980.

Amid the bewildering complexity of the moribund state and the overall collapse, religion does help people's force to endure life's hardships. However it does not offer a durable socio-political way out, whether through the established communes, the Pentecostal movements, the independent healing communes, or the ancestral institutions of divination and healing. Some of the young take their chance by engaging in 'bush economies' or illicit trade in dollars, diamonds, guns, narcotics and gasoline on the long land between Brazzaville, Kinshasa or Bujumbura and the diamond mines of Angola's Lunda Norte.[21] But most of the disillusioned Kinois resigned ('Kinshasa is burning like hell'; Yi: *Yitsaatsa kilemena mbwaawu*) but yet resist ('we'll not let the current famine or war exterminate us'; Yi: *tufwa lwoku*).

ACKNOWLEDGEMENTS

It is in the perspective of the mutational process in the 1990s that I look back at former periods, sharing the regrets or negative feelings of the Kinois subalterns themselves, who feel cheated by the predatory state during recent decades. I have personally become increasingly sensitive to the sufferings of people in Kinshasa, in particular the Yaka, exposed to the hardships and misery of their townships, as well as exasperated by the runaway inflation and disintegrating public services and institutions.

From 1965 to 1971 I studied philosophy and anthropology in Kinshasa and from January 1971 till October 1974 participated in the daily life of Yaka people in a settlement of villages in northern Kwaango along the Angolan border (in the Bandundu province of south-west Congo, some 450 km from Kinshasa). There, at the margins of the national political scene, I witnessed both enthusiastic nation-building and the abrupt 'Zairianisation'—the nationalisation of private property and enterprises owned by foreigners. Since 1986, for approximately three to four weeks annually, I have worked among the Yaka in the suburban shantytowns of Kinshasa, where many families live in destitution, and in particular with Koongo healing communes and Yaka healers.

The at times passionate analysis of life in Kinshasa offered here arises from participation in cultic healing sessions and prophetic healing communes, and in particular from being shaken by the widespread breakdown of civilisation in Kinshasa and other Congolese cities in late September 1991. In January and February 1993 I was present during violent looting by soldiers and gangs of youths, which has left me with the feeling that I should bear witness to what happened, yet without presuming to convey a message without hope.

Besides medical-anthropological collaboration in 1980–6 with family physicians in Antwerp and Brussels, research has extended to Tunis and southern Ethiopia. Supervision visits of doctoral research led me to Cairo, west Congo-Kinshasa, northern Ghana, southern Nigeria, north-western Tanzania, north-western Namibia, south-western Kenya, and Druze communities in northern Israel.

The present research is being carried out in the context of the programme of the Africa Research Centre, Department of Anthropology, Catholic University of Leuven (Louvain). It has been supported by the Fund for Scientific Research-Flanders, the European Commission Directorate-General XII (B4 Sector Health-STD2 0202-B and STD-TS3 CT94-0326), and the Harry-Frank Guggenheim Foundation, New York. I gladly acknowledge the valuable co-operation of my colleagues at the IMNC (Institute of the National Museums of Congo) and CERDAS (Centre for the Co-ordination of Research and Documentation in Social Science for Africa south of the Sahara; under the direction of Professor Lapika Dimomfu), both in Kinshasa. Bumbakini Ekwalama, Pascaline Creten, Jaak Le Roy, Matula Atul Entur, Muyika Musungu and Espérance Niku have all contributed to the research on the healing communes in Kinshasa.

NOTES

1. Throughout this article I use terms like 'the west, missionary, the whites', as ideological notions in daily use in present-day Kinshasa. 'White man' (*mundele*) is a term for the coloniser, for the expatriate development expert and for those who in politics, liberal professions and Christianity arrogantly display Western-style conduct and consumerist values. Colonial terms like 'elite, extra-customary, indigenous, paganism' and the like have been banished by the Return to Authenticity movement. Yet they still haunt people's representations of self and identity.

2. I employ the term 'imaginary' along the line of Lacan (1949), not with the primary connotation of 'fictitious'. In Lacan's approach, the imaginary register is a mode of unconscious feeling and understanding of other people as shaped by the partial projection of the subject's own affects of the body and psychic forces in the form of unconscious images or clichés, i.e. imagos (a notion evocative of Freud's *Sachvorstellung*). The imagos are transformed into the symbolic order in as much as they interpenetrate, in a shadowy in-between zone, with the register of language (cf. Freud's notion of *Wortvorstellung*), social time and space, social exchange and dialogical intersubjectivity.

3. Devisch 1993, pp. 90 ff.
4. Mbembe 2000, p. 269.
5. Society of Thrill-seekers and Elegant Persons; Friedman 1992, Gandoulou 1984, 1989, Martin 1995, Yoka 1991; compare with Mbembe 1992.
6. Bazenguisa-Ganga 1999.
7. Devisch 1995 and 1998.
8. See De Boeck 1996.
9. de Herdt and Marysse 1997.
10. de Maximy 1984, pp. 208 ff. and Pain 1984, pp. 105 ff.
11. Devisch 1995.
12. Comaroff 2000.
13. Devisch 1995.
14. Jewsiewicki 1992, my translation.
15. Devisch 1995, 1998.
16. Devisch, Lapika, Le Roy and Crossman forthcoming.
17. Devisch 1996.
18. Devisch 1993, Devisch and Brodeur 1999.
19. De Boeck 1996, MacGaffey 1987 and 1993.
20. de Dorlodot 1994.
21. De Boeck 1996, 1998, 1999.

BIBLIOGRAPHY

Bazenguisa-Ganga, R. 1999, 'Les Ninja, les Cobra et les Zoulou crèvent l'écran à Brazzaville. Le rôle des médias et la construction des identités de violence politique', *Canadian Journal of African Studies*, vol. 33, pp. 329–61.

Bourdieu, P. 1980, *Le Sens pratique*, Paris, Minuit.

Comaroff, Jean and John Comaroff 2000, 'Millenial capitalism: first thoughts on a second coming', *Public Culture*, vol. 12, pp. 291–343.

De Boeck, F. 1996, 'Postcolonialism, Power and Identity: local and Global Perspectives from Zaire', in R. Werbner and T. Ranger (eds), *Postcolonial Identities in Africa*, London: Zed Books, pp. 75–106.

——— 1998, 'Beyond the Grave: History, Memory and Death in Postcolonial Congo/Zaïre', in R. Werbner (ed.), *Memory and the postcolony: African Anthropology and the Critique of Power*, London: Zed Books, pp. 21–57.

———— 1999, 'Domesticating Diamonds and Dollars: Identity, Expenditure and Sharing in South-western Zaire (1984–1997)', in B. Meyer and P. Geschiere (eds), *Globalization and identity: Dialectics of Flow and Closure*, Oxford, Blackwell, pp. 177–209.

de Dorlodot, P. 1994, *'Marche d'Espoir' Kinshasa 16 février 1992. Non-violence pour la démocratie au Zaïre*, Paris: L'Harmattan.

De Herdt, T. and S. Marysse 1997, 'Against all odds: Coping with Regress in Kinshasa, Zaire', *The European Journal of Development Research*, vol. 9, pp. 209–30.

de Maximy R. 1984, *Kinshasa, ville en suspens*, Paris: Orstom.

Devisch, R. 1993, *Weaving the Threads of Life*, University of Chicago Press.

———— 1995, 'Frenzy, violence and ethical renewal in Kinshasa', *Public Culture*, vol. 7, pp. 593–629.

———— 1996, '"Pillaging Jesus": Healing Churches and the Villagisation of Kinshasa', *Africa*, vol. 66, pp. 555–86.

———— 1998, 'La Violence à Kinshasa, ou l'institution en négatif', *Cahiers d'études africaines*, vol. 38 (2–4), nos. 150–2, pp. 441–69.

———— and C. Brodeur 1999, *The Law of the Lifegivers*, Amsterdam: Harwood Academic Publishers.

———— Lapika Dimomfu, J. Le Roy and P. Crossman, forthcoming, 'A Community-action Intervention to Improve Medical Care Services in Kinshasa, Congo: Mediating the Realms of Healers and Physicians', in N. Higginbotham, R. Briceno-Leon and N. Johnsons (eds), *Applying Health Social Science: Best Cases from the Developing World*, London: Routledge.

Friedman, J. 1992, 'The Political Economy of Elegance', *Culture and History*, vol. 7, pp. 101–25.

Gandoulou, J. 1984, *Entre Paris et Bacongo*, Paris: Centre Georges Pompidou.

———— 1989, *Au coeur de la sape: moeurs et aventures des Congolais à Paris*, Paris: L'Harmattan.

Gaonkar, Dilip Parameshar 1999, 'On Alternative Modernities', *Public Culture*, vol. 11, pp. 1–19.

Jewsiewicki, B. 1992, 'Jeux d'argent et de pouvoir au Zaïre: la 'bindomanie' et le crépuscule de la Deuxième république', *Politique africaine*, vol. 46, pp. 55–70.

Lacan, J. 1949, 'Le Stade miroir comme formateur de la fonction du je', *Revue française de psychanalyse*, vol. 13, pp. 449–53.

MacGaffey, J. 1987, *Entrepreneurs and Parasites: the Struggle for Indigenous Capitalism in Zaire*, Cambridge University Press.

———— 1993, '"On se débrouille": réflexions sur la 'deuxième économie' au Zaïre', in J. Tsonda Omasomba (ed.), *Le Zaïre à l'épreuve de l'histoire immédiate*, Paris: Karthala, pp. 143–59.

MacGaffey, W. 1983, *Modern Kongo Prophets: Religion in a Plural Society*, Bloomington: Indiana University Press.

Martin, P. 1995, *Leisure and Society in Colonial Brazzaville*, Cambridge University Press.

Mbembe, A. 1992, 'Provisional Notes on the Postcolony', *Africa*, vol. 62, pp. 3–37.

────── 2000, 'At the Edge of the World: Boundaries, Territoriality, and Sovereignity in Africa', *Public Culture*, vol. 12, pp. 259–84.

Pain M. 1984, *Kinshasa: la ville et la cité*, Paris: Orstom.

Yoka, Lye Mudaba 1991, 'Système de la mode à Kinshasa. Culte du paraître', in Mashin Mazinga (ed.), *La Ville africaine et ses urgences vitales*, Kinshasa: Facultés catholiques de Kinshasa, pp. 31–7.

GREEN BOOK MILLENARIANS?
THE SIERRA LEONE WAR WITHIN
THE PERSPECTIVE OF AN
ANTHROPOLOGY OF RELIGION

Paul Richards

A PAN-AFRICANIST MILLENNIUM?

War in Sierra Leone between 1991 and 2001 is seen by many as nothing more than greed for diamonds or the barbaric excesses of drug-addicted youth. In fact the conflict has very specific political origins. The insurgency was begun by a small group of Sierra Leoneans embittered by exclusion from education and employment opportunities. The Revolutionary United Front (RUF) took much of its inspiration from the Green Book of Colonel Gaddafi.* A core group of fighters was trained in Benghazi, and received Libyan financial support for its military campaign. Libya first backed the insurgency of Charles Taylor in Liberia, but Taylor proved an unreliable revolutionary, more interested in business than ideology.

With its legacy of secondary and higher education dating back to the mid-nineteenth century, Sierra Leone was once the 'Athens of West Africa'. But by the 1980s its educational systems were close to collapse. The Green Book is an inspirational document addressing the frustrations of youth. With their high educational expectations undermined by political corruption and economic failure, young people in Sierra Leone offered more scope for a Green Book-inspired revolution than Liberian youth. The Libyan aim appears to have been a network of client states in the West African sub-region. Doubtless, the Libyan project had its *Realpolitik*, but it appealed to groups like the RUF as a millennial ideal. Green Book egalitarianism and the dream of a United States of Africa also spoke to some educated but marginalised diaspora elements, especially in America, whence the RUF drew most of its often muddle-headed overseas support.[1]

DEBATING THE RUF

There has been dispute about the origins and motivation of the RUF.[2] To Abdullah the movement was an opportunist uprising by '*lumpen*' youth, its 'politics' no more than a puerile perversion of student Green Book debate (something Abdullah helped launch in Sierra Leone). This offers us no explanation of why the RUF maintained its coherence and purpose for a decade against considerable odds—'drop-outs' clearly have an altogether unexpected capacity for long-term strategizing and coordination. Nor does it explain why the Libyans kept faith with the movement for so long. It is hard to imagine Colonel Gaddafi being so misinformed as to entrust any aspect of his foreign policy to a mere street gang.

The not-dissimilar argument that the RUF was a motley collection of young criminals motivated by 'greed not grievance' fails to get us much further.[3] There is incontrovertible evidence that the RUF was assisted by an international network of clandestine dealers in diamonds and weapons. But if diamond mining was the objective of the RUF (and not fighting against the injustices of the diamond economy, as the RUF has always claimed) then it is hard to understand why 'organised crime' and the alleged 'neo-Nazi' elements arrived on the scene so late (not until 1998). All armed insurrections need resources to survive, but there is no good evidence that diamond mining was the purpose of the RUF when it took the field in 1991. It might be easier to imagine why Sierra Leone radical intellectuals (Abdullah) would want to insist on the RUF springing from nowhere, or why World Bank neo-liberals (Collier) picture all African wars as economically motivated.

The outline of a rather different—sociological—argument is sketched in Richards (1996/8). There it is suggested that much of what was distinctive about the RUF derived from the fact that from early on (due to the counter-productive impact of indiscriminate violence by Liberian and Burkinabe mercenaries) it became a populist movement without popular support. Faced with adverse local reaction, movement intellectuals—to protect themselves, and save their dream—subsequently tried to re-organise the RUF, and disorganise rival social worlds, to conform to their theories about the nature of the political crisis in Sierra Leone. In effect the aim was to 'act out' rather than 'argue for' their revolution; ostracised by their own violence, and lacking good communications in the bush, the leadership could no longer get close enough to the intended audience to argue anything. The result was a classic enclave social formation,[4] with solidarities and potentialities to match.

This chapter revisits that argument, strengthening the theoretical interpretation by drawing more systematically on certain ideas from the anthropology of religion, and reviewing important new evidence. Recent developments confirm that the RUF retained more political coherence than is commonly believed. The movement's silence had long been misinterpreted as proof of lack of vision and ideology, and this had led to the threat it posed being underestimated. Blocked in its attempts to preach reform, the RUF turned instead to local cultural precedents—the shaping of social alternatives through management of secret knowledge. Forming durable associations around secrets is a long-practised social art in the region. This proved to have a certain effectiveness in the wider post-Cold War world, where there is little to be gained from proclaiming ideology from the rooftops. Having turned itself into a sect, perhaps almost by accident, the RUF seemed to have realised that a millennial vision shared by only a trusted few might prove a viable basis for prosecuting a revolutionary project beyond the 'end of history'.

THE RUF PROJECT: COAXING THE COLLAPSE OF STATE
AND SOCIETY

The methodology of the RUF was for a small group to exploit a long history of petty quarrels and injustices in the Sierra Leonean interior only weakly policed by a distant and effete state. RUF spies studied local communities assiduously, and a small and ill-equipped movement was subsequently able to manipulate local tensions to its strategic advantage. Sometimes this might have involved attacking a village and burning the houses of one faction in a chieftaincy or land dispute. In other cases RUF cadres might have disguised themselves as government troops, seeking to drive a wedge between civilians and the military. The RUF expended scarce resources in fighting only when strictly necessary. Much of the destruction and looting in Sierra Leone was self-inflicted; a divided society spooked by the RUF turned upon itself. As one group of villagers, in a chiefdom 'ninety-five percent destroyed' by fighting, has stated, the destruction was for the most part not the work of the RUF but 'of indigenous rebels'.[5] The RUF's theory of accession to state power was based on an understanding that (as Palmer [1992] puts it, in regard to Shining Path) it is not revolution that succeeds but weak government and civil society that fail.

Over nearly ten years some from the original RUF leadership group perished in fighting, were eliminated in internal power struggles, or broke with the movement. How many of the 'core' survived was in some doubt. But it may be larger than previously suspected (perhaps up to thirty-strong, with a handful of survivors from the original Benghazi-trained cohort). A good proportion was apparently detained, following events in May 2000, which drew key figures sheltering behind the movement's overt leader, Foday Sankoh, into Freetown, expecting to take part in a coup.

Meanwhile, this chapter revisits the issue of how much the movement depended on an ideological vision provided by a tiny leadership, and how much on 'functional' social processes that determined the actions of the rank and file. It is a puzzle to be explained how and why a largely abducted youth army was apparently willing to continue the revolutionary project even in its leadership's absence.

The explanation offered here of the durability of the RUF is couched in neo-Durkheimian terms,[6] regarding the movement as a species of sect (noting that pan-Africanism, more broadly, has millenarian aspects).[7] Sects—or enclaves, to use the term preferred by Douglas (1993), cf. Sivan (1995)—regularly manifest distinctive ideas (e.g. about the cleansing and reformative role of violence) and have unusual modes of organization (e.g. espousing egalitarianism and charismatic leadership). Normally ideology is thought to precede organization.[8] A neo-Durkheimian approach allows us to reverse the arrow of causality. On neo-Durkheimian reckoning a sectarian organizational dynamic requires certain modes of social accountability, as manifested in sectarian beliefs and values.[9] In the conditions described below—of abduction, forest incarceration, extreme violence, and abundant diamond resources—the organizational logic of the armed sect (it will be argued) becomes, to a degree, self-sustaining.[10] The RUF revolt may have been triggered by a pan-Africanist fantasy, but it continued according to a dynamic of its own, perhaps requiring sociologically 'smart' steps to halt or reverse. The consequences of a run-away sectarianism, in terms of the appalling violence that has overwhelmed Sierra Leone in recent years, should leave us in no doubt that sects without creeds are very unsafe sects indeed.

ENCLAVES IN THE FOREST: THE WORLD THE RUF MADE

The RUF launched its campaign at two points from across the Liberian border on 23 March 1991. With a force of only about 100 fighters the war was waged by rumour and terror. Village chiefs were sent letters predicting dates on which their settlements would be attacked. Houses were burnt, community leaders tortured and killed, and young people rounded up and inducted into the movement by force; many were tattooed to deter them from running away. The RUF also had lists of dissidents living in rural exile—including former members of Green Book discussion groups. Some dissidents were taken as hostages but perhaps found little difficulty in adapting to a movement embracing principles with which they were in sympathy. Some later joined the collective leadership of the RUF. Particular significance (for the later development of the RUF as a bush survivalist movement) is attached to a number of staff and students from the primary teacher training college at Bunumbu in Kailahun District. There were also some local volunteers. In the best-known case, groups of youths from families earlier displaced by the so-called Ndogboyosoi War rallied to the RUF in Pujehun District. Also, in parts of northern Kailahun District it was not uncommon for family heads to encourage older sons to join the rebels, as a kind of insurance, while families withdrew. In most places, however, the RUF was rejected by the rural populace, largely on account of the brutal killing of community leaders carried out by Burkinabe and Liberian 'special forces' loaned to the RUF from Charles Taylor's Liberian militia.

The Sierra Leone army and armed police units initially retreated towards Freetown, but with the assistance of local irregulars and anti-Taylor Liberian volunteers later pushed the RUF back towards the Liberian border (August–September 1991). 'Border guard' units trained by loyalist army officers strengthened government positions after an army coup in April 1992, and by the end of 1993 the RUF was hanging on by its fingernails in a remote area (Nomo Chiefdom) protected by an expanse of the Gola forest, the last great boundary wilderness separating Sierra Leone and Liberia.

With further retreat for the RUF blocked by a change in Charles Taylor's fortunes in Liberia, an accommodation then began to develop between army units and the RUF, which allowed both groups to engage in diamond mining and looting. Government soldiers had little or no political agenda (a few may have been loyalists of the deposed Momoh government anxious to undermine a new military regime) but the RUF was accumulating resources to pursue its political project.

It was at this juncture that the movement began to establish a chain of forest camps eventually stretching across the country almost as far as the capital. The RUF 'headquarters camp' was called the 'Zogoda', an allusion to the magic-drenched initiation processes through which forest peoples have long made 'society' in the region.[11] Whether it was a single place, or the camp in which Foday Sankoh and other leaders resided at any given time, is unclear. But at one stage the Zogoda was located adjacent to the boundary between the Gola West and Kambui South Forest Reserves. Here a 'war council' presided over the training of many young captives, and organised a model meritocratic community reflecting Green Book values and beliefs.

Deep in reserved forest, and well fortified, the camps could not be approached by army units not trained for jungle warfare. From time to time RUF and army leaders met to arrange a vigorous trade in diamonds and military supplies. After a year or so (i.e. by late 1994) the RUF was well enough supplied to launch what it termed its 'Phase Two struggle'. Eschewing roads, vehicles and heavy weapons, roving RUF columns infiltrated the countryside as far as the outskirts of Freetown, often taking many weeks to attain their objective. These were for the most part pin-prick raids on scattered defenceless communities, intended to spread terror, and convey an impression of much greater power and ubiquity than was in fact the case. The rebel columns would melt back into the forest as quickly as they had appeared, to rely upon the army to undertake 'clearing' (ostensibly mopping up rebels, but in fact looting). RUF raids were often designed to set neighbour against neighbour (e.g. only the houses of Christians might be burned in an attack, to set Muslim and Christian at odds). This helped ensure that cycles of revenge continued the war long after the RUF had withdrawn.

Young abducted cadres fought with surprising tenacity and determination—some because they responded positively to a movement that rewarded enterprise, promoted on merit, or promised access to fabulous riches allegedly hidden by a corrupt ruling elite, others because they had been implicated in atrocities or had no homes or families to which to escape.[12] Those who attempted to surrender were either killed by their own side, or summarily executed by government forces.[13] With a steady supply of diamonds (mined by conscript labourers) to exchange for arms and ammunition, and with few prospects for the rank-and-file to run away (see below), the movement settled in for a long struggle, banking on its cherished belief that a state as rotten and a society as riven by petty conflict as diamond-rich but utterly impoverished Sierra Leone would sooner or later implode. The reclusive leadership, sheltering behind the charismatic Sankoh, and the 'war council' on which some of the most prominent members were dissident abductees, did not need to show its hand. It simply sought to bide its time, believing state and society would fall apart under the stress of the terror campaign. Those who held the vision would inherit the political kingdom. A new age would dawn.

CULTURE OR CIRCUMSTANCE?—A FUNCTIONAL APPROACH TO RUF CAMPS

Humans have social intelligence which is never switched off, however arduous the conditions. We do not cease to be social because of the huge environmental deterioration labelled war, even if many social values and institutional arrangements are brought into question. In fact, it seems likely that social intelligence works overtime in times of war. We are positively challenged to get on with our social work. One aspect of social intelligence in a species with symbolic processing capacity (including language) is the capacity for religion. Broadly the anthropology of religion (on a Durkheimian reckoning) concerns itself with the way our social intelligence works on the raw material of social interaction to develop a world of spirit forces, symbols and rituals through which we interrogate, comprehend, defend or change key values, relationships and institutional arrangements. Meyer Fortes' classic account of how through death Tallensi ancestors emerge in such a way as to lock in place some of the key authoritarian ties that bind patrilineally regulated lineage society is but one well-known example of this perspective.[14]

The question here is what kinds of 'society' and 'religion' emerges under the conditions described for RUF forest camps. The line of analysis we shall explore is functionalism. Functionalism has a bad name among anthropologists, but it still has its uses. Any attempt to argue 'for' the RUF in terms of its history and identity (focuses of attention in contemporary cultural anthropology) is quickly condemned as 'excusing atrocity' (not least by those who seek to keep secret the identity of the 'real RUF' as a ploy in an unfinished political project). Thus what we try and do here is something different. A functional analysis does not attempt to justify. It simply seeks answers to questions about what has been created by social intelligence in specific, and in this case highly adverse, environmental circumstances. If we want to understand the behaviour of wild RUF abductees we shall have to look at the way their social worlds were pulled apart by social exclusion and capture, and put together again through initiation and subsequent social control, in a violent forest world organised around a degree of practical Green Book egalitarianism.

Such an exercise is not perhaps as strange as it might seem (though all who presume to write about current conflicts are vulnerable to misinterpretation of their motives). In the Netherlands you can find on the edge of each settlement a small 'camp' of so-called *woonwagenbewooners*—caravan-dwellers. Actually, the 'caravans' are small, usually wooden, bungalows or prefabricated houses. Many of the inhabitants work in the scrap trade, recycling car spares in particular. *Woonwagenbewooners* appear to be a kind of 'Gypsies'. But in fact they are entirely Dutch in origin. They were once itinerants, but not (as research has shown) because of any occupational specialization.[15] Their origins are very mixed. They are the descendents of a fairly arbitrary cross-section of Dutch society that just happened in the early years of the twentieth century to be living in mobile homes. From the 1920s onwards the state increasingly required mobile home dwellers to settle in one place in order to administer social welfare. (Real Gypsies were not constrained in this way, because the state assumed few responsibilities in regard to them; as foreigners they could always be moved on.) Having started out no different from any other set of ordinary Dutch families, *woonwagenbewooners* today have a distinctive cultural and occupational identity. They are the product of enforced immobilization and internal social elaboration of the space allocated by the state.

Dutch caravan-dweller culture is to be explained not by historical evolution or cultural essentials; rather it is a functional response to administrative fiat. This more or less serves as a model for a functional account of the RUF rank-and-file, as a group moulded by the circumstances of abduction, forest incarceration, state and movement violence, and civilian hostility.

CAMP SOCIETY

First we need to think about the raw materials of camp society. The camps were essential cogs in the RUF war machine from 1993 to 1997. Their inhabitants were leading fighters, rank-and-file combatants, fighters-in-training, medical or administrative support staff, sexual partners of fighters, and their children. Rank-and-file were mainly abductees, many seized from rural primary schools with only a smattering of literacy. These were the ones offered guerrilla training. Illiterates were kept as porters and camp servants. Some girl abductees were trained as fighters (but probably not as many as in Shining Path, where up to 50 per cent of combatants were female). Most abducted girls were assigned to the RUF 'combat wives unit' and 'combat support unit'.[16] Camps were not self-sufficient for food and labour, though the movement did maintain a large farm staffed by forced labour in Kailahun District (see below). Rural communities were either raided or placed under tribute for food and other essentials. These 'civilian' sectors also supplied slave labour, and were known as 'ideology zones' (a phrase that in RUF parlance means 'correction' or 'punishment' rather than 'inculcation of doctrine'). They were placed under the control of RUF civilian administrators known as 'town commanders'.

Each camp had its quota of hardcore RUF leaders. Some were Green Book veterans with a university background. Engineering graduate Philip Palmer (current whereabouts unknown), who challenged for the leadership of the movement in 1997, and Mohamed Rogers (detained in the May 2000 sweep), an economics graduate and secondary schoolteacher, would be examples. Both were combatants. Others were 'civilian' recruits—dissidents rounded up on the march and recruited into the 'war council'. Examples include Fayia Musa, a former agriculture student at Njala University College, in charge of RUF agricultural operations, and college lecturer I. H. Deen Jalloh and his wife Agnes Jalloh, a schoolteacher. Both Musa and Deen Jalloh had grievances with their educational establishments and were known before the war as radicals.

Benghazi-trained ideologues and civilian sympathisers constituted what might be termed the intellectual core of the movement, in charge of its strategy in the field. Despite a modest educational background, Foday Sankoh, the movement's elder, also belonged to the group of movement intellectuals. Schooled by the British army, he evinced a dogmatic streak duly noted by his trainers in early reports (one such document recording that he needed to make sure of facts before being allowed to instruct). Sankoh took charge of the Pendembu training base for the RUF in 1991 (at the time he described himself as the movement's spokesman, the leadership being collective). A trainee in Pendembu later recalled Sankoh's diatribes against a system in which the clients of politicians sat on jobs for which they had no qualifications while the qualified were denied jobs.[17] Sankoh had once belonged to a student Green Book club in Bo.

Around the intellectual core there was an outer circle of recruits trained locally or in Burkina Faso, some with a background as economic migrants or political exiles in Liberia or Côte d'Ivoire. Members of this outer circle tended to be noted fighters, but were less highly educated, and perhaps less familiar with (or privy to) the movement's political significance in the Libyan scheme of things. Two representative figures in the outer group would be Issa Sesay, appointed interim RUF field commander after the events of May 2000, and Samuel Bockarie, the infamous 'Maskita', who split from Sankoh and the RUF in 1999 to continue freelance military operations in Liberia and Guinea. Sesay was (like Sankoh) a Temne from the central-northern part of the country, and enjoyed the leader's confidence due to personal ties. Bockarie, the Temne-born adopted son of a Kissy from the Guinea-Liberia-Sierra Leone border, spent time in the Kono diamond fields, as a digger, later working as a dancer and hairdresser, before heading for Liberia and Côte d'Ivoire where he joined the nascent RUF (in his own account) on a whim. He trained at a foreign location which he was careful not to name (perhaps Libya or Burkina Faso). Steve Coll of the *Washington Post*, who visited Bockarie's domain in northern Kailahun late in 1999, found more stress on the Green Book's revolutionary programme than earlier accounts of the movement's apolitical excesses might have led one to suppose.[18]

We have as yet no statistical data on rank-and-file for RUF camps, but it is clear that most camp dwellers were very young people, in the main abducted from rural primary schools. Video footage of a camp rendering of the RUF 'anthem' (for text see Appendix below), filmed by a negotiator for the conflict resolution agency International Alert at the time of the release of a group of international hostages in mid-1995, suggests that perhaps 80 per cent of camp rank-and-file inmates would have fallen in the age range 10–15. The extreme youth of the RUF rank-and-file was a central fact about the movement's sociology.

The collectivist leadership, inspired by Libyan populism, initiated a trend towards an egalitarian way of life (e.g. planning camps as communes[19]), but a functionalist explanation of the sectarian tendencies of the RUF is usefully stressed at this point. As Mary Douglas and other neo-Durkheimian social theorists have argued,[20] there are only so many ways in which it is possible to resolve the challenges of bonding a social group, and managing its regulation (so called 'grid' constraints), and these tend to lead to a limited number of regularly recurrent social biases (attitudes, values and modes of accountability) labelled by neo-Durkheimians as 'hierarch', 'fatalist', 'individualist' and 'egalitarian' (alternatively 'enclavist' or 'sectarian') solidarities.

No social group (even a small total institution, such as a beleaguered guerrilla band in the forest) is ever totally dominated by one or other of these social solidarities, but (so neo-Durkheimians argue) a particular bundle of tendencies and attitudes will predominate depending on the precise ways in which circumstantial pressures bear down. In this case the relevant circumstances were large numbers of abducted and traumatised young people attempting to survive in isolated forest camps, and roaming the countryside for long periods in lightly-armed columns on dangerous hit-and-run missions with only a minimum of adult supervision. The situation is perhaps analogous to that envisaged by linguists for the emergence of a Creole language—restricted linguistic input, but unrestricted output (a full language conditioned largely by human functional capacities for language). The rank-and-file cadres absorbed Green Book discourse in fragmentary and partial form, but elaborated from it a functional hybrid 'culture' of their own practical, survival-oriented devising.

THE RUF AS CIRCUMSTANTIAL SECT

Evidence that organizational considerations reinforced the emergence of the RUF as an enclave or 'circumstantial sect' is mainly of three kinds. First, there is the issue of rank. Operational command among junior ranks was rotated (combatants were appointed 'commander for the day'). Promotion to more senior ranks was highly meritocratic. We know that this clashed with the normal 'birth order' or 'initiation order' rule of precedence widespread among young people in Sierra Leone, causing problems for some (older) abductees, who found it hard to accept the command of their juniors who had been more successful in battle.[21] Shining Path in Peru also motivated very young cadres through putting them in charge of raiding parties. This was often the first time marginalised young teenagers were taken seriously, and explains some of the determined inventiveness of these under-age fighters, even where they might barely understand the cause for which they were fighting.[22] One of the cadres in charge of the RUF attack on Bo on 27 December 1994 was a young woman, Alice. Those who witnessed her being beaten to death by vengeful civilians later that day remarked on her personal smartness when preparing for the attack. The trouble taken to braid her hair drew particular wonder, as indicating youthful self-confidence and bravado, not the fear or despair women are popularly thought to experience at the thought of war. This self-belief argues a more formidable sense of mission among RUF rank-and-file than conventional accounts of abducted, drugged teenage drop-outs allow. But the argument there is that this may have been more a matter of behavioural grooming than ideological instruction.

Second, there is clear significance in the fact that the RUF proved hard to divide in the field, despite several attempts by the government side to sabotage communications and sow the seeds of discord (most notably the attempt in 1997 to get Philip Palmer to take over the movement from the detained Sankoh). When asked about this, fighters explained that they had been trained to anticipate attempts to fragment the movement. They were to await a secret 'final command'. The millenarian overtones of the phrase are obvious. But equally impressive is the unshakeable commitment of cadres to the command, indicating a degree of internalisation of the movement's aims even among the very young rank-and-file. How such internalisation might have been achieved is a point at issue. Rank-and-file fighters report that ideological instruction was part of their training,[23] but a neo-Durkheimian approach suggests the movement's resolve may owe as much to organizational constraints as ideational stimulus. A key point about sectarian organization is that strength is achieved not through expensive hierarchical machinery (of command and control) but via what Durkheim called 'mechanical' forms of social solidarity (building up the group from equivalent and substitutable elements). Several RUF procedures seem to have been attuned to the support of mechanical solidarity. Rotation of command has already been mentioned, but we might also note the practical egalitarianism of camp life, and how it impressed itself upon young abductees. The movement maintained careful control over loot and looting. Items were used for redistribution according to need. One young woman reported being led into an Aladdin's cave of shoes, remarking that no one had ever given her shoes before. Another combatant described how the movement was always short of medicine, but that even though only a lowly fighter he would always be given whatever was available, down to a last aspirin.[24] In one perspective egalitarianism maintains solidarity by treating everyone the same. But in another perspective, an attack on one is an attack on all.

A third kind of evidence concerns Sankoh's leadership style. Originally, he claimed only to be spokesman for the RUF, denying leadership ambitions.[25] He executed several leading cadres in 1992, which Abdullah (1997) interprets as Sankoh the opportunist seizing control of the movement. But his long-term removal from the day-to-day running of the movement (he was absent in Abidjan on peace negotiations throughout 1996, detained by the Nigerians in 1997, jailed and condemned to death by the government in 1998, pardoned as a consequence of the Lome peace process in mid-1999 and briefly released, but jailed again in May 2000) seems not to have demoralised or fragmented his followers, which would have been an unlikely outcome if the RUF was no more than a cluster of traumatised abductees dominated by an opportunist demagogue. Sankoh (like Taylor) may have been an insincere revolutionary pursuing an agenda of personal aggrandisement, but he was also shrewd enough to understand the dynamics of sectarian 'leadership', and to have grown into the role required by the movement's forest enclavisation.

Both in the bush camps and in captivity, Sankoh manifested a crucial dimension of sectarian leadership—charismatic (or messianic) authority. He rarely if ever ventured out of the Zogoda. To many cadres in the other camps he was only ever a disembodied radio presence. However, he was assiduous in communicating with his young fighters, showing detailed knowledge of their achievements and concern for their predicament. If the radio went off air, the senior cadres would trek many miles through the forest to reach the Zogoda.

Sankoh is now well-known for his mercurial changes of position in negotiation, and his long and rambling mode of address. But we should hesitate before concluding uncertainty and incompetence. Sect leaders are delegates,[26] and demoralise their supporters if they do not consult at every phase. This accounts for much of their difficulty in hammering out deals in negotiations (though we should also add that Sankoh is also probably sticking to the central RUF proposition that victory depends on playing a long game). The lengthy harangue is a well-known tool of sectarian leadership, serving to cloak coded messages and prophetic gems accessible only to the faithfully attentive. The style can be assessed from the incoherent address Sankoh gave before the camera for the farewell of the international hostages in mid-1995 (as filmed for International Alert). One comment about prophetic incoherence is that a sect leader has great problems with the straight-to-the-point organizational approach of, say, an army commander in an operations briefing. Sect members must feel inspired (and bonded), but not controlled and manipulated (high group, low grid, in neo-Durkheimian jargon[27]). The belief and commitment must come from within.

That Sankoh (whether sincere sectarian or merely adjusting to circumstances) achieved much of the necessary oracular 'saintliness' in the eyes of his followers in the bush is evident in the fact that his leadership survived nearly four years of incarceration. When he was condemned to death in 1998 the government said it was 'cutting off the head of the snake', with the implication that this would disable the movement by striking at its source of command and control. Over-estimating the leader's executive authority is a common mistake in dealing with sectarian organisations. Where social solidarity is cellular or 'mechanical' the 'saint' enjoys boundless respect but little scope (or need) to command. The attempt to disable the RUF through a death sentence on the leader seems only to have inspired greater determination among the fighting cells in the bush, culminating in the attack on Freetown in January 1999. Much of the fighting, destruction, looting, and atrocities against civilians in that attack was carried out by dissidents from the disbanded government army (venting their anger at their dismissal by the government). The RUF followed up upon the chaos. Its own focus (as Samuel Bockarie at the time made clear) was not looting or revenge, but to rescue Sankoh from jail.

The end was not yet in sight. Even as subsequent peace negotiations got under way, there were several attempts by the government to claim that Sankoh had ordered his followers to put down their arms, but the RUF proved impervious to ruses and diversions. When the cadres from the bush eventually conferred with their leader face-to-face he seems to have convinced them to be patient once more. The RUF project (whether for the sake of a Green Book revolution or for Sankoh's personal glory) still required the state to collapse from within.

LEARNING WAR: FOREST CAMPS AS BUSH SCHOOLS

The RUF abducted and re-socialised large numbers of primary school children into a brave new forest world in which few adults played a part. As the movement expanded it was increasingly the case that youths trained youths. In this regard the RUF, in its forest-camp phase, constituted the kind of social experiment envisaged by William Golding in his novel *Lord of the Flies* (a story about the social dynamic of groups of schoolboys marooned on a desert island after a plane crash). Note should be taken of two points. First, abduction constituted a fundamental break with the wider society. The RUF 'core' viewed this as more than just a tactic to undermine the state, but as a means to rescue young people from a society corrupted beyond reform. The RUF anthem (see below) exhorts its singers to tell their parents (and the President) that they are 'fighting in the battlefield for ever', that their families will not see them again until victory is won. Second, RUF recruiters actively sought primary school children because literacy was vital to regulation of the movement in the bush. Limited access to radio meant considerable use of letters and written passes. The cadres dropped letters in villages they attacked explaining their motives and frustration. They sent messages to village chiefs warning of impending attacks. They plastered walls of wrecked buildings with unsubtle political graffiti. Camp commanders communicated via hand-written messages carried by cadres along bush tracks. The RUF war was a riot of basic literacy.

So if we are to understand what social tendencies were emphasised in the everyday life of camps we should ask William Golding's question: what kind of social worlds are groups of schoolchildren likely to create when cut off from the wider social influences received out of school hours? We are talking here about a strange situation, even by West African standards (where residential schooling is quite common). Forest camp life was in effect a kind of *primary boarding school*, with no prospect of parental visits. Furthermore, it was a primary boarding school *under siege*, where bigger boys and girls armed with guns maintained order while 'teachers' were absent for long periods on operations. Discipline involved not just detention and beatings, but also executions.

An important point about primary education is that it focuses on skills that are readily assessed by objective methods. You can read, write and count, or you cannot. All the pupils know where they stand. There are no nuances of quality. Even in regular primary school in Sierra Leone rank in class is unarguable (and assessed and published on a regular basis). Children report their position in class, where it is worth reporting, even to strangers, if they think that thereby they might attract some sponsorship. In bush camps made up largely of primary school children competing with each other to survive under the most atrocious and dangerous conditions it seems quite possible that meritocratic tendencies built into the primary classroom were picked up and amplified to a point of distortion. Perhaps the simple objectivity of primary school ranking infected children's ideas about how to wage their war, so that 'punishment beatings', sieved through a Darwinian regimen of terror and fear, escalated into the epidemic, subtractive violence of the 'cut hands brigade'. And perhaps this was a regimen first imagined by primary school graduates to deal with the refusal of adult society to 'learn'.

Although much remains to be discovered about the actual patterns of violence in the war and their precise authorship,[28] hypotheses about atrocity-as-communication merit consideration. It is currently not at all clear that amputation was premeditated and planned, however much respect for human rights and justice demands that perpetrators be brought to account. We may here need to recognise that we are confronting a *lan-*

guage of violence. Languages are intellectual products without individual authors. The language of atrocity may have been a collective and infectious response to the threat of extreme organizational dislocation, rather than the intentional product of an ideological fantasy.

'SING UNTO THE LORD A NEW SONG'

In 1999 the BBC World Service broadcast a remarkable interview with a woman who had been abducted by the RUF and served several years within the movement (Appendix). The interviewer was Tom Porteous, visiting Sierra Leone in 1998 to make a programme about child soldiers. 'Rose', a middle-aged woman who had worked as a secretary in Monrovia, was living in her village on the Liberia/Sierra Leone border when she was abducted, apparently sometime during 1994 (she states she was with the RUF for 27 months and escaped finally in an ambush by *kamajoi* [hunter] fighters—the *kamajoi* militia was not a major factor in the war until mid-late 1996).

Rose is asked what the RUF said they were fighting for:

They told us...they were fighting to move out the rotten system of the APC government...that we have so many minerals in our country, like diamonds, gold, bauxite, rutile, and even so many fishes in the sea, but they said we are suffering in this country...the government is taking care of the money...we don't have free education, even in the hospital people die because they don't have money to buy needles and tablets, pay hospital bills, or consultation fees to the doctor... they want free education, and everything to be good in the country.

The interviewer wonders whether this was sincere. Rose answers:

They told us this...but according to their actions...they were killing and threatening people...so we...it was bad for them...[laughs]...you will tell someone to stop doing something, then you are seeing him doing another one which is worse, eh? Then how can you believe that person?

The interviewer persists: 'So what do you think [the RUF was] fighting for?' Rose sums up the movement and its fate in a sentence: 'To me, maybe they were fighting for what they told us, but they never succeed[ed]... because of their bad acts.'

However the RUF was much more organised than some commentators assert. Literacy was prized, and after her capture Rose was put to work as a secretary-typist in the RUF War Office (adults without such useful skills became slave labourers[29]). The movement, she explained, made considerable use of record keeping. She typed monthly reports from various 'targets' and from all camps belonging to the RUF, detailing

…how many people have been captured in that month, how many women or children, how many died what kinds of sickness have breakouts in that month, how many combatants have died at the front line…so they send in all the monthly reports in the office and hand it over to Foday Sankoh.'

She also prepared passes to be signed by commanders controlling movements of both fighters and civilians outside the camps. The punishment for being caught without a pass was death. When there was no typewriter or ribbon Rose prepared reports and passes by hand.

The movement had its own courts ('they nearly formed their own government, because when you do any wrong they have their own supreme courts…you have to face in that court if you have done any wrong…if the court states that you will die, then you will die'). 'Rose' confirms this was not mob rule; people were judged before being punished ('in the jungle they judge you before they kill you'). The purpose of many of these trials was to control the behaviour of young combatants ('for the boys that can go at the front line, if they kill innocent people, when the commander comes in he has to bring in his report, so if you are caught, and you killed a civilian, or burned them up in a house, you will be killed'). But this draconian discipline also undermined the RUF. Rose explains:

Some of those boys, when they have done these acts, they will not go back in the combat camp…they will prefer to stay at the front line just fighting…of course, they know that they will be judged and be killed…so they will never turn back to the rear, they are always at the front fighting.

This goes some way to explaining the leadership's view of the RUF as a disciplined movement and the perception of outsiders, including victims of attacks, as nothing more than a murderous rabble ('Yes, they were disciplined…but some of them can't obey…').

Every day camp life began at 6 a.m. with compulsory prayers. Those who did not go were 'in jail for three days…in the guard room'. The prayers were both Muslim and Christian. 'They will appoint one person to pray. After you have prayed then you will say the Lord's Prayer, and then you will say the Alfatiyah'. The interviewer asks, 'how did you [long pause] reconcile the fact that these people were forcing you…were making you pray every day, and at the same time carrying out such terrible things, both to the people within the RUF, and to their enemy?' Rose seems at a loss for an answer.

Yes, when they…when they will…after the prayers, they have to pick…these boys from the strike force…to go at the front there, after the prayer…but when they go, really they are out of control, now, you see…because when they go they see these wines, this marijuana…so they got out of control, and even at times they won't obey their commanders.

After prayers camp inmates were also required to sing the RUF anthem (Appendix). Rose gives a note-perfect rendering. The interviewer praises her for singing so well. Rose explains her mastery in terms of the harsh beatings administered to those who stumbled. She had been beaten four times to acquire the song. Baffled, the interviewer wonders. 'How can you sing that song so beautifully, with that memory? You sing it very well, but with the memory that it was beaten into you...how can you sing it with such...?' Both laugh. 'Rose' answers 'They taught us that song because we have teachers among us...so after prayers you are just forced to sing, whether you are hungry, or you feel discouraged, or someone died from you that day, they don't want to know. All they know that you sing the song on the right time.... This is a revealing exchange. Painful memories ought, the questioner implies, to have interrupted the flow of the performance. But this is to assume that Rose has an intentional agent's rational control over the song. There is evidence that the acquisition and retention of music involves elements of conditioned response. Music may flow from areas of the brain quite different from the areas in charge of social intelligence. Her rendering was simply a performance to oblige the interviewer. It carried no political intentionality, despite the words. But even so it was the movement's hymn. It gives us an insight into how adaptable humans are to the harshest circumstances (how, as 'Rose' puts it, humans can be taught), and how even a concentration camp takes on a strange routine and normality of its own when other social realities are out of reach.

The leaders worked hard to make it impossible for captive populations ever to run away. It was their aim to wreck the social worlds outside the camps so as to undermine belief in any normality beyond the bizarre new reality they were busy shaping. Rose did escape from the RUF forest enclave world. Camps were for ever being shifted for strategic and defensive reasons, and Rose and her party were caught in an ambush by *kamajoi* militiamen in Kailahun sometime in 1996. She fled in the confusion, and was later reunited with members of her family (only nine members of the group of 24 people abducted from her village survived). She was unable to return home, since people vowed vengeance upon her, believing that in surviving she had somehow become a committed member of the RUF, rather than treating her as a survivor of an experience they could not comprehend. She subsequently dedicated her life to helping demobilised child soldiers. But her song speaks eloquently of the dilemmas and dangers of assuming that so much of what the RUF's abducted children did in the name of the movement stemmed from some kind of agency against which moral judgements can be obtained. It may be more reasonable to conclude that their actions cannot usefully be separated from the circumstances of camp life, and the functional values (rituals, music and worship) that emerged in the making of that camp life.

Thus Rose's testimony helps confirm that the civil war in Sierra Leone had a distinctive (though as yet largely unexplored) functional sociology, and provides clear evidence that, within a Durkheimian perspective, where there is 'society' then there will also be 'religion'.[30] There is, of course, no suggestion that any such 'religion' (based on coercion) has relevance or viability beyond the immediate cessation of the circumstances calling it into existence. But getting at and grasping cultural phenomena forged as a makeshift in the struggle for survival by RUF cadres may help re-orient our understanding of what it is that the promised Peace and Reconciliation Commission and war crimes court for Sierra Leone will have to address. It may help to recall, in arriving at judgements based on respect for 'universal human values', that such values also have their own functional history. John Locke—as author of the idea of persons as owners of themselves—was himself a direct beneficiary of the West African slave trade. In effect, he argued that slavery was justified because it led to a realisation of personhood through learning the meaning of hard labour. And yet Locke's arguments on individualism grounded in the labour theory of value are beliefs foundational to modern ideas about social contract and civil society. Religious beliefs, like human values, may first form in quite unpropitious and even embarrassing circumstances. Harsh necessity is the mother of religious as well as of technological invention. Hence, in debating the culpability of some of the youths abducted into the RUF we might wish to pay more than usual attention to the Biblical injunction about those without sin casting the first stone.

Of course it is important not to stretch neo-Durkheimian analysis to the point where it obscures the significance of creed altogether. There would have been no RUF without the wider millennial ferment of pan-Africanism. The events of May 2000 leading to the detention and placing on trial of the militant leaders of the RUF serve to remind us that the orthodox millenarian project may be much more in evidence than some commentators wish to claim. There are still plenty of believers in a United States of Africa, where it is hoped to find redress for the legacy of division and bitterness stemming from centuries of slavery, colonialism, poverty and exploitation, including many who utterly deplore the violence of the RUF. Like many actual renderings of broad millennial dreams the RUF project was bungled and violent from the outset, and responsibility for this clearly lies with the original leadership. Nor can one reject out of hand the economic explanation of the war in Sierra Leone. Over the years pressing issues of economic survival have pushed the RUF into diamond mining on an extensive scale, and many cadres now adhere to the movement either because they view it as a 'cargo cult' (believing the leadership's claims that successive corrupt regimes have salted away fortunes from diamonds which the movement will help them access) or because they can find no other job opportunities in a war-torn mining region.[31] But neither of these arguments seems fully to account for the emergent 'elective affinity' between the ideologically inspired but secretive leaders of the rebellion, and abducted rank-and-file who shelved or forgot their dreams of escaping to normality and began to live the millennial dream of their captors. It is here—among the abducted under-age rank-and-file—that it is useful to apply the neo-Durkheimian perspective, in which millenarianism is treated not as social action driven by a vision, but as a vision sustained by social organization (in this case the social organization of youthful combatants locked in a forest world of meritocracy and egalitarian redistribution, with little prospect of escape). The Judgement of Solomon handed down by Secretary-General Kofi Annan and the British ambassador to the United Nations, Jeremy Greenstock, that RUF under-age war criminals must face trial but will not face punishment may prove to be a fair and sensible response to the conundrum of millennial fervour as much induced by circumstances as inspired by belief.

APPENDIX

'Sierra Leone Rose', a programme broadcast by the BBC Africa Service in 1998, and in a revised version by the BBC World Service in October 1999 (interviewer Tom Porteous, text transcription by Paul Richards). Transcription published by kind permission of the BBC Africa Service.

Question [Tom Porteous]. *Can you start by telling me what you were doing before the war?*
Answer ['Rose']. I was in Liberia before the war. Then I came home in '92.

Q. *What kind of work did you do?*
A. I was a secretary at the Temple of Justice in Monrovia.

Q. *How did the war affect you?*
A. I was captured in my village by the RUF and taken away in the jungle forest.

Q. *Were you captured alone or with your family?*
A. I was captured with my family, about 28 of us, and only 9 survived and came home. The rest died in the bush with hunger and sickness.
[Editorial commentary on war in Africa.]

Q. *How long were you with the RUF?*
A. Two years and three months.

Q. *And what happened in that time?*
A. We were there, they carried us in the jungle. We used to suffer. They would threaten us. They command you to do anything, you don't do it, they kill you. For

example, like saying 'let's go, we are being attacked now', if you want to escape, but if you escape, they catch you and you will be killed.
[Editorial commentary on how Tom Porteous first encountered 'Rose']

Q. *What did you do in the RUF? What were your duties?*
A. I was a secretary in the RUF at the war office. The war office was one of the units. Everyone belongs to a unit.

Q. *What were your duties as secretary?*
A. We used to make passes [for journeys], like when you are moving from one camp to another in the bush, from one jungle to another. And the commanders have to sign the pass before you move.

Q. *What was the purpose of these passes?*
A. They don't want anyone to escape from the bush. If the other commandos meet you going without a pass you will be killed.

Q. *What else did you have to do? What other documents did you have to deal with?*
A. We received monthly reports from various targets. From all camps that belong to RUF. They would like to know how many people have been captured in that month, how many women or children, how many died, what kind of sickness have break outs in that month, how many chil[dren]...er...combatants have died at the front line. So they send in all the monthly reports in the office and hand it over to Foday Sankoh.

Q. *How did you write these reports? Were they written by hand, or...?*
A. At times we write it, at times we typed it. But where there is no ribbon, no type...write.

Q. *So was there a shortage sometimes of, er, ribbons and typewriters?*
A. Yes, because if you are attacked we leave everything there...at times they burn it up.

Q. *Normally, when you travelled from one place to another did you travel with a lot of material, like typewriters and other stuff?*
A. When they are moving they have interest in their weapons, they tied it up to the civilians, and the others women would carry it for them, but only few like, if they have portable typewriters they will carry it, but like the medium size ones they leave it there, or destroy it.

Q. *How did they get hold of them...these typewriters?*
A. From the big-big towns that they have attacked, like the Rutile Company and other places...they get all the stationeries and machines from those places.

Q. *From the mining company offices?*
A. [Emphatic] Yes, Rutile.
[Editorial commentary on mining and corruption in Sierra Leone, and the RUF's claim to be fighting to return mineral wealth to the people.]

Q. *Did you get the feeling while you were there that the RUF was a very well structured organization?*
A. Yes, they nearly formed their own government, because when you do any

wrong they have their own supreme courts. You have to face in that court if you have done any wrong. If the court states that you will die, then you will die.

Q. *When they kill people they kill them after judgement? Did they always judge people before they killed them?*
A. [Emphatic] Yes, in the jungle they judge you before they kill you.

Q. *How did that take place, that...those judgements, those trials, what kind of trials were they?*
A. Well, for the boys that can go at the front line, if they kill innocent people, when the commander come in [*sic*] he has to bring in his report, so if you are caught, and you killed a civilian, or burned them up in a house, you will be killed. But some of those boys, when they have done these acts, they will not go back in the combat camp. They will prefer to stay at the front line just fighting. Of course, they know that when they will be judged, and be killed...so they will never turn back to the rear. They are always at the front fighting.

Q. *Do you think that in some ways there is quite a lot of discipline within the RUF?*
A. [Emphatic] Yes, they were disciplined. But some of them can't obey. So they send them in the farm, in Kailahun, to stay in there and be making farm for the RUF.

Q. *How did you get your food when you were moving around in the bush? What kind of food did you have?*
A. We lived on bush yams, bananas, oranges, pineapples, and the civilians around...when they go and attack any place they have to loot the people's things, food, and carry it for us, and then we eat it...but at times we get our food through Kailahun, from the RUF farm.

Q. *Were you often hungry?*
A. Yes.

Q. *Were you always hungry?*
A. Yes, we are always hungry, because we can eat, but not enough for us.
[Editorial commentary: The RUF was a populist but never a popular movement. Lacking volunteers it turned to abduction for members. Its bases were concentration camps.]

Q. *So you say that you were part of the civilian group within the RUF. Was there a big distinction between the civilians and the fighters?*
A. Yes, they always keep the civilians in the forest, and the combatants in the forest, now they have a distance between them, but they have to take about...according to the population of the civilians...they have to take about 5 or 10 combatants to be guarding them, so that they won't escape. But if you are a hard working [*sic*.], or they know you have been to school, they will draw you near in the combatants' camp. So you will be writing, or working for them. Those who were nurses or doctors, they have been captured; they will be treating them, also.

Paul Richards

Q. *What was the role of the children within this organization?*
A. The children are there to be carrying their loads from them, from one place to another, or most of these children, they were command [sic.] even to kill, to beat people, to abuse their elders. Some were six years, some were two years, some were 5, 8, 9, 15-year-old boys.

Q. *So they used the children...they used the children...to carry out the punishments?*
A. Yes, to carry out the punishment, and to carry their loads, for them.

Q. *Were these punishments carried out in public, in front of everyone?*
A. Yes, if they want to punish anybody they punish you at the formation ground where we gather to pray in the morning and in the evening. They will tell you, this is the crime that this person have [sic.] committed, so you are going to be punished.

Q. *Were your days very formally structured? Did you have always to get up at a certain time, and eat at a certain time?*
A. No. The only thing, it is force [sic.] for us to get up before six, because at six o'clock everybody will be at the prayer ground. If they caught you, you don't go for prayers, you will be punished, you will be in jail for three days. They have their own guardroom. They made a guardroom there. So, apart from that you try for yourself for your feeding; at any hour you can eat, only that you can't make fire during the day. They don't allow it because of the smoke [so as not to give away the position to the enemy]. So we cook at night.

Q. *What kind of prayers did they have?*
A. Both Muslims and Christians. They will appoint one person to pray. After you have prayed then you will say the Lord's Prayer, and then you will say the Alfatiyah.

Q. *How did you...[long pause]...reconcile the fact that these people were forcing you...were making you pray everyday, and at the same time were carrying out such terrible things, both to the people within the RUF, and to their enemy?*
A. Yes, when they...when they will...after the prayers, they have to pick in these boys from the strike force to go at the front there, after the prayer, but when they go, really they are out of control, now, you see...because when they go they see these wines, this marijuana...so they get out of control, and even at times they won't obey their commanders.

Q. *Did the RUF tell you what they were fighting for?*
A. Yes, they told us that they were fighting to move out the rotten system of the APC government.

Q. *That was the government of the time? In the early '90s?*
A. Yes, the government in the '90s.

Q. *What did they say was wrong with it?*
A. They told us that we have so many minerals in our country, like diamonds, gold, bauxite, rutile, and even they were talking about the sea...that we have so many fishes in the sea. But they said we are suffering in this country. The government is taking care of the money. We don't have free education. Even in the hospital people die because they don't have money to buy needle and tablets, pay

hospital bills, or pay consultation fee to the doctor. So they want…need free education, and want everything to be good in the country.

Q. *Did you believe that really they wanted to change Sierra Leone for the better?*
A. They told us this. But according to their actions…they were killing and threatening people. So we…it was bad for them [laughs]…you will tell someone to stop doing something. Then you are seeing him doing another one which is worst [*sic*]…eh…then how can you believe that person?

Q. So what do you think they were fighting for?
A. To me, maybe they were fighting for what they told us. But they never succeed [sic.]. That's what I can think of. They never succeed because of their bad acts.

Q. *Do they ever have any anthems, or anything like that?*
A. Yes. We sing the anthem, after prayer we sing the anthem.

Q. *How did it go?*
A. [sings]:

> RUF is fighting to save Sierra Leone[32]
> RUF is fighting to save her people
> RUF is fighting to save her country
> RUF is fighting to save Sierra Leone
>
> Go and tell the president that Sierra Leone is my home
> Go and tell my parents they'll see me no more
> We're fighting in the battlefield, and fighting for ever
> Every Sierra Leonean is fighting for his land.
>
> Where's our diamond Mr. President
> Where's our gold, APC
> RUF is hungry to know where they are
> RUF is fighting to save Sierra Leone
>
> Go and tell the president that Sierra Leone is my home
> Go and tell my parents they'll see me no more
> We're fighting in the battlefield, and fighting for ever
> Every Sierra Leonean is fighting for his land.
>
> Sierra Leone is ready to utilize our own
> All our minerals will be accounted for
> The people will enjoy in their land
> RUF, the saviour we need right now.
>
> Go and tell the president that Sierra Leone is my home
> Go and tell my parents they'll see me no more
> We're fighting in the battlefield, and fighting for ever
> Every Sierra Leonean is fighting for his land.

Q. *How often did you have to sing that song?*
A. Every day after prayers.

Q. *Every single day?*
A. Yes.

Q. *And what happened if you got it wrong, or…you forgot the words, or something like that…what happened to you?*
A. Well, you will be punished…beaten. You are forced to learn it. You are forced to learn that, to sing that song.

Q. *How would they beat you?*
A. You hang, or you touch your toes, or you stretch your arms when they are beating you…you put your arms down they start again to beat you.

Q. *With what would they beat you?*
A. With sticks, medium size of sticks, or rubber, or wire or strong rope, or anything they feel like.

Q. *Just because you weren't singing properly?*
A. Yes.

Q. *How many times were you beaten like that?*
A. [Laughs] For the song? They beat me four times, to know this song.

Q. *How can you sing that song so beautifully, with that memory? You sing it very well, but with the memory that this was beaten into you…how can you sing it with such…?* [both laugh].
A. They taught us that song because we have teachers among us. So during…after prayers…for this anthem song, you are just forced to sing, whether you are hungry, or you feel discouraged, or someone died from you that day, they don't want to know. All they know that you sing the song on the right time [style].
[Editorial commentary: In a country with average life expectancy of 35 years statistically Rose aged 41 should have died 6 years earlier.]

Q. *Did a lot of people try and escape?*
A. Yes. People always tried to escape when we were in the camp. But they always planted land mines around the camp…the mines…So they can announce it in the formation, no one to go out of the camp without permission. And they have ambushes for the camp, for those who will escape. So most people used to die, when they try it. Some…some can go, but we can find some of them later…we heard…we saw that person lying down on the road. Maybe they can meet with the boys. They have no pass. And if you have no pass when you are escaping, they will kill you. So most of them died.

Q. *Did you try and escape?*
A. I never tried it. I am afraid to die.

Q. *Did many people die just because they were sick or hungry? Or you said that many of your family died in the camps?*
A. Yes. Many people died because of the hunger and sickness. There were those who used to capture tablets and injections from other towns. But if you don't have enough food how will the medicine work? So they died of hunger.

Q. *Is that how your family…the members of your family…died?*
A. Yes, of hunger. There was a little bit of medicine, but there was no food for them to eat.

Q. *Were you with them for most of the time in the same camp?*
A. We were together for eight months. Then I was taken away, because they said I can read and write...unless I had a message from these combatants...they said two or three per...family, from you, has [sic.] gone away from...that is why they told us they are going to 'look for bush yams'...'your people have gone to look for bush yams'...when they have died.
[Editorial commentary: on the failure of government to provide protection, the rise of *kamajor* (hunter) Civil Defence]

Q. *Did you witness a lot of fighting?*
A. No. I was always in the camp. Unless they bring in the reports. Or we fell in an ambush on our way going. But I have never been at the front.

Q. *So how many times were you ambushed?*
A. Twice.

Q. *What happened then?*
A. We were going to Kailahun. Then we fell in an ambush...with the *kamajors* [Civil Defence] ambush.

Q. *And was there a lot of fighting?*
A. Yes. A lot of fighting was there. Pregnant women died, sucking mothers, combatants, civilians, children...some of us died, some of us went to the *kamajors*.

Q. *How did you eventually escape? You fell into this ambush with the kamajors, and the RUF were defeated ands you ran away?*
A. Yes, I ran away, in the forest. I was there for some time and I don't know the whereabouts of my children. But later, when I went to surrender to the *kamajors*, I met my children there and we all came home.

Q. *So your children were with you all the time?*
A. Yes, they were there with me.

Q. *And did they all survive?*
A. Only one died later in Bo Government Hospital. Only one.

Q. *So you must have taken very good care of them to bring them through all that experience?*
A. Yes, the Lord helped me, and I brought them all home.

Q. *Do you feel uncomfortable among Sierra Leoneans, having been among the RUF? That they may suspect you are sympathetic to the RUF?*
A. Well [nervous laugh]...I am not sympathetic with the RUF. Because these boys have done so many wrong with people sic. You know we will forgive, but it will be very hard for us to forget about this war in Sierra Leone. Because these combatants...some were so nice...some were wicked...some can't obey...some can't obey...so you know...and we don't have to forgive everybody...and we don't know who to forgive...and we don't know who to be punished...and we don't know now who to be killed...

Q. *You are now living in Freetown...would you like to go home?*
A. I would like to go home, but I am afraid of the *kamajors*...

Q. *Why are you afraid of the kamajors?*
A. These *kamajors* are our parents. But they are angry with this RUF. And we have been captured. Most of the people have been captured by the RUF. Some of them fail to realise that we were forced to follow them...although anything...now they are against us...our parents...they even go on writing our names on cutlasses. So our relatives came in Freetown and told us 'don't go, or you will be killed'. So we are afraid to go home.

Q. *How do you think you can change that mentality?*
A. Now? We are looking at the government for peace. We are begging God...praying to God...so we will have peace. Then everything will finish. And they will take control over these *kamajors*. Then we will go home.
[Editorial commentary: In January 1999, a month after the interview was first broadcast, the RUF launched its attack on Freetown.]

Q. *What lessons have you learnt from your experience over the last four years?*
A. Well...we have learnt hardship [laughs], punishment. At times they take this advantage on you...you just have to overlook it, because you don't have power.

Q. *Have you learnt anything about your people...the people of Sierra Leone?*
A. Yes. I have learnt something about the people of Sierra Leone. You mean about the war? Everyone is looking for peace now. Everyone is tired now.
[Editorial commentary: The Lome peace accord of June 1999 was peace without justice, offering the RUF a blanket amnesty and bringing them into government.]

Q. *And you...what do you want to do with the rest of your life?*
A. I would like to be in peace...to stay home, or to work...for the mission.

Q. *For the mission?*
A. Yes. For the Catholic Mission. I have faith in God.
[Editorial commentary: revised broadcast, October 1999. 'Rose' survived the renewed fighting in 1999.]

NOTES

* This article was written in 2000, while the war was still current, and has not been revised since. The war was formally ended through the Abuja Accords and final demobilisation completed at the end of 2001. The Revolutionary United Front no longer exists, but has been replaced by a political party, the Revolutionary United Front Party (RUFP).
1. Coll 1999 provides a brief portrait of one diaspora volunteer, responsible for the RUF website and radio station.
2. Richards 1995; Abdullah 1997.
3. Cf. Collier 2000.
4. Douglas 1993.
5. Governance Reform Secretariat 2000.
6. Douglas and Ney 1998; cf. Durkheim 1912/1995.
7. Sundquist 1993.

8. But cf. Bromley 1997.
9. Richards 1998.
10. Cf. Richards 1998.
11. Bellman 1984.
12. Peters and Richards 1998.
13. Amnesty International 1992; Peters and Richards 1998; Human Rights Watch 1999.
14. Fortes 1965.
15. Cottaar 1996.
16. Richards *et al.* 1997; Peters and Richards 1998.
17. Richards *et al.* 1997.
18. Coll 1999.
19. RUF/SL 1995.
20. E.g. Douglas 1993; Douglas *and* Ney 1998; Sivan 1995.
21. Peters and Richards 1998.
22. Palmer 1992.
23. Peters and Richards 1998.
24. Peters and Richards 1998.
25. Richards 1995.
26. Douglas 1993.
27. Cf. Douglas and Ney 1998.
28. Human Rights Watch 1999.
29. Peters and Richards 1998.
30. Durkheim 1912/1995.
31. Fithen 1999.
32. The version printed in RUF/SL (1995) contains an extra verse: 'Our people are suffering without means of survival/All our minerals have gone to foreign lands/RUF is hungry to know where they are/RUF is fighting to save Sierra Leone'. Other differences include 'our people' for 'her people' and the line 'When fighting in the battlefield I am fighting forever' in the chorus, and 'NPRC' for 'APC' in the second verse.

BIBLIOGRAPHY

Abdullah, I. 1997, 'Bush Path to Destruction: the Origin and Character of the Revolutionary United Front (RUF/SL)', *Africa Development*, vol. 22 (3/4), pp.

Amnesty International 1992, *The Extrajudicial Execution of Suspected Rebels and Collaborators*, London: International Secretariat of Amnesty International, Index AFR 51/02/92.

Bellman, B. 1984, *The language of Secrecy*, Rochester University Press.

Bromley, D. G. 1997, 'Constructing Apocalypticism: Social and Cultural Elements of Radical Organization', in T. Robbins and S. J. Palmer (eds), *Millennium, Messiahs and Mayhem: Contemporary Apocalyptic Movements*, New York and London: Routledge.

Coll, S. 1999, 'The Other War', *Washington Post Magazine*, Http://washington-post.com/wp-srv/photo/galleries/sierra_leone/part_3.htm

Collier, P. 2000, *Economic Causes of Civil Conflict and their Implications for Policy*, Washington, The World Bank.

Cottaar, A. 1996, 'Kooplui, kermisklanten en andere woonwagenbewoners: Groepsvorming en beleid 1870–1945', PhD thesis, Free University, Amsterdam.

Douglas, M. 1993, *In the Wilderness: the Doctrine of Defilement in the Book of Numbers*, Sheffield: JSOT Press.

Douglas, M. and S. Ney 1998, *Missing Persons*, Berkeley: University of California Press.

Durkheim, E. 1995 (originally published 1912), *The Elementary Forms of Religious Life* (trans. Karen Fields), New York: Free Press.

Fithen, C. 1999, 'Diamonds and War in Sierra Leone: Cultural Strategies for Commercial Adaptation to Endemic Low-Intensity Conflict', PhD thesis, Department of Anthropology, University College London.

Fortes, M. 1965, 'Some Reflections on Ancestor Worship in Africa', in M. Fortes and G. Dieterlen (eds), *African Systems of Thought*, London: Oxford University Press, pp. 122–44.

Governance Reform Secretariat 2000, *The Wonde Chiefdom Consultation Report, 5th/6th July 2000*, Freetown: Ministry of Presidential Affairs, Government of Sierra Leone.

Human Rights Watch 1999, *Getting Away With Murder, Mutilation and Rape: New Testimony from Sierra Leone*, New York: Human Rights Watch, vol. 11 (3-A), June, 1999.

Palmer, D. S. (ed.) 1992, *Shining Path of Peru*, London: Hurst.

Peters, K. and P. Richards 1998, 'Why we fight: voices of youth ex-combatants in Sierra Leone', *Africa*, vol. 68 (1), pp. 183–210.

Richards, P. 1995, 'Rebellion in Liberia and Sierra Leone: a Crisis of Youth?', in O. Furley (ed.), *Conflict in Africa*, London: I. B. Tauris, pp. 134–70.

——— 1996, *Fighting for the Rain Forest: War, Youth and Resources in Sierra Leone*, Oxford, James Currey (reprinted with additional material 1998).

——— 1998/1999, 'La nouvelle violence politique en Afrique noire: sectarisme seculaire au Sierra Leone', *Politique Africaine*, vol. 70, pp. 85–104 (1998)/ 'New Political Violence in Africa: Secular Sectarianism in Sierra Leone', *GeoJournal*, vol. 47, pp. 433–44 (1999).

——— I. Abdullah, J. Amara, P. Muana, E. Stanley and J. Vincent 1996/1997, 'Reintegration of War-Affected Youth and Ex-Combatants: a Study of the Social and Economic Opportunity Structure in Sierra Leone', unpublished report.

RUF/SL. 1995, *Footpaths to Democracy: Toward a New Sierra Leone*, n.p. Revolutionary United Front of Sierra Leone.

Sivan, E. 1995, 'The enclave culture', in M. Marty and R. S. Appleby (eds), *Fundamentalisms Comprehended The Fundamentalism Project*, vol. 5, University of Chicago Press, pp. 11–68.

Sundquist, E. J. 1993, *To Wake the Nations: Race in the Making of American Literature*, Cambridge, MA: Belknap Press.

Yeebo, Z. 1991, *Ghana: the Struggle for Popular Power*, London and Port of Spain: New Beacon Books.

MASKED VIOLENCE
RITUAL ACTION AND THE PERCEPTION OF VIOLENCE IN AN UPPER GUINEA ETHNIC CONFLICT

Christian Kordt Højbjerg

This chapter aims at an understanding of the local perception of an act of political violence, which occurred in connection with a ritual performance, and to serve as a background for an assessment of the idea of religion as an idiom of violence. The focus is on a traditional masking tradition that has achieved a prominent role, momentarily at least, in an ongoing conflict between two ethnic groups in West Africa. As such it represents a standard example of the political uses of religious symbolism. Masks are some of the most powerful religious symbols among the Loma people, who live in the border region between Guinea and Liberia. These artifacts are occasionally used as a means of entertainment or as an object of ritual invocation in various contexts, ones ranging from religious ceremonies such as initiation and healing to civic such as political meetings and national holidays. Recently the mask performances have also been related to acts of political violence.[1]

Many refugees, Loma and others, have returned to their homes in Liberia since the end of the civil war in 1997. Yet in some areas the resettlement has not proceeded without difficulties. Lofa County, situated in north-western Liberia, has become the scene of a renewed violent conflict with indisputable ethnic overtones. At the moment of writing, armed conflict has spread to the entire borderland between Guinea, Liberia and Sierra Leone and caused several hundred thousand civilians to flee. This region is primarily the homeland of the Loma as well as of a considerable number of Mandingo who, despite their economic superiority, have been assigned a politically inferior position because they arrived in the area at a time when the Loma had already settled there.[2] The Loma are now overtly contesting the resettlement of the Mandingo in Lofa County. Since November 1998 Liberian and international news agencies have reported an increasing number of violent incidents in this region with victims among both ethnic groups. This conflict echoes the historic rivalry between the Loma and the Mandingo and confirms the fragility of their coexistence.[3] Likewise, there can be little doubt that the conflict results from the violent strife between the ULIMO-K, a Mandingo-dominated rebel faction, and the Loma during the civil war of 1991–7.[4]

However, the parties involved do not interpret the conflict solely in these terms. Some of the latest killings have been justified by citing the ULIMO-K rebels' violation of shrines and transgressions of prohibitions related to masking performances.[5] They can also be seen as a response to the desecration of sacred sites and cult objects which took place in the first half of the 1990s.[6] In late February 1999 two persons were killed and a mosque was burned down in Zowudomai (Söghödömai). The Loma who carried out the attack on a minority of returned Mandingo justified their action by saying that the Mandingo consistently refused to go inside their houses, as all other non-initiated people are expected to do when the supreme being named *afui* appears in a settlement. *Afui*, the highest ranking of all Loma masks and a real ethnic marker, is the emblem of the Loma male initiation society known as Poro. In this way an ethnic conflict, which is really an issue of access to land, resources and political power is turned into a symbolic conflict expressed through the manipulation and violation of religious symbols.[7] First-coming Loma are opposed to late-coming Mandingo, as sacred groves are opposed to mosques. The issue of conflict is typically veiled by the medium that gives expression to it in such political use of symbolism.

One of the questions the analysis ought to address is perhaps less the evident manipulation of symbols of group identity for political purposes than how the people involved perceive the conflict. In the present case this question in particular concerns the Loma who purposely stage political violence as cultural performance or this is, at the least, how it seems. The Liberian authorities have denounced the incident as organized crime that cannot be justified by reference to any cultural tradition.[8] Rather than taking this statement at face value, I believe it is important to ask whether Loma mask symbolism conveys a meaning that actually legitimizes radical violence or simply makes sense of it.

Recent studies of the civil war in Liberia have pointed to religion as an idiom of violence. They suggest a causal link between the traditional religion of people of the Hinterland and the atrocities committed by the parties involved.[9] It is assumed that the acts of terror experienced during the civil war are indirectly a consequence of the symbolic and real violence displayed in the rituals of the secret cult associations, including mask performances, which pervade the region. By contrast, a number of recent studies of masquerade in contemporary Africa also emphasize its pragmatic character in the politics of culture without necessarily interpreting it as a consequence of some reified tradition.[10] Accordingly, one should be careful not to draw premature conclusions about causal relations in such cases of particularly violent warfare, despite the urgent need to understand the cruel nature of the Liberian civil war. Observers of the Upper Guinea forest societies in present-day Sierra Leone, Liberia and Guinea have only rarely had direct access to local religious activities, notably because of the secrecy surrounding both male and female cult associations. Thus it is very speculative to generalise about belligerent behaviour from a few impressionistic descriptions of ritual practices, especially when they are second-hand accounts, and this type of reasoning furthermore implies an unfounded conceptualisation of Upper Guinea forest societies as 'cultures of violence' or 'cultures of terror'.

RECURRENT ETHNIC ENMITY AND SYMBOLIC CONFLICT

Violation of religious symbols and claims to land, resources and political power are recurrent themes in the history of the co-existence between Loma and Mandingo in northern Liberia and southeastern Guinea. The ongoing Loma-Mandingo enmity seems to be shaped by a variety of causes, including cultural and environmental constraints, which have been rejected in connection with the civil war in neighbouring Sierra Leone.[11] For instance, ethnic and religious identity, claims to land, environmental deterioration and the wish for revenge are among the most frequent causes alluded to by the people involved and by journalists and observers from various international humanitarian agencies.[12] However, in order to avoid essentialising the explanation of conflict it needs to be mentioned that the Loma-Mandingo enmity is only a sub-plot of and determined by a larger one, which is regional in scale. This blurred situation makes it much more difficult to understand the underlying causes of warfare and occasional acts of violence. Both Guinean and Liberian government soldiers were involved in fighting and looting on each side of the frontier and bands of armed rebels which were not initially part of the conflict have profited from the chaotic situation out of economic greed. It follows that in the course of events the kind of religiously inspired violence discussed here has become only one aspect of more generalized violence. It would be wrong, therefore, to see the atrocities committed during the Liberian civil war and afterwards as being articulated mainly through the medium of religion.

One regional historian suggests that 'the dominant theme in the recent history of the Toma is the gradual penetration of their forest habitat by Mandingo settlers and traders,[13] an immigration rich in conflicts which has caused 'time and again bloody clashes'.[14] Some authors even describe the two ethnic groups as 'hereditary enemies'[15] or as two peoples whose relationship is characterised as 'antagonistic' to the extent that some Loma villages have for a long time not even allowed Mandingo to settle.[16] Divergent views exist on the settlement history of the transition zone between savanna and forest in southeastern Guinea and northern Liberia, even though most scholars concur that the Loma arrived before the Mandingo of Konianké origin who are also known as Toma-Manya. Agreement also prevails on the fact that the area has been gradually populated by the present inhabitants since the early 16th century, when various Mande groups started a southward migration due to the decline of the Mande empire, situated in parts of contemporary Mali, Senegal and The Gambia.[17] Loma claims of first-comer status are confirmed most clearly by the idiom of matrilineal kinship that both ethnic groups use to conceptualize their relationship. They typically relate to each other as mother's brother to sisters' sons, thus assigning traditional political authority to the Loma.[18] On the other hand, this does not mean that actual power relations simply reflect ideology. The political landscape of the area has been continuously reconfigured since the first Mandingo immigration in the 17th century, entailing subordination of the Loma on several occasions. An intensified Mandingo expansion occurred in the second half of the 19th century, just before the first contact with colonial power, and was motivated by a variety of factors, such as control over the forest trade route linking the coast and the interior as well as access to fertile soils. A. W. Massing points to Islamic fundamentalism and holy war as yet another motive for Mandingo expansion into the region inhabited by pagan groups, including other Mandingo.[19] The Loma met this Mandingo quest for political, religious and economic supremacy with resistance and it was mainly due to the intervention of foreign powers in their favour that the Mandingo actually succeeded in dominating the 'autochthonous' population.[20] The Wubomai chiefdom in present Liberia has been described 'as the theater of an intensive colonisation by the Mandingo'.[21] People living in Lofa County, northern Liberia, still have a vivid memory of this relatively recent conquest of a Loma-ruled territory and it may partly explain the Loma resistance to Mandingo resettlement following the conclusion of the civil war in 1997 as well as why fighting and 'masked violence' has been more intense in this particular area than in others.

Symbolic conflict appears as a salient feature of the inter-ethnic enmity described here. Long before the current cases of desecration of sacred places and icons, both parties are reported to have committed similar acts of violence. For instance, during the 19th century emerging reformers of Islam were instrumental in promoting a renewed expansion of the Mandingo whose leaders invoked the spirit of the holy war to build territorial states.[22] These precursors of the great Mandingo chief Samori were opposed to pagan Mandingo, several of whom became allied with the non-Muslim Loma, at least until the conquest of the area in the second half of the century by Samori's army, known as the Sofa warriors. By contrast, Mandingo traders often found their routes blocked by other ethnic groups engaged in fierce warfare, in particular the Gola, Kpelle and Loma people, who felt threatened by the economic power and religion of the Mandingo. Contemporary oral sources also recount conflict, including the burning of Mandingo mosques.[23] On the other hand, Samori's Sofa warriors reportedly destroyed Malawu, a sacred Poro village in Gizima in the territory of the southern Loma.[24] Yet symbolic conflict can be more than simply competitive, destructive or expansive[25]; it may also imply the appropriation of essential symbols of group identity.[26] This is what happened, according to many Loma informants, when a Mandingo chief named Nakouma Kama Kamara was initiated into the Poro by his maternal uncles at the end of the nineteenth century. Being initiated, he later created a Poro grove (*savei*) of his own and made other Mandingo undergo the *pölögi* ritual with the additional aim, it is claimed, of enlisting the support of his Loma subordinates. Nakouma Kama's uncles were free to initiate their proper sister's son, but according to contemporary Loma opinion it amounts to profanation when unrelated Mandingo strangers become familiar with a main Poro ritual, be it male initiation or the sight of *afui* during a funeral ceremony, such as in Zowudomai in 1999.

THE SEMANTICS OF VIOLENCE

The question of the religious dimension of violence has been addressed explicitly in two recent studies devoted to the much-reported barbarous nature of the civil war in Liberia.[27] Both authors adopt a modified essentialist approach to violence in the sense that the causes for cannibalistic practices and other atrocities committed during the war can be indirectly explained as being a consequence of traditional ritual practices related to the so-called secret societies pervading the Upper Guinea forest region. There are few references to masking in these studies, although they draw considerably on an older study of Mano (and Gio/Dan) religious tradition and in particular the role of masks in a decentralized political environment.[28] This medical missionary reports some instances of human sacrifice in connection with the fabrication, transmission and use of masks by secret cults, which is then interpreted by contemporary scholars as the origin of the current proliferation of cannibalism in situations of war and among aspirants to political and financial power. Further evidence of human sacrifice and cannibalistic practices is derived from colonial court cases and travellers' accounts relating to Liberia and Sierra Leone. The reason for referring to this interpretation as a modified essentialist approach to violence is that the authors of these accounts do not claim the existence of a direct relationship between some reified traditional religious practice involving human sacrifice and a relatively widespread corresponding practice in recent times. By contrast, the argument is based on a presumed erosion of the ritual specialists' control over the practice of human sacrifice within the confines of secret religious cults. This highly valued violent source of power is claimed to have multiplied because it was 'privatised'[29] or became 'non-ritualised'.[30]

It may seem obvious to explain the atrocities of post-colonial civil war and Upper Guinea political culture with reference to cultural tradition. This is what Galy and Ellis do while emphasising that no immediate causal relation exists between the two phenomena. What causes the current perverse behaviour documented mainly by journalists is the unconstrained proliferation of supposedly traditional ritual practices. Yet the argument is fraught with difficulties regarding both the evidence on which it is based and the view of religion it purports to reflect, and moreover it produces a distorted image of Upper Guinea forest communities as 'cultures of violence' or 'cultures of terror'.[31] There is a certain ambiguity in the description of human sacrifice and cannibalistic practices in general, and specifically in relation to the mask cults and other secret societies to be found in the region. The ambiguity appears most clearly from the study by Ellis, since it is he who pays most attention to this alleged religious practice. On the one hand, Ellis is fully aware of the problems involved in assessing the value of available written and oral sources on such a contested topic. Especially since the past and present cases of human sacrifice referred to are either assigned to an undocumented pre-colonial past[32] or described as rumours and calumny.[33] Methodological precaution does not, on the other hand, prevent Ellis from putting forward the contradictory claim that 'the evidence that people were killed during the twentieth century for purposes of human sacrifice is so strong as to be overwhelming, although precisely how frequent such killings have been is impossible to determine.'[34] We do not deny the existence of ritual killings in this or other parts of Africa but simply reiterate that methodological scepticism is required for the investigation of local discourse on cannibalistic practices.[35]

It may be futile to disconnect discourse and reality, for as much poststructuralist theory has reminded us, and in anthropological thinking it is now recognized that more widely traditional forms of violence such as cannibalism, witchcraft and head-hunting must be reconceptualised as violent discourses as much as violent acts.[36] A personal experience at an early stage of field work is illustrative of this point. I had planned to do research on Loma religious life but, staying in the multicultural regional urban center known as Macenta, had not yet made any observations of religious performances. In the mean time, waiting to locate my 'real' field work site, I rather naively talked about the topic to all and sundry. My neighbour, a Toma-Manya, then explained to me that the Loma initiation ritual known as *pölögi* involved human sacrifice. Whether my interlocutor actually believed in this knowledge, which he had acquired when attending theatre plays during the state-governed 'demystification campaign' that aimed at suppressing traditional religious beliefs and practices during the 1960s and 1970s, was not clear.[37] The 'demystification campaign' was obviously an ideological project in which the end justified the means. It was a matter of changing peoples' minds and habits, and therefore the authorities probably cared less about the authenticity of the representations of Loma religion promulgated. Of course, Loma informants denied this representation of their male initiation ritual and also found it abominable. According to Rivière, human sacrifice among the Loma should not be assigned to custom and has never been part of initiation.[38] Notwithstanding the truth of this anecdote, a representation of Loma initiation as a 'criminal act' prevails and can indeed be characterised as an act that is just as violent as the physical desecration of Loma masks and other sacred objects. Ellis is not far from depicting a similar distorted image of the Poro initiation ritual, when continuously blurring the distinction between this tribal institution and the obviously anti-social secret societies known for practising ritual killings, such as the leopard or crocodile societies. It has been suggested by several authors that these associations may well have risen and prospered in reaction to colonial and other foreign pressures on local and relatively self-contained societies, rather than representing some widespread, traditional religious practice.[39]

There is little doubt that Stephen Ellis has produced one of the best background accounts so far of the recent civil war in Liberia. However, his approach to religion appears insufficient for an understanding of the relation between religion and violence, because it is at once reductionist and too generalizing. Religion is first of all viewed as an ambiguous source of power that may be tapped by individuals as well as being put in the service of society. Fear is the basic psychological mechanism underlying religious belief, which accounts for religious symbols such as masks being manipulated and used as efficacious instruments of social control. Furthermore, religion is characterised as an indispensable institution in societies devoid of a centralized power structure like those of the

Upper Guinea forest region in pre-colonial times. According to this interpretation of stateless societies, secret associations and masks in particular are used to counter and sanction any deviant social and cultural behaviour such as accumulating and abusing power, causing the shedding of blood etc. Due to a focus on checks and balances between reciprocally exclusive political and ritual offices, this model tends to overlook the dynamic potential of matrilateral kinship and patron-client relationships that more recent studies hold as a predominant organising principle of Upper Guinea political culture.[40] The lack of supporting evidence represents an additional problem with the functionalist view of masks and mask cults put forward. For instance, in Harley's description of Mano and Gio masking tradition, the social control mechanisms of masks are all assigned to a pre-colonial past. The 'law-enforcing' function of Mende masks is apparently also a thing of the past.[41] A further difficulty is that the representations and practices relative to secret associations are taken to represent those of a whole country, as when Ellis writes 'Liberians generally believe...'[42] We shall see that Loma mask cults do not reflect this picture of fear-generating and instrumental use of masking, at least not until very recently. Additionally, how is one to account for the fact that young Muslim ULIMO-K rebels have been reported to recur to cannibalistic practices, which have never been part of their religious tradition? I concur that it requires a certain degree of generalisation, when one tries to grasp the more or less subtle relationships existing between religion and politics at a national scale. It remains to be tested, however, whether the theory in question can bear the lack of evidence and conjecture that such generalisation implies. At present we are seeking a more differentiated approach to local religion in order to understand how Loma performers of masquerade perceive its violent use.

There are a number of approaches to the current episodes of gruesome and spectacular violence in Upper Guinea that contrast with the 'religion as idiom of violence' thesis. Richards, for instance, argues that the acts of terror committed by the young RUF rebels in Sierra Leone are rational and modern media-influenced ways of achieving intended strategic outcomes. Far from being random, the violence should be seen as the response of a group of marginalized educated exiles and dispossessed youth to the perceived corruption of a metropolitan patrimonial elite.[43] Likewise, both historical and present cases of accusations of cannibalism are interpreted as the 'weapon of the weak' directed against the leaders who through excessive individualism attempt to break egalitarian social contracts.[44] Ferme (1998) has addressed violence from yet another angle, by unveiling some of its less visible structural forms in the modern projects of state administration, rationalization and governance. Unfortunately the author suggests but never demonstrates how these practices may help to make sense of the more 'spectacular' manifestations of violence in the civil war in Sierra Leone.[45] It would appear to be a step in the right direction that these alternative ways of explaining extreme violence are careful not to depict past and often unverifiable religious practices as models of contemporary acts of terror.[46] On the other hand, there is a risk of eclipsing the rationality of violence as cultural performance, as in the case of Loma masquerade turning into harassment and killing, if one only looks for causes of violence that are external to the religious representations and the practices framing it. Sometimes violence is carried out with avowed reference to a religious code. Whenever this is the case, a phenomenological informed analysis must address the issue accordingly, without excluding the potential secular motives behind violent action.

LOMA MASK APPEARANCE

Loma masks display a great variety in style. Some are wooden artifacts which, in combination with animal skins and raffia skirts, cover the wearer's body; other non-wooden masks have a head cover which consists only of a piece of black-painted raffia network, for instance, or simply china clay disclosing the identity of the masked person. Despite stylistic differences, some recurring features can be found in the horizontally worn oblong wooden masks, which, on the one hand, display discernible human features such as a nose, eyes and a protruding front, and, on the other hand, are characterised by animal attributes such as horns, feathers and jaws. Common to all Loma masks is their presence during the male initiation ritual entitled *pölögi* when some of them are endowed with precisely defined functions. They also play a significant role in the life cycle of male individuals, most of whom are members of the various mask cults and perform in particular at the funerals of their adherents. For reasons of space, the following account of Loma masquerade is limited to a few cases that are of immediate relevance for the present analysis of religion and violence. Likewise, representations and attitudes associated with masks will be introduced only briefly in the subsequent paragraph.[47] Let it be emphasized that the following examples represent some of the least frequent occasions for performing masked rituals among the Loma.

The exercise of social control is represented as the epitome of masks and masked ritual in much of the older as well as some of the recent literature on this particular cultural aspect of Upper Guinea forest societies. Some of the incidents of mask appearance, collected during my own fieldwork, support the hypothesis that masks may function as a mechanism for social control. Yet this observation does not necessarily lead to the conclusion that this is an essential aspect of Loma masking, or its reason for existing. I endorse the point of view on masking in general that 'one cannot account for the whole by assigning coercion as the cause'.[48] Over the years I have only once come across an example of mask appearance that actually operated as a force of intervention intended to restore social order. In a small village the youth had been summoned by their elected leader in order to impose a fine on those who did not participate in the obligatory, collective village work which had just been carried out. As almost always happens on such occasions, a dispute broke out. This one, however, proved particularly violent. Two men started a fight that nobody was able to stop; the situation turned critical. It was then, as a last resort, that the Poro leaders took the decision to let *afui* come out. The women ran to hide once *afui*'s voice resounded from the sacred grove. As it appeared in the village shortly after, the two groups that had engaged on each side of the combatants ceased fighting immediately. Everybody knew and seemed to respect the rule never to fight or quarrel in the presence of *afui*. It ought to be added that this incident was finally resolved with the regional, administrative authorities and not, as one might have expected, by the *afui* and Poro leaders to whom the youth eventually presented a formal apology. The case illustrates how only extreme situations trigger a masked intervention that serves to maintain social order, and moreover it is still very different from the assumed 'police functions' of Mano and Gio masks.[49]

In contrast to the rare evidence of masking as a mechanism of social control in civil matters among the Loma, a considerable number of mask appearances suggests that this particular competence of masks is exercised more frequently within contexts which can be identified as exclusively religious and of which the masks are themselves constitutive. During a male initiation in 1995, no less than two incidents within a single month entailed the extraordinary appearance of the *afui* mask. In one case two Poro members had started a fight while the *afui* was singing and presiding over one of the initiates' coming-out ceremonies. This was an indisputable violation of one of the rules that applies to *afui*. A trial was organized the following night in the presence of the mask, and in addition to the fine imposed on the transgressors they had to 'tie the wings' of the mask, which is an allusion to the act of apologizing to *afui*. Only three weeks later one of the accused persons violated another Poro rule and thus provoked an immediate sanction by *afui*. The initiation period was coming to an end when the father of a young boy, who had not been included among the initiates from the very beginning of the ceremony, decided not only to take his child to the initiation camp, but also brought him back to his mother the very same night. This undermined the entire illusionary edifice which sustains the symbolic making of the Loma male, and gave great offence to the secret society. *Afui* appeared in the father's compound and imposed a severe fine consisting of a cow, a hen, a dog, 117 packets and seven single exemplars of traditional iron currency. As usual, the fine was reduced to a mere symbolic payment after elaborate negotiations and apologies to the cult leaders.

In a different setting *afui* appeared in a similar fashion in order to sanction the transgression of secret society law committed by an ignorant young Poro member. *Afui* had been heard singing in the sacred grove, but did not make any sign of entering the village. Then the young man began to cry the *sa-ô-sa* (death, death) that announces the coming of the mask and all the women quickly left the public space. Yet this signal must never be emitted as long as it has not been heard emanating from the direction of the sacred grove. The mask at last appeared in the village, but only to give a lesson in Poro law. Addressing the transgressor it declared that 'the stone is in your pocket', which is a typical example of a coded message signifying that the person was going to deal with the Poro leaders the following morning. It will never be mentioned in public that someone has violated a secret Poro rule, which would be the same as revealing the secret; it is only alluded to. The accused individual was given a heavy fine consisting of a dog, a hen, and 77 packets and seven single exemplars of traditional iron currency. Due to the intervention of an older relative who apologized for the ignorance of the young Poro member, the fine was finally reduced to a hen and 1,750 Guinea francs. Ostracism is a final illustration of the mechanisms of social control employed by mask associations within a strictly religious context. For instance, once it became known that an *angbaï zowoi* had sold his mask for public use, he was instantly denied access to Poro meetings in the sacred grove and excluded from participation in *afui* performances, in which he had held an important position due to his musical skills.

Modern secular ceremonies of both national and local character represent the most frequent occasion for Loma mask performance next to manifestations relating to the auxiliary function of the masks, which have been left out of the present account. This is mainly for entertainment, even though the masks, often alternating with other local artistic performances, may thereby serve to affirm the authority of the high-ranking civil servants and politicians present at Independence Day parades, national ballet performances, presidential visits, inaugurations of administrative centres and similar secular ceremonies. Despite the existence of one particular mask, *masaani*, that is sometimes referred to as the 'chief's skin' (*massawolai*), there is no mention of this or other masks assisting at the former nomination of a traditional chief (*taa-* or *zuimassagi*), which contrasts with the bringing out of masks at the installation of a chief among the culturally related Mende in Sierra Leone.[50] It is important that the masks performing at secular, public events are the ones that the Loma themselves primarily consider entertainment masks, such as *laniboï* and *onilégagi* and less frequently *kpakologi* and *angbaï*, whereas the rare ones, *masaani* and *savhélégi*, for instance, and *afui*, which is surrounded by complete secrecy and epitomizes Loma cultural identity, will never be manifested at such politically encompassing occasions.

A final and very exceptional type of mask appearance concerns the role of masking in the relationship between distinct societies and more specifically in inter-group conflict. Unlike other regional mask traditions, Dan, Mano and Kono for instance,[51] the Loma do not seem to associate any of their masks with warfare. In his study of the Mandingo conqueror Samori, Person notes that the Loma soldiers are assumed to have been accompanied by numerous stilt masks, probably *laniboï*, which were shot down by Samori's Sofa soldiers, but he adds that this is the only known reference to the military role of these masks.[52] Almost a century later, masking was evoked anew in relation to a multifaceted conflict between the Loma and the descendants of Samori's former ally Toma-Manya. In 1994 Poro members were summoned all over Guinean Loma country in order to decide on the action to adopt in the continuous and increasingly armed conflict between the co-resident Loma and Mandingo in general and, more particularly, the Loma and the rebel army ULIMO-K supported by the Toma-Manya. One strategy among others was to attribute an increased significance to the *afui* mask because of its presumed ability to frighten and chase away all non-initiated people.[53] To my knowledge, the utility of *afui*'s intimidating character in ethnic interaction was put to the test only four years later when, according to informants and news reports, the mask 'besieged' administrative headquarters at Zorzor in Liberia, 'caused' residents to flee, 'stopped' cars and finally 'staged' the killing of two Mandingo and the desecration of the mosque in the town of Zowudomai.[54] A similar incident took place shortly after in the provincial capital Voinjama, where secret society leaders and masked figures awaited the government investigation of the event in Zowudomai.[55] There is no further information about the actual organisation of these highly unusual mask performances by the *afui*, though it is well known that the Loma outnumbered their adversaries considerably at the time of the incidents. Since then the ethnic clashes have increased without any further mention of masked harassment.

From all the historical information one can gather about the association of masks and warfare, there is little doubt that the instrumental use of the supreme Loma mask in recent ethnic conflict is not only exceptional, but probably constitutes a very modern phenomenon as well. Person does not indicate the source of his reference to Loma stilt masks serving in a nineteenth-century battle. Moreover, when asking contemporary informants directly about the function of masks, they only invoke the role of mask in entertainment, i.e. in addition to mask performance with religious contexts. One may put the recent use of masks in violent conflict in perspective by referring to the rather anecdotal description of a traditional dispute settlement between a Loma and a Kpelle village by means of a 'mock battle' carried out between two masks from the respective villages.[56] This type of combat appears more as fair game than the intimidating strategy of the Lofa County *afui*, whose action recalls a military strategy in a state of emergency, rather than ordinary occasions and modes of masked performance.

THE WORK OF MASKS

Irrespectively of thematic focus and theoretical approach, most recent studies of African masking seem to agree that the work of masks consists above all in their transformative role.[57] The preceding account of mask appearances sustains the assumption that masking serves as a vehicle of transformation and a means of coping with change. In a very general sense, all Loma mask performances relate to situations of transition from one state to the next. This is the case when a mask appears in a thanksgiving ritual occasioned by the acquisition of a new wife, at the death and funeral of an individual, during the initiation of boys into men, when masks settle violent disputes, and punish the transgression of secret society law, or when they appear in an entertaining role during the visit of a newly elected political leader. Passages from one state to the other are typically associated with some sort of danger. They represent critical situations in need of mediation and masks are apparently well suited to this task.

It has been argued that 'since masks are themselves transformations they are used as metaphors-in-action, to transform events themselves or mediate between structures'.[58] This statement is based on a concept of masks as expressions of paradox and ambiguity, the most basic being the act of covering, so that the concealment of identity is simultaneously the revelation of a new identity. Notwithstanding the accuracy of such general characteristics of the nature of masking, one ought to be more specific in the description of cognitive mechanisms involved in this type of ritual action. In the case of Loma masking tradition it is possible to identify a particular style that does not necessarily conflict with the general characteristic of masks as paradoxical and ambiguous. This style consists of a systematic juxtaposition of opposing values and roles, or of contradictory modes of behaviour, which recur in both tales about masks and in ritual action.[59] The pairing of opposites is found in the majority of composite, wooden masks which are both zoomorphic and anthropomorphic. In addition, stories of mask provenance not only evoke the natural origin of supernatural forces that are brought into the life of human beings who guard and provide them with physical form; they epitomize to an even greater extent the opposition and complementarity between the sexes, perhaps most significantly in the tale describing how the men succeed in inventing the illusory device of the supreme deity *afui* from which the women are completely excluded. Some of these stories also illustrate, the antagonistic relationship between the Loma and their Mandingo neighbours, especially in the case of the *savhélégi* mask that speaks their language and celebrates their Muslim festivals and yet rejects their presence. Mask performance and sacrificial techniques deployed in association with masks provide further illustration of the symbolic style that consists in linking of opposites. Masks that are considered original Loma, such as *masaani, savhélégi* and *kpakologi*, all communicate in foreign languages. Others simply invert ordinary rules of speech. The numbers three and four as well as left and right hand symbolism associated with the respective sexes are frequently inverted, most notably in the case of the *angbaï* mask, which in contrast to ordinary human behaviour is also seen walking backwards, as it enters and leaves a building. The performance of auditory, secret masks in a human settlement and public masks hiding secret miniature masks under their costume, or just celebrating a secretly held sacrifice, are yet more significant instances of the coincidence of contradictory forms in the context of masking. Mask symbolism rests on a tension between opposites, as does the change of states between life and death, childhood and manhood etc. that occasions mask appearance. It does not seem unreasonable, then, to conclude that it is precisely this analogy between distinct orders of reality which renders masks cognitively apt to mediate and solve such critical situations. Yet there is more to masking than serving as a cognitive bridgehead.

By means of differentiation Loma mask symbolism also serves to construct identities as well as to fashion certain types of social relationships. The creative dimension of mask symbolism follows logically from the outstanding importance of secrecy in religious organisation and communication. On the other hand, individuals and groups are sometimes found to make deliberate use of mask symbolism in order to manipulate social relationships.[60] In the case of most Loma individual destiny is determined by the presence of a category of supernatural agencies which materialize in the form of a mask. In addition to the intimate relationship existing between a person and his or her tutelary spirit, Loma mask symbolism displays a series of oppositional social relationships, among which the one related to gender figures most prominently. The opposition and complementarity between men and women are a recurrent theme in both stories of masks and in their actual performances. Masking is a male prerogative singled out in more or less autonomous cult groups from which the women are excluded. It should be added, for the sake of completeness, that Loma women too possess a considerable number of equally exclusive religious cults not associated with masks except for the disguised *bowoi* figure.

Masking is instrumental in the ordering of other essential social relationships in Loma society. Such social arrangements are not simply represented in tales and symbolic gestures, but rather emerge in ritual actions that entail mask appearance, such as sacrifice and funerals. It is important to note that mask associations recruit and assemble individuals from different patrilineal descent groups, which is an organizational form known from other parts of West Africa.[61] Mask activities also emphasize and reiterate the divisions between initiated and non-initiated, on the one hand, and between elders and youth, on the other. These social divisions tend, however, to diminish outside the ritual context. The authority of powerful ritual leaders rarely extends beyond the realm of the secret society. At present (if at any time at all) only a few such persons are endowed with considerable secular influence.

Finally mask associations, the Poro in particular, serve as a means of relating to an outside world. The antagonism between Loma and their Mandingo neighbours is a recurrent theme in the symbolism of masking in both discourse and practice and it is spelled out even more explicitly in the context of tribal male initiation. *Pölögi* belongs to the Loma. It is a symbolic marker that forges cultural identity and distinguishes this ethnic entity from other groups, notably the Mandingo, who do not share this cultural practice. One still hears Loma people deploring the theft of the *pölögi*, their symbolic capital, by a nephew of Toma-Manya origin (Nakouma Kama) at the end of the 19th century. The recent process of democratization in Guinea has sustained the discriminatory effect of initiation and masking in general. During their election campaigns throughout the 1990s candidates for Parliament and the Presidency repeatedly reassured the Loma of their freedom to initiate their children and feed their tutelary spirits by blood sacrifices. In a similar fashion both the Liberian and Guinean authorities have singled out the secret mask associations in their policy of controlling the Loma, either as an evil to be suppressed in the name of modernity, or as an ally. It is precisely this strategy that has been adopted by a recent traditionalist movement (*Gilibai*), inaugurated by an urban elite, in the ongoing tense relationship between the Loma and the Mandingo.[62]

RECAPITULATION

The survey of actual mask performances shows the existence of at least five different occasions in Loma society for the use of masks which relate, in turn, to their auxiliary role for individuals, to periodical rituals, to the violation of secret society law, to secular ceremonies and to the management of conflict between societies. The frequency of the various mask appearances provide little evidence supporting the assumption that masks serve as a strategic means of exercising social control beyond the context of secret society organisation. This does not prevent the mask institution in general from symbolizing male authority or, for instance, from affirming the political superiority of landowning lineages during initiation rituals. But these are rather unintended consequences of masked ritual and mask symbolism; they do not reflect the situations that require masked performance and cannot, therefore, be taken as the reason for the existence of the Loma mask institution. The assertion that Loma masks do not serve as a mechanism of social control is in line with a survey by Siegman of the interaction of spiritual forces and socio-political life in the central West Atlantic region. This scholar writes that in the Poro area and in contrast to the use of masks among other societies in the same region

Dispute settlement is normally affected by secular means but intractable disputes and especially those involving violations of sacred law and public morals may necessitate the involvement of the Poro. In such cases the disputes are heard in secret and this secrecy militates against the involvement of spirits in the direct public settlement of disputes. Thus, masks are normally never seen settling disputes, and in fact, in many areas where the Poro is found there are no visible manifestations of masked spirits at all.[63]

Such attention to the sub-regional differences of mask traditions is a rare critical qualification of both former and recent misleading studies of the use of masks in Liberia.[64] To sum up the work of masks we should emphasis that Loma masking tradition provides little basis for an instrumental understanding of the use of masks in the current ethnic conflict between Loma and Mandingo in northern Liberia, even though this case seems to represent a prototypical example of politically motivated manipulation of religious symbolism.

In order to reach a more satisfactory explanation of this instance of political violence one has to compare an ordinary masked event with one resulting in violent action, and then try to identify some of the differences that may illuminate the question concerning an atypical use of Loma masks. Tonkin suggests a useful parameter of comparison, when drawing attention to the fact that 'Every Mask [mask-in-action] is part of an event, which can only be intelligible when understood as a performance with complex interactions between Masks and non-maskers'.[65] The present context concerns funerary rituals for Poro leaders, which comprise masked performance of *afui*, the highest-ranking Loma mask. In addition to the performing auditory mask, the relational field of ritual action includes, on the one hand, non-maskers who participate actively in the ritual and, on the other, 'non-participants' of different categories who are acted upon and expected to follow the event at a distance, secluded behind closed doors.

At the funeral (*saagbai*) of a Poro leader in a purely Loma settlement, the *afui* appeared already at dusk. Later at night it was joined by *gazelégi*, another secret auditory mask, and they performed together until early morning. Meanwhile, the women and non-initiated children stayed in complete silence inside the houses. A considerable part of the initiated male population was present right from the start of the ceremony, which also comprised relatives of the deceased leader and members of the *afui* cult from neighbouring villages. Many of the participants, however, left the scene of the ritual before midnight. From then on, the active participants in the ritual consisted almost exclusively of other members of the deceased person's mask association. This and similar events are rich in information about Loma culture in general, but here we shall simply emphasize two aspects. Not all Poro members necessarily participate in the ritual consecrated to their leader and many of those who do so retire after a few hours. As a consequence, the ritual rather turns into an act of self-affirmation of the performing *afui* cult, which in a sense represents the most exclusive of all Loma cults.

We only possess scarce information about the episode of masked violence among the Loma in northern Liberia, but it has been reported that it was part of the funerals of those, including a high-ranking Poro leader, who had died in the course of the civil war and that the event was attended by a large number of Poro members from different settlements. The scene of the event was a village with a mixed population of Loma and Mandingo, though only a small group of Mandingo was present, because of the general Loma hostility to resettlement of their former co-residents. The Loma have justified the killings of two people as well as the burning of houses, including a mosque, on the grounds that the Mandingo had violated Poro law by refusing, as non-members, to hide in their houses as they used to do before the break-out of the conflict between the two factions.

This episode differs in several respects from a standard *afui* performance. First, *afui* and other Loma masks usually do not act as a coercive means of power. Second, masking seems to have been used as a means to act upon persons who were not only non-maskers, but also non-participants in the ritual and, moreover, who could not be considered ordinary members of the social and religious community. The Mandingo simply do not share the local religious tradition that they have succumbed to; a fact which challenges the idea of the mask as a non-disruptive force in the settling of conflict because of the executioner's concealed identity.[66] It is beyond doubt that the Loma have used an essential symbol of group identity in this political conflict. This represents a rather common mode of political action, if one considers it in broad terms. Anthropology and related disciplines abound with studies of the manipulation of cultural representation for political purposes. There are, however, salient aspects of this case which merit a few more words of explanation. The violent use of mask performance is first of all atypical of Loma masking tradition as such, and secondly, many other recent cases of violent confrontation have occurred between the two ethnic groups without recourse to similar symbolic means. I we will review a series of more or less overlapping answers to this apparently exceptional incident of Loma political action.

There may be several reasons for interpreting the political use of religious symbolism as a premeditated act. A similar intimidating use of secret auditory masks occurred only a few months before the funerary ceremony in Söghödömai, which means that a precedent in fact existed for such a practice. Moreover, it is widely known that the Loma have long nourished a desire to avenge the loss of lives and property in the civil war, for which the Mandingo rebel faction named ULIMO-K is held responsible. Three aspects of the ritual event suggest that it actually served as a pretext for the attack on a small group of Mandingo. First, the strong presence of Poro members from various sites; second, the unusual punishment of transgression of secret society law by death; and third, the choice of ritual participants to act upon people considered non-participant foreigners. We will probably never know how much of the action was decided beforehand and by whom, but the punishment of an enemy in the name of religious tradition obviously became both a physical and a symbolic expression of Loma sovereignty. In this, as in other instances, the performance of the secret *afui* mask transforms into an act of self-affirmation. However, one is still left with the question why the Loma should kill in the name of 'tradition', since this was evidently never going to be recognized by either the authorities or other outsiders, including the victims.

One may argue, on the other hand, that the violence was a result of the ritual action itself rather than vice versa. This interpretation reflects the Loma people's own justification for relying on violence and is, moreover, supported by contemporary theory of ritual behaviour as well as by contextual factors. Houseman argues for a dissociation of ritual actors' commitment to action and their conceptualization of ritual episodes. In the author's own words,

The participants' attribution of meaning to the ritual episodes they undertake is subordinate to a perceptual grasping of these episodes, and specifically of the interactive patterns they entail. It is the actors' active participation in such episodes, rather than their reflection upon them, that underlies their commitment to the realities these episodes enact.[67]

This view of interactive constraints on ritual performance applies amazingly well to the present case. It does not imply that the ritual participants are in any way unconscious of their actual behaviour, but when nonparticipants deliberately offend against the rules laid down for this particular ritual performance, they are inevitably subjected to the performers' regularization of the situation. However, it surely does not justify the radical means of regularization from the point of view of the victims as well as that of the Liberian authorities who rule according to a different code. In addition, the violent behaviour committed by the ritual actors will still remain unintelligible as long as no reference is made to the tense relationship existing between the two ethnic groups and, in particular, to the emotions emerging in a ceremony that commemorates relatives who had perished when the ULIMO-K army ravaged the region. This leads to the inference that in the present case it is 'tradition' which has been informed by the brutal behaviour of rebels and government soldiers, rather than vice versa. In contrast to the 'religion as idiom of violence' theory, the agents of acts of terror do not seem to have acted according to the prevalent model of Loma masked performance. Moreover, neither the accused party nor the present author's informants have suggested that the ritual performance leading to the acts run out of control. Apparently, ritual specialists were present from beginning to end.

One final remark on the dynamics and persistence of religious traditions. A number of recent mask studies have demonstrated that African masking has a history. The meaning and function of masks develop concurrently with changes in the society that uses them.[68] It is generally acknowledged too that ritual symbolism involves improvisation and continual redefinition of the situation,[69] and that cultural categories 'submitted to risk' in actual performance may entail both transformation and reproduction.[70] It may be that the recent atypical incidents of Loma mask performance reveal a change in use and meaning, but the fact that it is malleable to fit new situations at the same time illustrates the durability of this particular West African religious institution—provided it still is a religious institution.

NOTES

1. The information presented in this chapter was collected over a period of ten years. Fieldwork in the region of Macenta in Guinea was carried out in 1990–1 (thirteen months) and intermittently from 1993 to 1999. I wish to express my gratitude to the Danish Research Council for the Humanities, the Scandinavian Institute of African Studies, Uppsala, and the Council for Development Research (DANIDA) for generously financing my research in Guinea. I also thank Niels Kastfelt for valuable commentary on the material presented here and Tim Geysbeek for providing me with Liberian and international news reports relating to the conflict in the borderland between Liberia and Guinea.

2. Højbjerg 1999a.

3. Bouet 1912; Weisswange 1969.

4. The full name of ULIMO-K is United Liberation Movement for Democracy in Liberia. General Albert Karpeh formed ULIMO at the beginning of the Liberian civil war in 1991. It subsequently split into two main factions known as ULIMO-K (under Alhaji Kromah) and ULIMO-J (under Roosevelt Johnson). Ellis has provided a detailed description of this and other factions in the Liberian civil war (Ellis 1999, especially chapters 2 and 3).

5. Star Radio daily news, March 3, 1999; *The News*, March 16, 1999.

6. Ellis 1995, p. 195; Ellis 1999, pp. 229–30; IRIN *Background Report on Lofa Country*, 31 August, 1999.

7. Harrison 1995.

8. *The Inquirer*, April 6, 1999.

9. Ellis 1995; Ellis 1999; Galy 1998.

10. De Jong 1999; Englund 1999; Jordán 1993; Mark 1992; Isichei 1988.

11. Richards 1996 and Richards 2001. I have treated some of the political, environmental and demographic aspects of the conflict in more detail in an unpublished paper entitled 'Claims to Land and Desecration of Religious Symbols: Background Account of the conflict between Loma and Mandingo in Liberia and Guinea'.

12. BBC News, August 20, 1999; IRIN *Background Report on Lofa Country*, 31 August, 1999; USCR Report, vol. 20, no. 10, 1999; 1999 State Dept. Report on Human Rights Practices; Ellis 1999.

13. Massing 1978–9, p. 60.

14. Weisswange 1969, p. 87.

15. Bouet 1912, p. 5; Person 1968, pp. 49, 28.

16. Weisswange 1969, p. 63; Weisswang 1976, pp. 4–5.

17. Person 1971; Rodney 1970.

18. Geysbeek 1994; Højbjerg 1999a, p. 551; Leopold 1991; Weisswange 1969, pp. 62, 87.

19. Massing 1978–9, p. 49.

20. Beavogui 1995.

21. Massing 1978–9, p. 55; Person 1968, p. 564.

22. Massing 1978–9, pp. 52, 60.

23. Konneh 1996, pp. 20–2; see also Weisswange 1969, p. 87.
24. Massing 1978–9, p. 56.
25. Harrison 1995.
26. Harrison 1999.
27. Ellis 1995; Ellis 1999; Galy 1998.
28. Harley 1950.
29. Ellis 1999, pp. 223, 248, 266.
30. Galy 1998, pp. 539, 550.
31. Harley 1950; Walter 1969.
32. Including Harley 1950, pp. 5, 8–9, 11, 17, 25.
33. Ellis 1999, pp. 255–6.
34. Ellis 1999, p. 256.
35. Cf. Abraham 1976, Gardner 1999, Richards 2000.
36. Ferguson and Whitehead 1999, p. xxv; cf. Brinkman 2000.
37. Højbjerg 1999b.
38. Rivière 1971, p. 263, see also Bouet 1912, p. 9.
39. Jackson 1989, p. 114, Joset 1955, p. 179, Richards 2000.
40. See Højbjerg 1999a for an overview.
41. Phillips 1995, p. 56.
42. Ellis 1999, p. 276.
43. Richards 1996, pp. xx ff.
44. Richards 2000.
45. Ferme 1998, p. 556.
46. Cf. Leach 2000, p. 588, on the role of hunter-warriors in the civil war in Sierra Leone.
47. I have written a fuller account of Loma masking tradition, which is going to appear in a monograph on Loma religion and politics.
48. Cf. Tonkin 1979, p. 244.
49. Harley 1950.
50. Little 1948, p. 3.
51. Fischer 1977–8; Harley 1950; Holas 1952.
52. Person 1968, p. 581.
53. Højbjerg 1998.
54. Star Radio daily news, November 21, 1998 and March 3, 1999; *The Inquirer* December 1, 1998.
55. Star Radio daily news, March 7, 1999.
56. Bellman 1980, p. 63.
57. This aspect of masking is highlighted in various general studies of masks (Napier 1986; Pollock 1995; Tonkin 1979) and of African masquerade in particular (de Jong 1999; Förster 1993; Jordán 1993; Kasfir 1988; Picton 1990).
58. Tonkin 1979, p. 242.
59. Houseman and Severi 1998 points to the systematic juxtaposition of differences as a hallmark of ritual action. A number of mask studies also illustrate such interlinking of opposites (Binkley 1987, p. 82; Förster 1993; Jordán 1993, p. 52).

168   *Christian Kordt Højbjerg*

60. Højbjerg 1998.
61. Horton 1972.
62. Højbjerg 1998.
63. Siegman 1980, p. 93.
64. Cf. Tonkin 1979, p. 244 and Jedrej 1986.
65. *Ibid.* p. 243.
66. Ellis 1999; Harley 1950; Horton 1976; Walter 1969 and many more.
67. Houseman 1999, p. 3.
68. Kasfir 1988, p. 10; de Jong 1998; Jordán 1993; Mark 1992; Rea 1998, for instance.
69. Houseman and Severi 1998, for instance.
70. Sahlins 1985.

BIBLIOGRAPHY

Abraham, A. 1976, *Topics in Sierra Leone History: A Counter-Colonial Interpretation*, Freetown: Leone Publishers.
BBC News 1999, 'Chaotic borderlands where three countries meet', by Marc Doyle, 20 August 1999.
Beavogui, F. 1995, 'Place et rôle de Gamé Guilavogui dans la naissance d'un nationalisme loma pendant la colonisation française', *Histoire et Anthropologie*, vol. 11, pp. 138–45.
Bellman, B. L. 1980, 'Masks, Societies, and Secrecy Among the Fala Kpelle', *Ethnologische Zeitschrift*, vol. 1, pp. 61–77.
Binkley, D. A. 1987, 'Avatar of Power: Southern Kuba Masquerade Figures in a Funerary Context', *Africa*, vol. 57, pp. 75–97.
Bouet, Lieutenant F. 1912, *Les Tomas*, Paris.
Brinkman, I. 2000, 'Ways of Death: Accounts of Terror from Angolan Refugees in Namibia', *Africa*, vol. 70, pp. 1–24.
De Jong, F. 1999, 'Trajectories of a Mask Performance: The Case of the Senegalese *Kumpo'*, *Cahiers d'études africaines* , no. 153, pp. 49–71.
Ellis, S. 1995, 'Liberia 1989–1994: A Study of Ethnic and Spiritual Violence', *African Affairs*, vol. 94, pp. 165–97.
——— 1999, *The Mask of Anarchy: The Destruction of Liberia and the Religious Dimension of an African Civil War*, London: Hurst.
Englund, H. 1999, 'Murderers, rapists, and thieves: arguments about "Chewa religion" in a Malawian township', paper presented at the workshop Religious Reflexivity, University of Copenhagen, 15–16 September, 1999.
Ferguson, R. B., and N. L. Whitehead (eds) 1999, *War in the Tribal Zone. Expanding States and Indigenous Warfare*, Oxford: James Currey.
Ferme, M. 1998, 'The Violence of Numbers: Consensus, Competition, and the Negotiation of Disputes in Sierra Leone', *Cahiers d'études africaines*, nos. 150–152, pp. 555–580.
Fischer, E. 1977–78, 'Dan Forest Spirits: Masks in Dan Villages', *African Arts*, vol. 11, pp. 16–23.

Förster, T. 1993, 'Senufo Masking and the Art of Poro', *African Arts*, vol. 26 (1), pp. 330–41, 101.

Galy, M. 1998, 'Liberia, machine perverse. Anthropologie politique du conflit libérien', *Cahiers d'études africaines*, nos. 150–2, pp. 533–53.

Gardner, D. 1999, 'Anthropophagy, Myth, and the Subtle Ways of Ethnocentrism', in L. R. Goldman (ed.), *The Anthropology of Cannibalism*, Westport, CT: Bergin and Carvey, pp. 27–49.

Geysbeek, T. 1994, *Fala Wubo and the Wòmò (Kònò) in Loma Oral Traditions of Origin*, Liberia Working Group Papers no. 11, Berlin; Liberian Working Group.

Harley, G. W. 1950, *Masks as Agents of Social Control in Northeast Liberia*, Peabody Museum Papers, vol. 32, no. 2, Cambridge, MA: Peabody Museum.

Harrison, S. 1995, 'Four Types of Symbolic Conflict', *Journal of the Royal Anthropological Institute*, vol. 1, no. 2, pp. 255–72.

Harrison, S. 1999, 'Identity as a Scarce Resource', *Social Anthropology*, vol. 7, no. 3, pp. 239–51.

Holas, B. 1952, *Les masques Kono. Leur rôle dans la vie religieuse et politique*, Paris: Paul Geuthner.

Horton, R. 1976, 'Stateless Societies in the History of West Africa', in J. F. A. Ajayi and M. Crowder (eds), *History of West Africa*, vol. 1, London: Longman, pp. 78–119.

Houseman, M. 1999, 'The Social Perception of Ritual Actions', ms. published as 'La percezione sociale delle azioni rituali', *Ethnosistimi*, vol. 7, January 2000, pp. 67–74.

Houseman, M. and C. Severi 1998, *Naven or the Other Self: A Relational Approach to Ritual Action*, Leiden: E. J. Brill.

Højbjerg, C. K. 1998, 'Tradition invented and inherited: The construction of Loma cultural identity', paper presented for the EASA Conference 1998, Frankfurt am Main.

———— 1999a, 'Loma Political Culture: a Phenomenology of Structural Form', *Africa*, vol. 69 (4), pp. 535–53.

———— 1999b, 'Inner iconoclasm: Loma ways of resisting iconoclast movements', paper presented at the workshop Religious Reflexivity, University of Copenhagen, 15–16 September, 1999 (forthcoming).

Inquirer, The 1998, 'Mandingos, Lormas fuss: tensions building up in Lofa again', December 1, 1998, Monrovia.

Inquirer, The 1999, 'Lorma, Mandingo conflict resolved. 5 To Face Trial', April 6, 1999, Monrovia.

IRIN (Integrated Regional Information Network) 1999, *IRIN Background Report on Lofa County*, UN Office for the Coordination of Humanitarian Affairs 1999.

Isichei, E. 1988, 'On Masks and Audible Ghosts: Some Secret Male Cults in Central Nigeria', *Journal of Religion in Africa*, vol. 17 (1), pp. 42–70.

Jackson, M. 1989, 'The Man Who Could Turn into an Elephant', in M. Jackson, (ed.), *Paths toward a Clearing, Radical Empiricism and Ethnographic Inquiry*, Bloomington: Indiana University Press.

Jedrej, M. C. 1986, 'Dan and Mende Masks: a Structural Comparison', *Africa*, vol. 56, pp. 71–80.

Jordán, M. A. 1993, 'Le masque comme processus ironique. Les makishi du nord-ouest de la Zambie', *Anthropologie et Sociétés*, vol. 17 (3), pp. 41–61.

Joset, P.-E. 1955, *Les sociétés secrètes des hommes-léopards en Afrique noire*, Paris: Payot

Kasfir, S. L. 1988, 'Introduction: Masquerading as a Cultural System', in S. L. Kasfir, (ed.) *West African Masks and Cultural Systems*, Tervuren: Koninklijk Museum voor Midden-Afrika, pp. 1–16.

Konneh, A. 1996, *Religion, Commerce, and the Integration of the Mandingo in Liberia*, Lanham, MD: University Press of America.

Leach, M. 2000, 'New Shapes to Shift: War, Parks and the Hunting Person in Modern West Africa', *Journal of the Royal Anthropological Society* (N. S.), vol. 6, pp. 577–95.

Leopold, R. S. 1991, 'Prescriptive Alliance and Ritual Collaboration in Loma Society', PhD thesis, University of Indiana.

Little, K. 1948, 'The Poro as an Arbiter of Culture', *African Studies*, vol. VII (1), pp. 1–15.

Mark, P. 1992, *The Wild Bull and the Sacred Forest: Form, Meaning, and Change in Senegambian Initiation Masks*, Cambridge University Press.

Massing, A. W. 1978/79, 'Materials for a History of Western Liberia: Samori and the Malinké Frontier in the Toma Sector', *Liberian Studies Journal*, vol. VIII (1), pp. 49–67.

Napier, A. D. 1986, *Masks, Transformation, and Paradox*, Berkeley: University of California Press.

News, The 1999, 'Eight Wounded In Clashes', 16 March 1999.

Person, Y. 1968, *Samori. Une Révolution Dyula*, Dakar, Mémoire de l'IFAN.

—— 1971, 'Ethnic Movements and Acculturation in Upper Guinea since the Fifteenth Century', *African Historical Studies*, vol. 4, pp. 669–89.

Phillips, R. B. 1995, *Representing Woman: Sande Masquerades of the Mende of Sierra Leone*, Los Angeles: UCLA Fowler Museum of Cultural History.

Picton, J. 1990, 'What's in a Mask', *Journal of African Languages and Cultures*, vol. 3 (2), pp. 181–202.

Pollock, D. 1995, 'Masks and the Semiotics of Identity', *Journal of the Royal Anthropological Society*, vol. 1, pp. 581–97.

Rea, W. R. 1998, 'Rationalising Culture: Youth, Elites and Masquerade Politics', *Africa*, vol. 68 (1), pp. 98–117.

Richards, P. 1996, *Fighting for the Rain Forest. War, Youth and Resources in Sierra Leone*, Oxford: James Currey.

—— 2000, 'Chimpanzees as Political Animals in Sierra Leone', in J. Knight (ed), *Natural enemies: people wildlife conflicts in anthropological perspective*, London, Routledge.

—— 2001, 'Are "Forest" Wars in Africa Resource Conflicts? The Case of Sierra Leone' in N. Peluso and M. Watts (eds), *Violent Environments*, Ithaca, N.Y., Cornell University Press.

Riviére, C. 1971, *Mutations sociales en Guinée*, Paris: Éditions Marcel Riviére.

Rodney, W. 1970, *A History of the Upper Guinea Coast 1545–1800*, Oxford: Clarendon Press.

Sahlins, M. 1985, *Islands of History*, London: Tavistock Publications.

Siegman, W. C. 1980, 'Spirit Manifestation and the Poro Society', *Ethnologische Zeitschrift*, vol. 1, pp. 89–95.

Star Radio daily news 1998, Local news bulletin aired in Monrovia on Saturday, 21 November 1998 and 3 and 7 March 1999.

State Dept. report on Human Rights Practices 1999, *Liberia. Respect for Human Rights. Country Reports on Human Rights Practices*. Released by the Bureau of Democracy, Human Rights, and Labor, US Department of State, 25 February 2000.

Tonkin, E. 1979, 'Masks and Powers', *Man* (N. S.), vol. 14, pp. 237–48.

USCR 1999, *Post-War Liberia Starts Over Again Toward Fitful Peace, Economic Hardship*, by Jeff Drumtra, US Committee for Refugees Report, vol. 20, no. 10, 1999.

Walter, E. V. 1969, *Terror and Resistance. A Study of Political Violence with Case Studies of Some Primitive African Communities*, New York Oxford: University Press.

Weisswange, K. I. S. 1969, 'Feindschaft und Verwandtschaft. Konflikt und Kooperation im Zusammenleben von Loma und Mandingo in dem Ort Borkeza in Liberia', master's thesis, Johann Wolfgang Goethe-Universität, Frankfurt am Main.

—— 1976, 'Mutual Relations between Loma and Mandingo in Liberia According to Oral Historical Tradition', paper presented at the Eighth Annual Liberian Studies Conference, Indiana University, 1976.

'SURVIVAL, REVIVAL AND RESISTANCE'
CONTINUITY AND CHANGE IN ZIMBABWE'S POST-WAR RELIGION AND POLITICS

David Maxwell

The Zimbabwe African National Union/Patriotic Front (ZANU/PF) swept to power in April 1980 following more than two decades of nationalist activity and a costly armed struggle against Southern Rhodesia's white minority regime. The new ruling party won 57 out of a possible 80 parliamentary seats and 63% of the votes cast. Its victory was a shock to many external observers but not to rural Zimbabweans who had experienced the extent of ZANU/PF control of the communal lands.

The victorious party quickly constructed a new system of rural local administration. At a rhetorical level at least ZANU/PF advocated social transformation on an international socialist model. It had little time for 'patriarchal' authorities—traditional leaders who had supposedly collaborated with the colonial regime. Moreover, in practice guerrilla support committees and party committees had emerged as representatives of local opinion in many rural communities. Hence the new regime removed chiefs' judicial and political powers. Chiefs and headmen were simply to act as 'guardians of traditional culture'. And in their stead, ruled the party. Organised from the most elementary level of the village through branch and district to the province and nation, it was deemed to represent the will of the people. Alternative institutions, Village Development Committees (VIDCOs), were also created in 1984 for the purpose of fostering development at a local level.

Christian leaders were also fearful of what the new regime would bring. The widespread suspicion, fed by Zimbabwean nationalism, that mission Christianity had too easily collaborated with colonialism caused many clerics to fear that mission institutions would be seized by the state. Moreover, although many rural Christian communities across the church spectrum aided the liberation armies,[1] there had been too many attacks by guerrillas on missionaries and black Christians to leave the rural churches comfortable at the prospect of a Marxist-Leninist government.[2]

However, the first two decades of Zimbabwean independence have witnessed a flourishing of religious life. While the major urban experience has been the explosion of the global born-again movement,[3] rural society has seen innovation and revival across the whole religious field. In the Katerere chiefdom of Nyanga district, Northeast Zimbabwe, with which this chapter is largely concerned, religious change took a number of forms. After a brief lull in activity *mhondoro* mediums reemerged, in alliance with chiefs and headmen, as popular leaders. This rehabilitation of royal ancestor cults was matched by the blossoming of Pentecostal churches, characterised by their extensive practice of exorcism, healing and witch cleansing. There was also growth in adherence to possession cults of avenging spirits, *ngozi*, and an increase in the practice of witchcraft and witchcraft accusation.

There has been a tendency to explain these religious phenomena as legacies created by the liberation war.[4] While this perspective certainly offers valuable insights, this chapter, drawing on in-depth research of over a century of social and religious change in Katerere, analyses religious developments within two further perspectives. First, it explains religious adherence in terms of long-term and persistent tensions within rural society, which manifest themselves along lines of gender, generation, faction and status. Secondly, the religious efflorescence will also be understood as a response to the rapid transformations in Zimbabwean rural society since independence.[5] This broader approach, which is both sociological and explanatory while still historical,[6] allows for a more nuanced understanding of religious innovation in post-colonial Zimbabwean society. It also highlights continuities in religious adherence and practice as they respond to the changing political economy.

KATERERE AND THE WAR OF LIBERATION

Because the war was a major engine of change in Katerere it is first necessary to describe the region and its social dynamics and then consider how these were affected by processes of popular mobilisation and political violence. This provides a baseline from which to assess post-war developments.

The Katerere chiefdom lies in the north of Nyanga district, in the eastern province of Manicaland.[7] By the mid 1970s Katerere exhibited complex socio-political dynamics which reflected the significant variations in the zone's social make-up, economics and geography. The region had two missions: the first, Avila, was founded by Irish Carmelite Catholics; the second, Elim, was founded by Elim Pentecostals from Ulster. The two movements had very different histories of missionization and theology, and these affected their modes of interaction with local culture and religion. African elites staffed each station's schools and hospitals. Also in operation was a distinct ethnic hierarchy. At the top were the migrant Christian elites of Manyika people, favoured by the local administration and missionaries for access to land and employment. Next came the autochthonous Hwesa, and below them refugees from Barwe in Mozambique. None of these groups can be studied as an undifferentiated whole; all need to be disaggregated in terms of gender and generation. Furthermore, those living in the particularly isolated and mountainous border area also experienced disadvantages in access to resources and ability to influence the Rhodesian state in matters like chiefly succession.

The territory's mountainous terrain made it relatively easy for ZANLA—Zimbabwe African National Liberation Army, the military wing of ZANU—to seize control of communications. By the end of 1976 all the major roads leading to Katerere had been mined,[8] and numerous bridges destroyed.[9] The comrades controlled virtually all civilian movement by forcing travellers to move along the road beside the Mozambican border where they were easily monitored.[10] The comrades also replaced the local political structure. State-imposed headmen were killed.[11] In contrast, other 'traditional' leaders whose positions were the product of hereditary succession and thus endowed with 'traditionally' legitimate status, were merely relieved of their badges of office, and local committees were formed in their place.[12] These committees channelled resources to guerrillas from stores, missions and the peasants themselves. Uncooperative store-owners were killed, or their stores burnt down.[13] Some committees had responsibility for agriculture, health and women's affairs. A ruthlessly effective intelligence network was constructed using *mujiba*—teenage boys who worked in alliance with guerrillas.[14]

The guerrillas' control of Katerere was extensive. By early 1977 they had created a semi-liberated zone between the Ruenya River, and the Chirenje (Majenjere) and Ruangwe ranges. The police camp perched on the top of the Ruangwe range was effectively in a state of siege from that point onwards. As the guerrillas became more firmly established, their mobilization rallies—*pungwe*—grew in size, so that as many as ten villages could be brought together at one time.[15] At mobilization rallies peasants were subjected to regular indoctrination with guerrilla politics. Despite their revolutionary credentials, there is little evidence that ZANLA guerrillas preached or even understood Marxism-Leninism. Instead they spread the message of Shona cultural nationalism, which was an attempt to gain political legitimacy by appealing to a particular version of African culture. Their vision of restored lands, political autonomy and all the benefits of the modern world had millenarian overtones.[16] Pungwe were also remembered as the arena where those accused of being sell-outs were beaten or killed.

Given their relative freedom of access to the local population ZANLA were able to work out locally specific strategies in response to the differing agendas they perceived amongst the peasantry. These varied not only in relation to gender, generation, ethnicity and social stratification, but also geographical location. Strategies also changed over time as political ascendancy shifted from one group to another. The *mujiba* were initially powerful before guerrillas and elders curbed their activities. In the early stages of the war they took the opportunity to get even with the rich, and give vent to their ethnic prejudices. They beat and stole from the inhabitants of Gande village, a group of outsiders of Jindwe origin, who were socially mobile by virtue of their proximity to the Elim mission.[17] To begin with the guerrillas also chose to work with the more educated and politically sophisticated Manyika elites but gradually they came to favour the autochthonous Hwesa, who had been humiliated by years of missionary and Native Administration preference for the Manyika. Seizing their opportunity to gain back grazing land given to the immigrants, the Hwesa sold-out one Manyika village to a group of comrades, accusing them of being too close to the missionaries.[18]

The comrades were acutely aware of the existence of zones of popular religion, 'traditional' and Christian, and of the varied ability of the holy men who controlled them to act both as peasant leaders and as agents capable of bestowing political legitimacy upon them. Missions were a great source of logistical support to ZANLA, providing them with food, medicines, money and indirect access to the towns and cities. Certain guerrilla commanders were sympathetic towards the church because of their own mission education. Some were seeking self-legitimation through their Christian faith. Others used the Christian idiom as a means of mobilisation. Drawing on a long tradition of creativity and innovation in Shona protest song, hymns were rewritten to carry a political message for *pungwe*.[19] Traditional religious input was different but certainly more significant in its capacity to bestow legitimacy on the guerrillas. Of central importance was the Katerere dynasty's most senior medium—Diki Rukadza, host of Nyawada, whose remarkable capacity to re-imagine Hwesa history provided the mythic basis for the alliance between the people and guerrillas. Throughout the period of the war, local politics and religious belief were more prominent than guerrilla ideology.

The guerrillas were heavily influenced by local agendas because their ideology of cultural nationalism, although rhetorically effective, lacked immediately realizable goals. It offered only the deferred gratification of land, universal suffrage and modern comforts with little hope of instant gain. And by 1979, when the guerrillas were well established in Katerere, their concern for legitimacy began to subside. They deferred instituting a political programme which would transform the structures of rural society. Instead they were content to bide their time, living off the resources generated for them by the local committees. When such supplies failed they resorted to coercion, bringing about a crisis of legitimacy. Thus while ZANLA did initially secure a popular following, their lack of a concrete political programme meant that they lost the opportunity to bring about lasting change in rural society.

CHANGING FORTUNES: THE DEMISE OF THE RULING PARTY AND THE REVIVAL OF MALE GERONTOCRACY

Immediately after the cessation of violence in 1980 there was a brief hiatus in rural social relations. ZANU/PF formalised its control of local politics, and some women and youth, empowered by their wartime mobilisation, asserted their interests at political meetings. Chiefs and headmen were initially marginalised. However, even in this moment of political flux there were signs that these male gerontocrats were not finished.

At a national level, government policy towards chiefs was contradictory. Chiefs sat as *ex-officio* members of the new councils, and along with headmen retained their salaries. Some key ZANU/PF politicians and officials publicly defended the continued recognition of chiefs in terms of the government's policy of reconciliation and its desire to preserve culture. Like politicians of the Rhodesian Front era, Prime Minister Mugabe held a series of *indaba*—meetings—with chiefs in 1980.[20]

Within Katerere too there were signs of hope for traditional leaders. It is true that they had been the focus of some popular opposition during the war. Commenting on the political position of Chief Njanji Katerere in early 1980, the outgoing District Commissioner wrote: 'He was subject, along with all his followers, to the control of *mujibas* and terrorists. This included their judicial and financial movement systems.'[21] But Njanji's instincts for survival were well honed and he did avoid the gruesome fate that his populist successor had experienced. Moreover, towards the end of the war, political ascendancy began to shift back to both Christian and traditional elders, as with the help of guerrillas, they began to rein in the excesses of the *mujiba[s]* Equally important, the war caused the re-sacralisation of the royal ancestors—*mhondoro*—and the growing influence of their mediums—*masvikiro*.[22] These important traditional religious authorities were to help chiefs and headmen claw back power and dash the hopes of radical change that many of their subjects believed the nationalist victory would bring about.

In his influential account of wartime religious mobilisation in Dande, Zimbabwe, researched immediately after the end of hostilities, David Lan argued for the post-war demise of chiefs at the expense of *mhondoro* mediums. Chiefs had become increasingly associated with the white settler state. They were associated with its unpopular agrarian policies and were representatives of a 'neo-traditionalism' which was intended as a counter to the nationalist movement. Thus in the war many chiefs and headmen were killed by guerrillas, and new administrative structures run by party committees were set up in their place[23].

In contrast to chiefs, mediums as hosts of *mhondoro* represented a tradition of resistance. They embodied an age of past chiefs, who were heroes and conquerors at a time of African pre-colonial autonomy, hence they dissociated themselves from patterns of rural land use and conservation which contemporary chiefs were obliged to enforce. Mediums rose in significance to become 'the focus of political action' in Dande. During the war they transferred the legitimising power of their spirits away from their royal descendants on to the guerrillas, who offered a means of return to a more glorious age.[24]

Lan's analysis may well have been accurate for Dande in the early 1980s but his case-study cannot be generalised, nor does it stand the test of time. In Dande the prior reality of weak chiefs before the colonial occupation gave him greater cause to argue for a dichotomy between them and mediums.[25] There is also the issue of scale. Lan refers to super-tribal spirits such as Nehanda and Chaminuka while those in Katerere have a local clientele, and are more entangled in the affairs of the chieftainship. Hwesa *mhondoro* have a strong interest in the chief, acting as his benign ancestors. Once installed he acts as their personally appointed descendant, through whom they exert influence. Lan's characterisation of chiefs as colonial stooges underestimates their significant populist role under colonialism, in the invention of tradition, the imagination of ethnicity, and the defence of local interests against an interventionist state. In Katerere mediums along with chiefs have consistently been involved in local affairs, particularly in their critique of an interventionist state.

Lan cited evidence of some occasions when mediums made their presence felt at local party committee meetings, and of others when some were elected as councillors in post-war Dande.[26] In Nyanga District there were no examples of spirit medium involvement in local party politics, rather evidence of exclusion at district level. Although, possessing a popular legitimacy, Hwesa mediums were rapidly excluded from party politics after independence.[27] But they did not hesitate to mobilise opinion against the ZANU/PF. In 1989 Katerere's leading medium, Diki Rukadza, expressed disgust at the ruling party: 'The government does not respect the ancestor spirits. They have taken part of their power for their own. The spirits can no longer give judgements through the chief.'[28] Other mediums felt that the government owed them a debt for the help they had provided during the armed struggle. They argued that members of the local party should come and present them with gifts, such as cloth and hoes, as tokens of respect. They were quick to make populist statements about slowness of development and criticise the paucity of drought relief in the late 1980s.[29] Mediums like Rukadza used the idiom of tradition to depict community courts as alien:

Community courts are misplaced because they are operating in land which belongs to the chief. Since the chief is the owner of the land he should try the case. The job of the community courts is taking place in the forests because the land is not theirs, it is the chief's land.

Q. What do you mean by 'taking place in the forests'?
A. It is because what the government did is unlawful. The acts of the community courts are just wild.[30]

Their public proclamations were well placed. Many people *did* complain about the inability of community courts to dispense quick and effective justice. Mediums also skilfully exploited public opposition to villagization and dams, which involved displacement and concentration of people, and an increase in witchcraft accusations.[31] Their utterances were both populist and patriarchal. The chief's court offered the best hope of enforcing conservationist taboos, which often underpinned elite control of resources such as firewood and water.[32] Furthermore, as Andrew Ladley notes, community courts were popularly perceived as 'women's courts', used to chase men for the maintenance of children born outside marriage. Women could thus potentially replace their dependence on men with a dependence upon the state, destroying the whole basis of marriage as a union of kinship groups.[33] When the medium Rukadza spoke of his opposition to community courts he prefaced his remarks with the words: 'It is impossible to have two cocks in one hen run. The two fight for the hen.'[34] In this context his use of gender-laden imagery was striking.[35]

But by far the most powerful illustration of the patriarchal alliance between traditional religious authorities and chiefs was the involvement of Hwesa *mhondoro* mediums in a long-running succession dispute from 1988 to the present. This competition between factions for the office of chief was a vast and complex drama whose key players were mediums and traditional leaders with claims to the royal succession, but which also involved the territory-wide mobilisation of commoners and outsiders. The dispute itself was fought out in the rhetoric of 'tradition' and involved the manipulation of myth, legend, genealogy and custom.[36] Rukadza, the medium who worked most closely with the guerrillas during the liberation war, became the most effective player in these politics, the trump card in the hand of the dominant faction. During the liberation war he had offered prophetic advice to the comrades and placed taboos on them to protect local people. Most important, he had placed a key ancestral myth at the disposal of the guerrillas as a discourse of resistance. During the succession dispute this story of military heroism and ancestral benevolence was transformed into an establishment charter to legitimise the dominant faction's claims to succession.[37]

In their opposition to the ruling party Katerere's *mhondoro* mediums were by no means lone voices crying in the wilderness. Their critique was based on the well-founded perception that the ruling party was collapsing at local level. Out of the revolutionary committees established in the war emerged the first wave of ZANU/PF branch officials, often women and youth.[38] Yet this rural dynamism, which characterised local politics in the early 1980s had vanished by the closing years of the decade. Party structures such as Village Development Committees (VIDCOs)—arbitrary collections comprising 100 villages—were imposed from above, replacing 'previous communities and affiliations'.[39] Local control over development diminished as authority was transferred further up the party hierarchy from village to ward level.[40] As elderly males consolidated their control of the branches, popular participation declined. The local turn-out for rallies and branch level independence celebrations steadily decreased in the latter years of the 1980s, and only male elders, local dignitaries and missionaries were invited to the sumptuous meals which often followed such events.

Judith de Wolf's 1996 study of the practices of local government in Katerere, and more broadly Nyanga district, paints an even grimmer picture of centralisation by both the ruling party and district level bureaucrats. On VIDCOs she found '[they] do not seem to function as independent local government institutions in Ru[w]angwe ward. They exist more on paper and in official government records…'.[41] WADCO (Ward Development Committee) meetings in Ruangwe were

primarily an opportunity for the councillor and ministries to inform people on government policies. Regularly local government issues are mixed with ZANU(PF) issues … the councillor acts as a representative of the government, 'selling' policy to the people rather than representing the people at the grassroots in the RDC [Rural District Council].[42]

Worse still, communal councillors deferred to bureaucrats who, despite claims to the contrary, formulated 'most of the policy'.[43]

Worried by its waning influence at local level, the ruling party revived the colonial strategy of using traditional leaders as its rural representatives. By the end of the first decade of independence the state had returned to chiefs their judicial powers and guaranteed that they would be involved in the process of land allocation.[44] It was also seeking to neutralise a potentially dangerous opponent. As one rural district council bureaucrat commented, 'it is good that they are in the council, because sometimes they accuse the government and now they are part of government.'[45]

Within Katerere local councillors both courted and sought to form alliances with traditional leaders in order to advance their party political agendas. Thus traditional leaders slowly came to influence party politics. By the end of the 1980s the local party was controlled by kraal heads, faction leaders and other elderly men, who may also have been successful builders, store owners or farmers. Party politics were localised to reflect local patterns of gerontocratic authority.

Moreover, at both the national and the local levels politicians and their bureaucratic allies paid greater attention to the language and practices of 'tradition'. As senior ministers were convicted on charges of corruption and public disaffection grew over rising unemployment, inflation and the slowness of development, the ruling party needed to be able to command a new language of legitimacy. Its discredited Marxist-Leninist rhetoric and its failing gospel of modernisation caused it to seek a legitimacy based on appeals to authenticity. In 1989 the Provincial Administrator for Manicaland sent a minute to all district offices complaining that some chiefs and headmen had not been properly installed and that no action seemed to be planned to improve the situation.[46] Other circulars devoted much attention to traditional leaders having the correct regalia—state-invented symbols of chiefly authority. Such administrative attention to the status of chiefs points to their full rehabilitation as local leaders. This restoration of gerontocratic elites had far-reaching effects throughout the rest of society, in particular in reshaping local expressions of Christianity.

NEW CHRISTIAN MOVEMENTS IN KATERERE

In the 1980s a new movement of Pentecostal churches appeared in Katerere: ZAOGA (Zimbabwe Assemblies of God Africa) Mugodhi, Torpiya, Zviratidzo, Rujeko, Borngaes-Njenje and Samanga. A number of the movements have existed for two or more decades but all were new in the sense that they appeared in Katerere after independence. Although they look like what some scholars would categorise as 'Christian Independence' their memberships describe themselves as Pentecostal. All except Torpiya, whose origins remain uncertain, have clear lines of descent from the Western-derived Pentecostal church, the Apostolic Faith Mission of South Africa.[47]

With the exception of ZAOGA the churches share a number of characteristics. They have no central place of worship, gathering at a number of sites, usually under shady trees in the vicinity of the leader's or his members' village. They practice taboos or Levitical-style laws concerning food and bodily cleanliness and their members wear white garments, either in full or in conjunction with normal clothes. They are particularly noteworthy for their practice of exorcism, divine healing and possession by the Holy Spirit. Their dominant concern is purity, empowerment and personal security. They also have the reputation for being churches of women and youth.

Despite their modest figures of adherence and fluid memberships these churches' impact far exceeds their numerical size. Numerous people outside the movement have come into contact with it through curiosity, witnessing its night dances or vigils, or experiencing its aggressive style of evangelism. The best measure of its impact is not figures of church adherence but the sheer intensity of the debates which it creates in schools, churches and among elders participating in 'traditional' religion, particularly *mhondoro* cults. The core of this debate is new-wave pentecostalism's critique both of traditional religion and of other forms of Christianity. The first line of explanation for this new movement relates it to legacies created by the war.

'BINDING UP THE WOUNDS': PENTECOSTALISM AND THE LEGACIES OF THE LIBERATION WAR

As with traditional religion, the war was also a great engine of change for rural churches. While many Christians did turn their backs on the church during the violence, others retained their faith and were empowered in the process. As missionaries were killed or withdrew to towns, or their home countries, church leadership was rapidly Africanised and church government de-institutionalised. At independence many churches were revived by a core of the faithful, strengthened by their defence of the faith during the war.

But the war had been double-edged for the church. In the Catholic case new-found freedom at parish level was short-lived. The state centralisation was matched by a similar process within the established church. Urban clerics who controlled the ecclesiastical hierarchies seized back religious authority from the grass roots.[48] The dynamism exhibited by the local established churches during the war withered away.

The rapid Africanisation of mission church leadership also had its down-side with the unexpected outcome of drawing African Christian leaders away from the people. The new ZANU/PF government immediately sought to increase access to health care and education. The missions were to be key players in this strategy and quickly had to crank up services, which had either ceased or deteriorated during the war. Moreover, black church leaders felt morally disadvantaged by the taint of their churches' former association with colonialism and hence had little room to contest the ruling party's ideology of development. Avila and Elim's secondary schools had closed down and their hospitals were operating at the level of clinics.[49] Thus, Avila's black nuns and priests and Elim's pastors found themselves, like the missionaries before them, running large institutions with little time to devote to evangelism and church work. The rapid Africanisation of mission leadership also contributed to rural class formation, again leading to the distancing of leaders from their flocks in terms of wealth and social status. The rapid untying of missionary 'apron strings'[50] left African mission personnel initially ill prepared for the exigencies of the 1980s, particularly the existential concerns of rural Zimbabweans.

The most significant legacy of the war was the trauma caused by the memory and experience of violence. The range of post-war demands for healing was extensive. Healers, both traditional and Christian, helped ex-combatants from both sides to come to terms with their memories of violence, and often with their sense of guilt. Parents were directed on how they were to mourn their children who had not returned from the fighting.[51] But the greatest spiritual legacy among civilians occurred at an inter-family level. This is the crisis of *ngozi*-avenging spirits. Numerous informants described how, when the war ended, their village was plagued by angry spirits of the dead who had been killed after being falsely accused by neighbours of being a witch or a sell-out:

After the war many bad things started to happen… There are avenging spirits of people who were murdered for no justifiable reason. Many people were killed during the war for no reason. Those unjustly killed [during the war] came out as spirits against those who had ordered the comrade to kill them… There was much guilt after the war.[52]

Ngozi is the most feared of all spirits among the Shona. As the spirit of someone unjustly killed, improperly buried or mistreated when alive, it is believed to kill members or descendants of the offending family before revealing its identity. Through a host in the offending family it demands that fines be paid to its kin in the form of money or cattle and often a young girl.[53] Coming to terms with a *ngozi* is costly, not only for the host, but also for the offending family. Hence many have sought an alternative option, not always successful—its exorcism by one of the new-wave Pentecostal churches.[54] Indeed, the Mugodhi church, which emerged just after independence in Katerere, comes into its own in response to the crisis of *ngozi*. Its leader described the symptoms of many of his clients:

> Some men and women start crying alone, others act[ed] as if they are cooking *sadza* others try to take things and run with them. They pretend to have guns implying that [the person with] that spirit died whilst performing that act. Old women crawl like Guerrillas [in the battle field]...when possessed...by bad spirits and men have to restrain them...[55]

He claimed to have exorcised numerous *ngozi*; the Torpiya church also appears to meet this need. Those with the ministry of casting out demons wear a white robe and red belt.[56]

The need to come to terms with both guilt and the memory of violence was most profound amongst the war's principal actors, the combatants and the *mujiba*. Born-again Christianity seemed to provide one of the most conceptually satisfying means of coming to terms with former deeds by offering a complete break with the past. One *mujiba* whose wartime experience had been a 'high' of sex, violence and drugs explained the logic of conversion:

> Since we were young boys we would go with girls. And if we found out that the father was refusing his daughter to go with us, that's the very time we would find ways of creating enmity between that man and the Boys [comrades] ... During the war I had become a notorious guy and had forgotten all about the Bible. But after the war, when the Word was preached to me again, I could see that ... I had backslid. And I had to repent and after repenting I can say that all that happened in the war had nothing to do with me.[57]

For others whose violence was more grievous, such as the platoon of guerrillas who stabbed, bludgeoned and hacked to death nine Elim missionaries and their four children in Vumba in June 1978, conversion was not enough. All eventually became evangelists and pastors appearing to directly replace those they had killed.[58]

These post-war Christian reprieves were also mirrored in the traditional idiom. In an article on trauma and healing, Pamela Reynolds notes that on returning from the war, men and women who had fought on either side sought out traditional healers for 'rituals of expurgation'. Many came fearing retribution from *ngozi*, the avenging spirits of those they had wrongly killed as witches. This form of healing differed from the Christian examples. It involved external as well as internal cleansing, and exhibited no evidence of acts of restitution. However, both forms possessed a striking similarity in the central importance of confession.

Reynolds observes that unless the patient tolds the truth the ritual was ineffective.[59]

Those who had experienced the effects of violence often struggled in the years following to find meaning in it. Thus the martyrdom of the Elim missionaries became an inspiration to their heirs living under the threat of RENAMO (Resistencia Nacional Moçambicana) incursions in the late 1980s. More generally numerous *pungwe* songs were transformed into hymns, turning painful wartime memories into a vivid message about the sacrificial nature of the Christian faith.[60]

It is important to stress that there were real limits to the process of healing. Often the perpetrators of past violence or their families were not in the community, so direct restitution could not work. Others were unwilling to face up to their past actions. Tensions still run deep in rural society, as victims of violence are forced to live with neighbours who have wronged them but have made no attempt at reconciliation. Some who have found no satisfaction have moved away, while others, having no opportunity to leave, remain with the bad memories.

Enduring tensions are apparent in wider Zimbabwean society too, and manifested themselves throughout the first two decades of independence. During the war the rural population were not only subject to the terror of the Smith regime but also had to endure the intolerance of the liberation armies. This intolerance was perhaps most apparent in the culture of the *pungwe* where an authoritarian and unitary version of nationalism was enforced on supporters, and where dissenters were punished. This *pungwe* mentality became evident in the immediate post-colonial period when state-directed violence was unleashed upon the inhabitants of Matabeleland in which as many as 20,000 Ndebele people lost their lives for their association with ZAPU (Zimbabwe African People's Union), the second nationalist movement. This was popularly known as *Gukura-hundi*—'the sweeping away of rubbish'. Richard Werbner has described the civil war as a 'quasi-nationalist' project, characterised by the state bringing 'authorised violence down ruthlessly against the people who seem to stand in the way of the nation being united and pure as one body'.[61]

Violence and intolerance have prevailed against other groups who transgress the ruling party's definition of the nation and challenge its political programme: in the repressive measures taken against strikers and demonstrators, in Robert Mugabe's prejudice against those with a different sexual preference, and in the violence against opposition parties during elections. In the face of its failed developmentalist politics, economic downturn, growing corruption and an unpopular war in the Congo, ZANU/PF has increasingly sought to bolster its legitimacy by reviving memories of the armed struggle and the promises of Shona cultural nationalism. In the 2000 parliamentary elections ZANU/PF sought the support of rural dwellers by rekindling the politics of land, arguing that 'indigenous' blacks alone had the sole historical claim to ownership. As well as silencing white opposition, it dismissed urbanites who supported the opposition movement as *'mabwidi'*: totemless blacks. Disloyal Zimbabweans living in Matabeleland were threatened with a second *Gukurahundi*.[62]

NEW CHRISTIAN MOVEMENTS AND THE REVIVAL OF OLD TENSIONS

Returning to the local case study the war left other tangible legacies, which explain the rise of new Pentecostal churches. There were initially considerable gaps in mission services. The running down of mission hospitals meant that bio-medicine was often out of reach. In a process, which mirrored the decline of mission churches during the Great Depression of the 1930s, Christian prophets arose to take on the missionaries' task.[63] The new Pentecostal churches which practise divine healing through the laying-on of hands or the use of holy water offered a powerful alternative to scarce technical solutions. Furthermore, the initial collapse of bio-medical care in rural areas after the war led to increases in infant mortality rates. The death of children remains one of the pretexts for witchcraft accusation.[64] The perpetuation of witchcraft and witchcraft accusation in rural Zimbabwe also prompts a line of analysis, which considers new Pentecostal movements in terms of continuities.

The war of the 1970s caused a brief pause in normal social relations. Some women and youth *did* experience empowerment through the mobilisation process. The record of Katerere's first meeting with a state official in 1980 portrays an assertive peasantry demanding new resources to bolster agricultural production. Among them were women insistent upon improved health facilities, women's organisations and adult education, and youth demanding access to schooling.[65] Yet because those shifts in local power relations, which brought women and youth to the fore, were never institutionalised, their new-found status was short-lived. As we have seen, elder male 'traditional' leaders clawed back power. And those who placed their faith in the transformative potential of the local party were also to be disappointed. Like the local institutions considered above, the state's bureaucratic centre was initially shaken by the war but nevertheless held. It soon demobilised the party at local level, stripping it of its autonomy. The collapse of peasant expectations in the transformative capability of the state through the party led not so much to their depoliticisation as to a change of focus back on to local struggles.[66]

Pentecostalism again became the idiom through which such struggles were fought out. The new churches perpetuate gender, generational and ethnic struggles that raged in Katerere throughout the twentieth century, and which were first made explicit to the Hwesa with the arrival of their first Pentecostal church, the Apostolic Faith Mission in the 1940s. The new churches thus represent Katerere's second Christian movement. They are also the Christian heirs of older witchcraft eradication movements.[67]

The stage was set for a second Christian movement on the dawn of independence. Elim had already become bureaucratised in the 1960s, and the brief revival in the early 1970s indicated that many church members had returned to 'idolatry'. Moreover the liberation war had caused the closure of five of the mission's outstations, leaving space for new movements. The war had left a new African leadership but they were now patriarchs in their own right, albeit Christian ones. They discouraged renewal, fearing that they would thereby lose control. Theirs was a logical response to the universalising of authority which can accompany such movements. The other main Pentecostal force in Katerere, the *Vapostori*—Apostles—of Johanna Marange, also became dominated by an elder male fraction which had drawn inspiration from its entrepreneurial ethic and thrived as local businessmen. Although it did not lose its pentecost—signs and wonders continued—its potentiality for women and youth could no longer be realised. In response to the emergence of Christian patriarchs and a more widespread post-war revival of rural patriarchy, groups comprising women and the next generation of young men founded the latest sequence of Pentecostal churches. This is not to contend that *all* members of the same social category acted in unison or had an identical set of interests. They had multiple identities of status, gender and ethnicity, and moved between different institutions and ideologies. Christianity simply offered women and youth the opportunity to reformulate social relationships in ways that were more conducive to their interests.

Pentecostal churches are popularly perceived as being churches of women and youth, but this perception has little to do with the proportion of these social categories attending the churches relative to other groups such as older men and women. The first reason for the strong association of women and youth with the new Pentecostal movement is that it was women and youth who were its founders. They had less of a stake in the old order and were more willing to break away and challenge it. The second reason is the Pentecostals' explicit challenge to patriarchal religion. Their contest with male-dominated ancestor cults occurs in graphic ways. Not only are all traditional spirits demonised, but a struggle takes place for control of the spiritual landscape. The contest usually concerns holy mountains.[68] For traditionalists these are associated with *mhondoro* spirits as they are the burial sites of past chiefs. For Pentecostals they are a place of pilgrimage, fasting and prayer. The brash young leader of Mugodhi explained: 'We go there to challenge them. Suppose they say "That mountain is holy" and we don't go, they will be challenging. We go to the mountain to prove them wrong and demand they repent.'[69] The traditional response is condemnation. Katerere's leading *mhondoro* medium announced: 'It seems as if they have no rules at all. They just climb mountains as if they are mad people.... They are quarrelsome and even live in places which are prohibited to them....'[70]

The medium's remarks signal a struggle between young men and elders for land and political power. *Mhondoro* mediums and their acolytes and allies seem to have been caught off-guard by the aggression of the new Pentecostals. One medium spoke of the confusion they caused,[71] and an elder suggested that their arrival signalled the end of the world.[72] Such images of order being turned to chaos are reminiscent of those used by mediums to express their disapproval of the empowerment of youth during the liberation war.

Women and youth benefit from this contest with male ancestor religion. In Pentecostal churches possession by the Holy Spirit is open to all members. Although the leaders are young married males, they have no monopoly on revelation.[73] Women and youth can prophesy, heal and testify within the loosely structured framework of the service. The status and sense of empowerment in healing, and the struggle against witchcraft and affliction gained by some adherents of the new Pentecostal churches, spilled over into the Elim mission, bringing with it a desire for revival as well as concern from church leaders regarding the activities of schoolboy prophets.

Although the new Pentecostal gatherings are characterised as places of debauchery and sexual immorality by the elders in neighbouring churches, new Pentecostal adherents profess to have a highly structured set of rules which attempt to discipline their bodies and speech, and control their sexuality. As Matthew Schoffeleers observes, such codes of conduct are not so much decreed by the male leaders as demanded by the membership.[74] Thus fidelity and sexual loyalty benefit women on the receiving end of a migrant labour system. In a similar vein women and youth gain materially from the eradication of drunkenness in husbands and fathers. The church gathering, usually a tight local community, maintains itself in a state of purity. The rules are enforced by prophets with an ear to the ground, who compel backsliders to confess and repent. The collapse of the Samanga church in 1989 occurred because the leader transgressed these codes of conduct.

The new Pentecostal churches also appeal to women as sources of witchcraft cleansing. As outsiders in a patrilineal society, women bear the brunt of witchcraft accusation. Instead of having to partake of the dangerous *muteyo*—poison—ordeal, or be shunned, they can confess, be exorcised and reintegrated into the community.

The issue of witchcraft cleansing or eradication brings us to the last continuity which the new Pentecostal churches embody. Witchcraft is not merely an idiom through which members of a community negotiate social stress. Individuals *do* practice sorcery, buying medicines in order to gain an advantage over their relations or neighbours, or to gain protection from them. The cost of witchcraft accusation within a community can become too high. In such circumstances public demand arises for an alternative means to redress fears of sorcery. Eradication movements are movements of absolution operating at communal level and those who participate in the rituals, particularly the imbibing of a medicine, are cleansed of witchcraft.

It is possible to reconstruct a trajectory of witchcraft eradication movements which have traversed the north-east of Zimbabwe throughout the twentieth century.[75] In the 1930s agents of the Central African Mchape movement entered Katerere and dispensed their medicine. In 1976 a movement, which according to aged informants made many resonances with Mchape, swept the region. It was led by a man called Makombe, and individuals were compelled, on pain of sudden death, to bring out their horns and charms for destruction.[76]

This trajectory of witchcraft eradication flowed into the Pentecostal churches which have arisen in sequence since independence. Witchcraft eradication has increasingly become a Christian idiom. When the Mchape agents entered the north-east of Rhodesia in the 1930s, they found scant Christian tradition in which a more Christianised message could resonate.[77] This was not true of the second movement led by Makombe in the 1970s. Although informants stress that a good deal of the praise and adulation at Makombe's campaigns was directed at himself, hymns and prayers were also directed to God, especially intercessions for the sick.[78] Moreover, the spatial design of the service, a near complete circle with an opening marked by the presence of two choirs through which attendants had to pass, resembles the lay-out of certain Apostolic services such as their *penta*-communion.[79]

Thus the Mugodhi and Torpiya churches are heirs of Makombe. They should be strictly characterised as *cleansing* rather than eradication movements because they deal with a multitude of individual cases and their cure is not collectively administered, although they were certainly more communal in their founding stages when whole villages gathered together to witness a new spectacle. Nevertheless, as sources of witchcraft cleansing, their existence undercuts the possibility of witchcraft eradication movements. In Pentecostal services women who have inherited witchcraft can be exorcised of evil spirits, and those who practice sorcery can bring their magic for destruction before being baptised. Accusations of witchcraft, or conscious lapses into it, can be overcome through continual acts of confession.

WITCHES AND PROPHETS: NEW-WAVE PENTECOSTALISM, THE STATE AND SOCIAL TRANSFORMATION SINCE INDEPENDENCE

The proliferation of Pentecostal churches in Katerere must also be explained in terms of more recent social processes, in particular the popularly perceived rise in witchcraft accusation since 1980. In her 1992 study of the war on Mutoko district in the north-east, Norma Kriger explains it by short-term conflicts created by the war.[80] Although these may be a consideration, the persistence of witchcraft accusation through the first decade of Zimbabwe's independence must also be contextualised in the rapid social transformations in the country since 1980.

Since independence Katerere has experienced a rapid increase in differentiation, as some families reaped the benefit of high urban income whilst others experienced unemployment, particularly the youth. This differential access to remittances also transformed the possibilities for productive farming, because the initial acquisition of livestock, grain, a plough etc. depended upon having a cash income. New sources of differentiation also emerged within rural society itself. The expansion of health, educational and agritex staff created a rural salariat. The arrival of the party (ZANU/PF) also produced new sources of power, status and patronage, or exaggerated existing power relations where recipients were already established rural patriarchs.[81]

This social differentiation led to an increase in witchcraft accusation. Informants spoke of a 'spirit of jealousy', elaborating how jealous neighbours and relatives put spells on them. One man offered examples of how the spirit worked:

My relatives can become jealous when I have more wealth than them and they get magic from the *n'ganga* and will later send bad spirits to me. The idea will be that of killing me or destroying my wealth...

Q. Are there also bad spirits between neighbours?
A. Yes [for example] that man up there...has a car. I do not have a car and a good house. I may hate him because he may seem to be proud and live luxuriously like a *murungu* [white man]. Consequently I may send spirits to such a neighbour.

Informants also often mentioned *chikwambo*, a spirit associated with unpaid debts.[82] Pentecostal churches like Rujeko actively engage in witchcraft accusation. Other new churches, like the Apostolic Church of Johanna Marange before them, do not directly accuse for fear of prosecution. Instead they detect those who practise sorcery and offer confession to those who have inherited witchcraft.[83] In the Mugodhi church a prophet, in similar manner to a traditional healer, will remove *zvitsinga*— bones or charms placed inside someone by a witch.[84]

The presence of the state in the countryside has indirectly stimulated the proliferation of new Pentecostal churches. Its piecemeal support for peasant agriculture and channelling of development money through male gerontocratic elites have led some families to prosper whilst others have not benefited. Pentecostal churches have responded to the social effects of rural differentiation. Given the fact that many of these movements coincided with the rise of Zimbabwean civil society and a growing democratisation movement at the end of the 1980s they must also be examined in terms of their direct relation to the state and its agendas.

But as the argument of this chapter suggests, viewing these movements in terms of a civil society/state focus obscures their major intentions. Local struggles appear more salient than the national ones. The state is 'not the critical referent' for these new-wave Pentecostals.[85] It is clear that their critique is directed first and foremost at other local institutions, though not to the exclusion of the state's current regime. They define themselves in critical relation to 'traditional' religious institutions and associated male gerontocratic power, and also to mission Christianity. At independence, mission churches in Katerere were unable to provide the healing, liberation from locally perceived evil, and sense of community that rural people require. The new Pentecostal churches have the ability to direct themselves 'at problems which are of immediate relevance to the faithful'.[86]

Moreover, the intensely localised new Pentecostal churches in Katerere, characterised by their charismatic leadership and fissile tendencies, barely resemble the urbane, bureaucratised associations of bourgeois industrialised cultures from which the concept of civil society is derived. More accurately, they should be understood as *movements*. They embody a systematic attempt by young men, women and youth to restructure rural social relations in the face of the intransigence of male elders. And more generally, they represent the continuing search of the wider community for healing and liberation. As such, these rural Pentecostal churches seek a local rather than a national accountability.

Moreover, it is the state's gradual demise in the late 1990s which in part explains the latest development in the religious field: the revival of mission Christianity. As the state's welfare and educational provision shrinks in the face of World Bank and International Monetary Fund ordained liberalisation policies[87] missions have become increasingly important for their resources. Moreover, as donor organisations grow suspicious of the state, so missions are seen to represent viable forms of civil society through which to channel aid money. In a sense mission churches have become 'NGO-ised', but their power to influence definitions of human development has increased as the government's has diminished.[88] President Mugabe's 1991 entreaty to the church to help renew the nation's moral fibre is an indication of his party's waning moral authority.[89] Thus, like the institution of chieftainship, Christian missions have recovered from the nationalist slur that they were collaborators with colonialism. In contemporary Zimbabwe, as in colonial Rhodesia of the 1930s, they are viewed as stabilising influences, vicarious sources of political order for a ruling party increasingly insecure in its hold over the people.[90] Moreover, in order to bolster their declining flocks, the mission churches have come to look more like their rural (and urban) Pentecostal rivals, through encouraging their youth to lead revival or charismatic renewal and instituting a variety of ministries and associations.

This chapter seeks to demonstrate the patterned nature of religious and political change in north-east Zimbabwe. It stands recent developments in Katerere's social and religious institutions not only in the context of changes brought about by the upheavals of the liberation war and political transformations since independence but also in the light of social tensions and waves of revival that have been working themselves out in the region over the last century.

The chapter illustrates how the struggle between male gerontocratic elites for control of the chieftainship is an important internal dynamic in Hwesa social history and one mediated by changing political contexts. In the pre-colonial period, faction leaders' success in part depended on their ability to ally with the leaders of adjacent polities. In contemporary Zimbabwe a successful faction leader needs to understand bureaucratic power and make connections with local and national party leaders and civic associations. As the chief benefactors of 'development' projects these 'old boys' have consistently been the most active supporters of the ruling party throughout Shona areas, and shored up its vote in the 2000 elections.

The chapter also highlights the continued importance of local cultural idioms as a means by which Hwesa people conceptualise social and political change. State intervention in peasant agriculture under both the colonial and post-colonial regimes has met with a consistent popular critique couched in the ecological idioms of *mhondoro* cults. Similarly, those same mediums offered Hwesa people conceptual control over the nationalist movement during the liberation war by drawing upon a well-established tradition of resistance and symbolic innovation: a mixture of myth, ritual, folk tale and custom. But it is apparent that in their present meaning such idioms have been localised. Whereas they were deployed in a territory-wide religious movement of popular mobilisation during the liberation war, they are now involved in a local ethnically-based struggle.

The consideration of the changing forms of Christianity as they interact with each other and traditional religion draws out further continuities, and highlights how Hwesa society is animated by a series of waves of enthusiasm which lead to its periodic renewal. While it is possible to link the religious movements which have spread across the region to the stresses of the colonial experience or modernisation, De Craemer, Fox and Vansina are right to assert that they are primarily religious in nature.[91] The meaning of good fortune and misfortune has changed with Katerere's evolving political economy but nevertheless the process of renewal occurs every twenty to thirty years with regularity.[92]

The periodic process of societal cleansing is linked to the resurgence of sorcery and witchcraft and the revival of ancestor religion, but also to the ageing of Christian churches. As the church leaders of the first generation grow old they become tired of the ceaseless battle against real and imagined spiritual enemies. They become reconciled to the fact that many have remained in idolatry and some begin to acquire magical substances themselves. This ageing process is often accompanied by a bureaucratization of the church. Angered by the resultant loss of adversarial zeal and egalitarian potential the next generation of Christians embraces the new religious movement. In the case of Katerere the resacralisation of ancestor cults during the liberation war and the ageing of the first generation of Pentecostal leaders made conditions ripe for a second Christian movement in the late 1980s.

The means of renewal has been increasingly Christianised. Where the destruction of charms and other magical substances was carried out by Mchape acolytes in the 1930s, it was performed by church leaders and Christian prophets in the 1950s and late 1980s. As a form of renewal, Pentecostalism has introduced new possibilities into the religious field. For women and youth it has a potential beyond other Christian movements. This is due to its overt challenge to patriarchal religion through the idiom of exorcism which is central to Pentecostal practice, and because of Pentecostalism's capacity to reformulate social relationships. The notion of exorcism and the associated idea of witch cleansing transform the options for those accused of practising sorcery and for those who have inherited the spirit of witchcraft. These qualities are particularly pertinent for post-independence rural Zimbabwe, where possession by avenging spirits can prove costly, and witchcraft accusation is rife.

With the collapse of expectation in the revolutionary capacity of the state, it is hardly surprising that new wave Pentecostalism should thrive, holding as it does the potential to transform the nature of local struggles. While religion, both Christian and traditional, has helped rural Zimbabweans find some sense of meaning in their experience of violence, and some means to heal its traumas through acts of confession, reconciliation and restitution, its limits have to be stressed. At a national level a powerful culture of violence runs counter to the policy of National Reconciliation. President Mugabe's infamous speech to the trade union movement in 1998 in which he reminded them that ZANU/PF have 'degrees in violence' points to the dangerous tendencies in states which are conceived, and conceive of themselves, through revolution or war.

NOTES

1. See various essays in Bhebe and Ranger (eds) 1995, and Hallencreutz and Ambrose Moyo (eds) 1988.
2. See Maxwell 1995 and Janice McLaughlin 1996.
3. See, for example, Gifford 1991, 1998 and Maxwell 1998.
4. See for example Kriger 1992 and Reynolds 1990.
5. This approach derives from Ranger 1991, p. 155.
6. I am aware of the limitations of this model, and take a more interpretive approach to Pentecostalism in my more recent research. See Maxwell 2001.
7. The district was called Inyanga in the colonial period. Today only its major town is known by this name.
8. EAC (Elim Archives, Cheltenham), file, Reports and notes South Africa and Rhodesia, J. C. Smyth and L. Wigglesworth, Report of Delegation's Visit to Southern Rhodesia and South Africa 13 June–6 July 1976.
9. Diary in possession of Elim Pentecostal missionary, Brenda Griffiths, 14 September and 15 October 1976.
10. *Ibid.*, 28 July 1977.
11. Diary, Brenda Griffiths, 4 August 1976, 7 October 1976. Diary in the possession of Elim Pentecostal missionary Joy Bath, 7 June 1976. Headmen Chifambe and Mungezi and another unnamed headman in the Ruangwe area were killed. Mungezi was unpopular for collecting contour ridge fines; his headmanship had been the creation of the ultra-traditionalist Rhodesian Front Government. The other two assassinated were probably 'kraal' heads.
12. DAI (District Administration Inyanga) file, Chief Katerere, D. C. (District Commissioner), Inyanga to Secretary for Home Affairs, 31 March 1980, file, Headman Sachiwo, minute from D. C. Inyanga, 16 October 1980. Interview, Herbert Turai (Comrade Sam Zvaitika), Chitungwisa, 9 August 1988. Interview, Augustine Mabvira (Comrade Ranga), Elim Mission, 31 May 1988, personal correspondence from Augustine Mabvira 12 May 1992. Interview,

Corporal Archibald Maziti, Dakota Barracks 25 July 1991. Interview, Richard Simbi, Elim Mission, 10 August 1988.

13. Diary, Brenda Griffiths, 4 August 1976, 28 July 1976. Diary, Joy Bath, 24 June 1976.
14. DAI, file, Chief Katerere, D. C. Inyanga to Secretary for Home Affairs, 31 March 1980.
15. Interview, Sister Michael Nyamutswa, Avila Mission, 31 May 1991.
16. Lan 1985, pp. 200–1.
17. These were the Gande people, who were of Jindwe origin. Interview, Martin Gande. Interview, Councillor Todd Mazambani, 1 June 1991. Conversation with David Mazambani, Oxford, 2 May 1992.
18. Maxwell 1999, pp. 124–5.
19. Maxwell 1995, p. 75.
20. Alexander 1993, pp. 169–71.
21. DAI, file, Chief Katerere, D. C. Inyanga to Secretary of Home Affairs, 31 March, 1980.
22. See Maxwell 1999, chapter 5.
23. Lan 1985, p. 211.
24. Lan 1985, pp. 136–8. See also Ranger 1985, pp. 200–2.
25. Lan 1985, chapter 8, particularly pp. 144–5 and p. 152.
26. Lan 1985, p. 210.
27. Daneel also found this in Masvingo Province, see Daneel 1991, p. 20.
28. Interview, Diki Rukadza, medium of Nyawada, Chifambe, 22 January 1989.
29. Interview, Aquiline Kaerezi, Nyamagoromondo village, 18 April 1989.
30. Interview, Diki Rukadza, medium of Nyawada, Chifambe, 15 August 1991.
31. For instance, the initial opposition of medium Kaerezi to the dam in the Mbiriyadi area. Interview, Aquiline Kaerezi, Nyamagoromondo village, 18 April 1989.
32. Daneel 1991, p. 4.
33. It is not always clear where Ladley is drawing his data from, but much of his argument seems focused on urban courts. However, it is my impression that much of the time of the Katerere community courts was taken up with 'women's' issues. Ladley 1990, p. 15.
34. Interview, Diki Rukadza, medium of Nyawada, Chifambe, 15 August 1991.
35. The cock symbolises a Hwesa chief.
36. See Maxwell 1999a, chapter 6.
37. *Ibid.*, chapter 6. Interviews, Diki Rukadza, 22 January 1989, 12 August 1989, 31 May 1991, 15 August 1991.
38. Interviews, Richard Simbi, Elim mission, 10 August 1988; Councillor Todd Mazambani, Elim mission, 21 May 1988.
39. Alexander 1995, pp. 183–4.
40. Dr P. A. Smyly, Oxfam Progress Reports, 1985 and 1986, Elim mission hospital. Dr Smyly found that the local health committee was dissolved into a ward development committee. Further, resources from a cooperative development project were only channelled into the homes of prominent people.
41. De Wolf 1996, p. 66.

42. *Ibid.*, p. 84. More generally for Zimbabwe see Alexander 1995.
43. *Ibid.*, p. 51.
44. DAI, file, Meetings and Assemblies, Minutes of the Manicaland Provincial Council of Chiefs [dates]
45. De Wolf 1996, p. 319.
46. DAI, file, Succession Claims and Disputes, Minute from the Provincial Administrator to all DAs Manicaland, 7 February 1989.
47. On the Pentecostal missionary origins of 'Independency' and the history of secessions from the Apostolic Faith Mission see Maxwell 1999b.
48. McLaughlin 1996, p. 272.
49. Adrian Smyley, Oxfam Progress Report, Elim Hospital, 19 February, 1984.
50. This phrase is taken from Kerkhoffs 1982. Though this chapter paints a less simplistic picture of the de-institutionalisation and re-institutionalisation of the church.
51. For more detail see Maxwell 1994, pp. 360–2.
52. For example, interviews, Elizabeth Pfunguro, Gotekote, 16 August 1991; Rumbidzai Bhande, Dumba, 25 November 1987.
53. See Bourdillon 1987, pp. 233–5.
54. It should be stressed that exorcism and healing sessions are not entirely the province of Pentecostals. On Jesuit responses to war trauma see Ranger 1987, pp. 154–5. On Anglicans see Weller 1991, p. 29.
55. Interview, Tobias Kasu, Nyamudeza village, 2 May 1991.
56. Interview, Elizabeth Pfunguro, Gotekote, 16 August 1991.
57. Interview with Michael Mudzudza, Elim Mission, 8 Nov. 1987.
58. Maxwell 1995.
59. Reynolds 1990, pp. 12–14.
60. Maxwell 1995, pp. 87–8.
61. Werbner 1991, p. 159. On 'surrealist re-enactment' of the *pungwe* see pp. 169–70.
62. For the above section I am indebted to Brian Raftopoulos 2000.
63. Hastings 1994, pp. 530–1, Ranger 2002.
64. See Ranger 1991, p. 161.
65. DAI, file, Chief Katerere, 'Development needs of the Mangezi Area', 1980.
66. See also Kriger 1992, p. 234.
67. On the early Pentecostal history of Katerere see Maxwell 1999a, chapters 3 and 4.
68. See 'Sermons on "Sacred" Mountain', *Sunday Mail*, 3 September 1989 for examples of this contestation outside Katerere. In Shurugwi, Zionists attempted to pray on a holy mountain to 'dethrone' the spirits of the Shiri people.
69. Interview, Tobias Kasu, Nymudeza village, 2 May 1991.
70. Interview, Diki Rukadza, medium of Nyawada, Chifambe, 22 June 1989.
71. Interview, Razau Kaerezi, medium of Chikumbirike, Nyamudeza village, 4 May 1991.
72. Interview, James Kaerezi, Gande village, 27 May 1989.

73. On interviewing the husband and wife team leading Torpiya, my impression was that the wife was *de facto* leader of the church. Interview, Elizabeth and Nicholas Pfunguro, Gotekote, 16 August 1991.
74. Schoffeleers 2002.
75. Similar trajectories of witchcraft eradication can be traced for other regions of Central Africa, see for instance Mark Auslander 1993, pp. 176–77.
76. On Mchape, see NAZ, S1542 W6, NC Mtoko to CNC, Salisbury, 14 October 1933. On Makombe, discussions with David Mazambani, Harare, 3 September 1991, and Ernest Masiku, Ruangwe, 5 September 1991.
77. This is not true for other parts of central Africa where Mchape agents operated. See Ranger 1982, p. 16.
78. Discussions with Joseph Chitima, 19 August 1991, Pious Munembe 5th September 1991, Ernest Masiku, 5 September 1991.
79. Murphree 1969. Makombe's ritual was similar to that of Dr Moses in Zambia and the more famous Chikanga. For a wide-ranging account of the symbolic meaning of Dr Moses' campaigns see Auslander, 1993.
80. Kriger 1992, chapter 6.
81. Alexander 1993, chapter 9; De Wolf 1996, p. 66 *and* chapter 6 passim.
82. For incidence of witchcraft accusation and *chikwambo* outside Katerere see *Sunday Mail*, 16 June 1991, on Muzarabani where 'Development in the district has ceased because people are afraid of doing anything that is better than a witch [neighbour]'.
83. Daneel 1971, p. 325.
84. Interview, Davis Matambo, Nyamudeza village, 29 April 1991.
85. Marshall 1993, p. 216.
86. Schoffeleers 2002.
87. For useful statistics on the impact of structural adjustment in Zimbabwe, see Chakaodza 1993, pp. 68–71.
88. These are also the conclusions of Paul Gifford's study of 1998.
89. Oskar Wermter, 'Time to Choose', *Moto*, Nov.–Dec. 1992.
90. See Fields 1985.
91. W. De Craemer *et al.* 1976, p. 467.
92. *Ibid.*, p. 472.

BIBLIOGRAPHY

Alexander, Jocelyn 1993, 'The State, Agrarian Policy and Rural Politics in Zimbabwe: Case Studies of Insiza and Chimanimani Districts, 1940–1990', DPhil thesis, Oxford.
——— 1995, 'Things Fall Apart; The Centre *Can* Hold: The Process of Post War Political Demobilization in Zimbabwe's Rural Areas', in Ngwabi Bhebe and Terence Ranger (eds), *Society in Zimbabwe's Liberation War*, Oxford: James Currey, pp. 175–91.
Auslander, Mark 1993, '"Open the Wombs"!: The Symbolic Politics of Modern Ngoni Witchfinding', in Jean Comaroff and John Comaroff (eds), *Modernity*

and its Malcontents: Ritual and Power in Postcolonial Africa, University of Chicago Press, pp. 167–92.

Bourdillon, Michael 1987, The Shona Peoples: An Ethnography of the Contemporary Shona, with Special Reference to their Religion, 3rd edn., Gweru: Mambo Press.

Chakaodza, Austin 1993, Structural Adjustment in Zambia and Zimbabwe: Reconstructive or Destructive? Harare: Third World Publishing Co.

Daneel, Martinus 1971, Old and New in Southern Shona Independent Churches, vol. I: Background and Rise of the Major Movements, The Hague: Mouton, Afrika-Studiecentrum.

——— 1991, 'Healing the Earth: Traditional and Christian Initiatives in Southern Africa', Utrecht, ms.

De Creamer, W., R. Fox and J. Vansina 1976, 'Religious Movements in Central Africa: A Theoretical Study', Comparative Studies in Society and History, vol. 18, 4, pp. 458–75.

De Wolf, Judith 1996, 'Practices of Local Governance: A Sociological Study into the Functioning of Local Government in Nyanga district, Zimbabwe', MSc thesis, Wageningen Agricultural University.

Fields, Karen 1985, Revival and Rebellion in Colonial Central Africa, Princeton University Press.

Gifford, Paul 1991, The New Crusaders: Christianity and the New Right in Southern Africa, London: Pluto.

Hallencreutz, Carl and Ambrose Moyo (eds) 1988, Church and State in Zimbabwe, Gweru: Mambo Press.

Hastings, Adrian 1994, The Church in Africa 1450–1950, Oxford: Clarendon Press.

Kerkhofs, J. 1982, 'The Church in Zimbabwe: The Trauma of Cutting Apron Strings', Pro Mundi Vita Dossiers, January.

Kriger, Norma 1992, Zimbabwe's Guerrilla War: Peasant Voices, Cambridge University Press.

Ladley, Andrew 1990, 'Just Spirits? Chiefs, Tradition, Status and Contract in the Customary Law Courts of Zimbabwe', unpublished ms.

Lan, David 1985, Guns and Rain. Guerrillas and Spirit Mediums in Zimbabwe, London: James Currey.

Marshall, Ruth 1993, "Power in the Name of Jesus": Social Transformation and Pentecostalism in Western Nigeria 'Revisited' in Terence Ranger and Olufemi Vaughan (eds), Legitimacy and the State in Twentieth-Century Africa, London: Macmillan in association with St. Antony's College, Oxford, pp. 213–46.

Maxwell, David 1994, 'A Social and Conceptual History of North East Zimbabwe 1890–1990', DPhil. thesis, Oxford.

——— 1995, 'Christianity and the War in Eastern Zimbabwe: The Case of Elim Mission', in Ngwabi Bhebe and Terence Ranger (eds), Society in Zimbabwe's Liberation War, Oxford: James Currey, pp. 58–9.

——— 1999a, Christians and Chiefs in Zimbabwe: A Social History of the Hwesa People c. 1870s–1990s, Edinburgh University Press for the International Africa Institute.

—————— 1999b, 'Historicizing Christian Independency: The Southern African Pentecostal Movement c. 1908–60', *Journal of African History*, vol. 40, pp. 243–64.

—————— 2001 'Sacred History, Social History: Traditions and Texts in the Making of a South African Transnational Religious Movement', *Comparative Studies in Society and History*, vol. 43.

McLaughlin, Janice 1996, *On the Frontline: Catholic Missions in Zimbabwe's Liberation War*, Harare: Baobab Books.

Murphree, Marshall 1969, *Christianity and the Shona*. London: Athlone Press.

Raftopoulos, Brian 2000, 'Nationalism, Violence and Politics', unpublished ms.

Ranger, Terence 1982, 'Mchape: A Study in Diffusion and Interpretation', unpublished ms.

—————— 1985, *Peasant Consciousness and Guerrilla War in Zimbabwe*, London: James Currey.

—————— 1987, 'Concluding Summary', in Kirsten Holst Petersen (ed.), *Religion, Development and African Identity*, Uppsala: Scandinavian Institute of African Studies, pp. 145–62.

—————— 1991, 'Religion and Witchcraft in Everyday Life in Contemporary Zimbabwe', in Preben Kaarsholm (ed.), *Cultural Struggle and Development in Africa*, London: James Currey, pp. 149–65.

—————— 2002, '"Taking on the Missionary's Task": African Spirituality and the Mission Churches of Manicaland in the 1930s' in D. Maxwell (ed.) (with Ingrid Lawrie), *Christianity and the African Imagination. Essays in Honour of Adrian Hastings*, Leiden: Brill, pp. 93–126.

Reynolds, Pamela 1990, 'Children of Tribulation: The Need to Heal and the Means to Heal War Trauma', *Africa*, vol. 60, no. 1, pp. 1–38.

Schoffeleers, Matthew 2002, 'Pentecostalism and Neo-Traditionalism: The Religious Polarization of a Rural District in Southern Malawi', in D. Maxwell (ed.) (with Ingrid Lawrie), *Christianity and the African Imagination: Essays in honour of Adrian Hastings*, Leiden: Brill, pp. 225–70.

Weller, John 1991, *Anglican Centenary in Zimbabwe 1891–1991*, Mutare: Zimbabwe Newspapers Ltd.

Werbner, Richard 1991, *Tears of the Dead: The Social Biography of an African Family*, Edinburgh University Press.

INDEX

Abboud, General, 55
Acholi, 13, 51
Adwor, 64
Akol, Lam, 61–2
All Africa Conference of Churches, 93, 95
All People's Congress (APC), 133
Alliance of Democratic Forces for the Liberation of Congo (AFDL), 111
Amba, Frederick, 73–4
ancestor worship, 176, 177–9, 192
Anglican/Episcopal churches, 41, 42, 51, 55, 59, 64–6, 67–73, 76
Angola, 1, 114, 115
Annan, Kofi, 137
anti-colonial revolts, 3, 4–7
Anyanya, 54–6, 69–70
Apostolic Faith Mission, 181
arms, 33–5
Arusha, 96
'Authenticity' (Zaire/Congo), 107–8, 110
Aweil, 64
Azande, 15, 69–72, 76

Bagaza, President Jean-Baptiste, 91, 94
Baggara, 32, 33, 47–8, 59
Bahr-el-Ghazal province (Sudan), 28–9, 32, 37, 45, 47, 56, 58, 59, 60, 61, 63–5
Bandundu province (Congo), 103, 115
Bari language, 72, 79 (n. 26)
Barwe, 176
Basic Christian Communities, 91
BBC, 133–5, 137–44
Belgium, 103, 104, 111

Benghazi, 119, 121
Biafra, 3–4
Bishop Allison Bible School (Uganda), 68
Bo, 127, 128–9
Bockarie, Samuel, alias 'Maskita', 127, 131
Bol, Father Zachary, 66
Bor (town and region), , Bor Dinka, 15, 29, 37, 42, 59, 60, 61–5, 71, 76
Bor massacre (Sudan), 37
Brazzaville, 107, 114
Britain, 127, 137
Burkina Faso, 120, 123, 127
Burundi:, 17, 82–98, 114; civil war, 17, 96–7
Butare, 85, 89, 98
Buyoya, President Pierre, 91, 97

Camp Luka (Kinshasa), 103–15
cannibalism, 11, 152, 154
Catholic Church, 3–4, 17, 41, 42–3, 43–4, 49, 55, 63–8, 70, 76, 83–98, 144, 173–4, 181
cattle in Sudan war, 38, 45, 48, 75
Central African Republic, 69–70
children: soldiers, 131–2, 136; victims of war, 35–6
China, 30
church-state relations, 82–98
Cold War, 121
Comboni (Verona) Fathers, 55, 65, 69, 77 (n. 6)
Congo (Democratic Republic, formerly Zaire), 3, 20, 55, 70, 95, 102–15, 184; economic crisis, 108
Côte d'Ivoire, 127

199